"Michael Yapko shows how the benefits of mindfulness and hypnosis are increased when both approaches are considered and effortless learning contexts are created. He showcases the power of experiential or first-hand learning and urges the reader to learn a variety of strategies to skillfully apply suggestion, focus, and dissociation into the helping process. This book is a 'must-read' for all therapists regardless of work setting or theoretical orientation." —Jon Carlson, PsyD, EdD, ABPP, Distinguished Professor, Governors State University

"Attune to the lively way in which Michael Yapko eases guided mindfulness meditation (GMM) and hypnosis into the 21st century, elucidating fundamental structures and interpersonal processes. Become ever mindful of entrancing ways to apply GMM and hypnosis in clinical practice. For the tyro; for the expert." —Jeffrey K. Zeig, PhD, Director, The Milton Erickson Foundation

"Michael Yapko's *Mindfulness and Hypnosis* challenges myths about hypnosis and artfully links trancework to mindfulness in clinical work. Given the rising interest and research on mindfulness in psychotherapy, this book is bound to be a popular addition to the literature." —Bill O'Hanlon, author of *A Guide to Trance Land* and *Solution-Oriented Hypnosis*

"Attempting the integration of two separate but related experiential approaches, clinical hypnosis and mindfulness, based on scientific evidence as well as clinical judgment, is a formidable challenge. With this new book, Dr. Michael Yapko has succeeded. Through his ability to integrate neurobiology with cognitive, social, and community psychology, he provides compelling reasons to consider the powerful role of suggestion in facilitating therapeutic shifts in attention. Dr. Yapko's book is practical and clear, and will be an indispensable resource for those therapists who are mindful of their clients' needs for focus and inner development." —Jacinto Inbar, PhD, Bar Ilan University, Ramat Gan, Israel, clinical psychologist and couple and family therapist (Jerusalem)

"In this landmark text, Michael Yapko deftly weaves the complementary threads of clinical hypnosis and guided mindful meditation (GMM). Linking the juxtaposed insights and methods of both fields, he constructs a brilliant tapestry to consider new possibilities for benefiting clients. With remarkable clarity, Yapko analyzes the 'art and craft' of hypnosis and illuminates how GMM scripts share identical pragmatic structures. Practitioners from both fields and beyond will undoubtedly gain new skills in designing individualized goals and tailoring suggestions to best meet the needs of a particular client." —Pamela Kaiser, PhD, CPNP, Co-director, National Pediatric Hypnosis Training Institute (NPHTI)

"At last! A book that merges two of the great, but long separated, healing traditions of the east and west. And who better to do this than Michael Yapko? With a lifetime of professional experience in the areas, a commitment to evidence, a down-to-earth practical approach, a crisp clarity of writing, and the warmth of human caring, he has produced a timely, pragmatic, process-oriented and powerful work that should be in the hands of all caring and responsible therapists, now." —George W. Burns, clinical psychologist, therapist trainer, and author of 7 books, including *Happiness, Healing, Enhancement*

Mindfulness
and Hypnosis

Mindfulness
and Hypnosis

THE POWER OF SUGGESTION
TO TRANSFORM EXPERIENCE

Michael D. Yapko, PhD

W. W. Norton & Company
New York • London

For information about permission to reproduce selections from this book, write to
Permissions, W. W. Norton & Company, Inc., 500 Fifth Avenue, New York, NY 10110

For information about special discounts for bulk purchases, please contact W. W. Norton
Special Sales at specialsales@wwnorton.com or 800-233-4830

Manufacturing by Quad Graphics, Fairfield
Book design by Bytheway Publishing Services
Production manager: Leeann Graham

Library of Congress Cataloging-in-Publication Data

Yapko, Michael D.
    Mindfulness and hypnosis : the power of suggestion to transform experience / Michael D.
Yapko. — 1st ed.
        p. cm. — (A Norton professional book)
    Includes bibliographical references and index.
    ISBN 978-0-393-70697-0 (hardcover)
1. Hypnotism.   2. Mental suggestion.   3. Mindfulness-based cognitive therapy.   I. Title.
    BF1156.S8.Y36 2011
    615.8'512—dc23   2011018733

ISBN: 978-0-393-70697-0

W. W. Norton & Company, Inc., 500 Fifth Avenue, New York, N.Y. 10110
www.wwnorton.com
W. W. Norton & Company Ltd., Castle House, 75/76 Wells Street, London W1T 3QT

1   2   3   4   5   6   7   8   9   0

With love to Wendy, Richard and Megan,

the best and closest of friends. I am forever mindful

of how extraordinary you are and deeply grateful

for all we share together.

ALSO BY MICHAEL D. YAPKO, PhD

Books

Depression Is Contagious: How the Most Common Mood Disorder Is Spreading Around the World and How to Stop It

Hypnosis and Treating Depression: Applications in Clinical Practice (Editor)

Trancework: An Introduction to the Practice of Clinical Hypnosis (3rd edition)

Treating Depression With Hypnosis: Integrating Cognitive-Behavioral and Strategic Approaches

Keys to Understanding Depression

Hand-Me-Down Blues: How to Stop Depression From Spreading in Families

Breaking the Patterns of Depression

Essentials of Hypnosis

Suggestions of Abuse: True and False Memories of Childhood Sexual Trauma

Hypnosis and the Treatment of Depressions: Strategies for Change

Free Yourself From Depression

Brief Therapy Approaches to Treating Anxiety and Depression (Editor)

When Living Hurts: Directives for Treating Depression

Hypnotic and Strategic Interventions: Principles and Practice (Editor)

Audio CD Programs

Focusing on Feeling Good: Self-Help for Depression

Calm Down! Self-Help for Anxiety

Sleeping Soundly

Managing Pain With Hypnosis

Contents

Acknowledgments

I am deeply grateful to all those special individuals who helped make this book possible. I would like to express my gratitude to them for their wisdom and support.

First always is my wife, Diane. Her rock solid steadiness, her loving nature and her sense of humor make the hard times much easier and the good times much better. I'm a very lucky man, and I know it.

In researching and writing about mindfulness, I had many occasions to consider all that I am grateful for in my life. I have been most fortunate that my work has taken me all over the world, allowing me the opportunity to meet and befriend many different people, learn about different cultures, and observe the wonders of life from many different vantage points. I value all the experiences and people that have contributed to my life, but most important is my family. My mom and dad, Madeline and Jerry Harris, were deeply mindful in raising their children. Their focus on our strengths encouraged each of us to develop into the unique individuals we became. Knowing I have their solid foundation of love and support is a gift I treasure. I am thankful that I have a close and loving relationship with my siblings: Brian Yapko and Jerry Groner, Ken and Jackie Harris, and Mitchell Harris. I am also mindful of my parents, Gerda and Benjamin Yapko and all they contributed to my amazing life. They would have been proud to hold this book in their hands.

My editor at Norton, Deborah Malmud, was immediately supportive of this project and never waivered. My thanks to her for making it possible to write this book. Karen Fisher, my copyeditor at Norton, used her remarkable patience, skillful use of language, and attentiveness to detail on my behalf, for which I am grateful. Vani Kannan, my "go to" person at Norton, has always been amazingly polite and efficient, which I appreciate very much.

Steven Jay Lynn, PhD, deserves a medal for contributions made above and beyond the call of duty. I'm grateful to Steve for his detailed feedback, expertise and generosity. I'd also like to thank Stuart Zola, PhD, and Pamela Kaiser, PhD, for their valuable support and helpful suggestions for improving my work. Rick Hanson, PhD, and Tara Brach, PhD, were especially gracious in granting permission to quote and analyze transcripts of their guided meditations.

Foreword

Lama Surya Das

I am always interested and even slightly bemused when people ask me to compare or find similarities between fields, especially with my own chosen field of study and practice, Buddhist meditation and related disciplines leading to awakened enlightenment. This occurs more and more often today in our shrinking, interconnected world and Age of Information Overload. Buddhism has influenced our culture in many ways over the last half-century and more. It has contributed significantly to fields as diverse as health and healing, hospice and end-of-life care, conflict resolution and mediation, nonviolent social activism, poetry and the fine arts, architecture and landscape design, performance coaching (sports, theater, physical training), consciousness studies, and mental disciplines including philosophy and higher education. Nowhere has it affected more of a transformation than in the fields of psychology and psychotherapy.

Here in this thoughtful, provocative, and well-researched book, psychologist Dr. Michael Yapko shows that mindfulness is both spiritual in nature and clinically effective, reinforcing and building upon what Jon Kabat-Zinn and other pioneers in this field have demonstrated as well. My primary questions about the encounter between Buddhism and psychotherapy are: How can this help directly awaken and illumine the heart and mind? How can we better work on improving ourselves and enriching our interactions with each other? I've found that each discipline helps support the strengths and ameliorate the limitations of the other, if used continuously, conscientiously, and intelligently. Is there really a distinct difference—an almost impermeable membrane of some sort—between the psychological search for personal fulfillment, mental health, and well-being, on the one hand, and the striving for transformative spiritual self-realization and sublime enlightenment through contemplation and meditation on the other? Are not both paths to free our mind of limitations and open our hearts, becoming more self-aware and relationally mindful and attuned in the process, for the betterment of one and all?

Being present in the moment with acceptance is more than just a practice; it is a key research-proven strategy that promotes health in the body, in the mind, and in our relationships with one another, revealing a new way of well-being and joy. Mindfulness is the essence of Buddha's path to the wisdom of enlightenment, and the essence of awakening. In fact, according to tradition it is the main ingredient in Buddha's own recipe for great awakening. The recipe also includes other factors such as investigation, balance, nonjudgment, flexibility, and concentration. Mindful awareness helps us see things just as they are—which is the essence of discerning wisdom—and not as we would like them to be: as they are, not as we are, with our projections, imagination, and interpretations. It is the open secret to living more fully and completely in the here and now, entirely present and accounted for.

As Buddhist teachings and modern psychotherapy rapidly converge, the notion of compassion and the applications of altruism for raising our happiness quotient and feelings of well-being—through intentional attention training—are revolutionizing our understanding of the path to emotional freedom. Throughout the 2,500 years that mindfulness has been a part of the Buddhist contemplative tradition, it was never intended to strictly be an awareness or attention-regulation exercise. Rather, it was always cultivated while concomitantly evoking the heartful, soulful quality of attunement, including tenderness, care, loving-kindness, wishing well for others and oneself, unselfish love, and compassion.

Compassion may be understood as a quantifiable skill that allows us to handle and hold seemingly unbearable suffering and misery. How do these interpretations play out in the practice of psychotherapy? And what are we learning about compassion from modern science, especially brain imaging and clinical research? I am not a psychologist, nor even particularly psychologically astute, but have been delighted to learn and begin to understand more about myself, and have become increasingly interested in the emergent new field I call NeuroDharma, which is the frontier and interface of brain science and Buddhism. I am also aware now of the limits to cognitive insight and talk therapy in actually changing behavior, and the need for deeper and more far-ranging practices to really address our issues along with their origins and implications for our present and future health and well-being. Although Buddhist philosophy and meditation practice offer many tools for profound spiritual development, they do not address all the psychological concerns of Westerners. Without more culturally appropriate interventions such as psychotherapy, including hypnosis, so richly described in Dr. Yapko's book, even some advanced meditators continue to suffer from anxiety, depression, isolating narcissism, or numbing and disengagement.

Certainly, moments of release and relief from obsession with self-image in psychotherapy can open windows into the type of samadhi or meditative release realized in Buddhist practice. In this regard, Michael Yapko states, "When someone has been fighting against the reality of what is, then striving for acceptance and attaining it is a powerful therapeutic intervention. In clinical practice, though, the decision of whether to act and *how* to act in the next moment following mindful acceptance is critically important in determining whether someone makes a good, bad, or irrelevant decision. In order to make better, more adaptive choices, and do so more automatically, the client does need to face "reality," but must sense the ability to choose as well as taking the responsibility for choosing wisely." Here Dr. Yapko captures the very essence of the mindful emotional mastery techniques many of us teach in the Buddhist mindfulness tradition.

Dr. Yapko's book provides a fascinating and well-documented synthesis of hypnosis and mindfulness-based guided meditation. He points out the inevitable role of suggestion in each, amplified by the structure and intent of the experiential process used. He is exceedingly clear and convincing in stating the following: (1) guided meditations are different in structure and intent than solo meditations; (2) guided meditations in a clinical context for therapeutic objectives are different than those employed for personal or spiritual growth; (3) the linguistic, neurophysiological, and social psychological overlaps between guided mindful meditation and hypnosis are evident (as described throughout the book); and (4) therapists using guided mindful meditation approaches in their treatments would benefit greatly from studying hypnosis for its deeper consideration of the role of suggestion and other interpersonal dynamics in catalyzing experiences that clients in treatment find helpful and enlightening.

Hypnosis and mindfulness are not the same, differing in philosophical foundations and stated intentions. Despite these abstract differences, they do share a common practical foundation, methodology, and therapeutic orientation, including altruistic core values and concentration practices. Change is the goal of therapy, as spiritual transformation and conscious evolution is the goal of the path of spiritual enlightenment. To know the world is knowledge, and as Lao Tsu said long ago, "to know oneself is wisdom."

Self-deception is the most pernicious affliction, from my point of view. Let this be my touchstone today. How is individual reality created? How are our symptoms and problems created and sustained over decades of time? Through a groundbreaking integration of Eastern philosophy and Western psychotherapy, Michael Yapko presents us with a highly original and immensely accessible answer. He demonstrates that entirely subjective states of absorption and a focus on questionable self-suggestions are the glue that binds our symptoms together—the vehicle that selects how we perceive, interpret, and internalize our subjective world. Our attention/intention and every word we say to ourselves and others serve as virtual posthypnotic suggestions that alter our perceptions of reality—and thereby reality itself—for good or ill. It is exciting to me to realize that much of the world is out of touch with the power we all have to create the kinds of realities we desire, but that this does not have to be so. We can actually change reality, each and every one of us, and shift our consciousness and the consciousness of the whole planet to a higher level.

One of my favorite Asian parables is from the seminal Taoist sage Chuang Tzu. He was walking across an arched footbridge with a friend one day and mentioned that he had dreamed the previous night of being a butterfly flitting about above that stream, and so now he was wondering whether he was a man remembering having dreamed of being a butterfly or was actually a butterfly dreaming he was a man. How can we awaken from the trances we live and find ourselves in? What are the similarities between waking and dream, or the afterlife for that matter or other somewhat psychic states, meditative absorptions, mystical epiphanies, and experiences of unity with all things? How to see around the corners of our own minds and undo the tangled skein of self-deception that we are habitually captive to and victim of? Is not this the essence of inner freedom and autonomy, psychological integration, spiritual enlightenment, self-realization, and self-mastery?

How to really *live*, for this is truly the time of our lives. How to awaken? Are we asleep? Who knows the truth, for sure? How to be oneself when one already is, actually getting from here to totally *here*? I call it being there while getting there, every single step of the way. Striving contentedly. This is the secret. Are we simply living entranced by the sirens' call like sailors within a dream within Being's imagination, or perhaps more like a gleam in the Buddha's eye? We are all thinkaholics. I think I think too much, and know and understand too little.

In the old cemetery here in historic Concord called Author's Ridge where I like to walk, the tombstones are all but covered by December's first snow.

Once upon a time I was no more. It lasted not, but I must live as it were true.

Things are not what they seem to be, nor are they otherwise. Everything changes, but . . . but. . . .

Nothing remains. Mirrors are revolutionaries.

We are not what we think.

Lama Surya Das
December 2010
Dzogchen Center
Cambridge, Massachusetts
www.surya.org

Foreword

Arreed Franz Barabasz

Focused attention is a key component of both clinical hypnosis and mindfulness meditation. Although it was late in the evening when I began my read of *Mindfulness and Hypnosis*, just when my focus was starting to wane, I found I could not put it down. Repeatedly, I told myself "just one more chapter." Hours into the early morning, I finally retired. Dr. Michael Yapko's scientific insight and intuitive understanding of the intrinsic integration of hypnotic involvement in mindfulness practices will effortlessly focus your attention, just as it did mine. As you will undoubtedly discover, this book is a very special guide into a greater awareness.

Guided mindfulness meditations, applied in the service of therapeutic goals, have long been viewed by those well-informed about hypnosis as resting within the domain of hypnotic approaches. As a hypnosis researcher into the nature of attention, a hypnosis journal editor eminently familiar with the advances in the neuroscience and clinical applications of hypnosis, a teacher of methods of hypnosis, and someone with recent experiences learning from Buddhist monks in the Kumbu region of Nepal, it has been easy for me to appreciate the merits of mindfulness as they relate to the merits of hypnosis. I am not alone in that, for national and international meetings on the subject of hypnosis have occasionally chosen conference themes featuring mindfulness meditation as a focus. Yet, somehow the conferences on mindfulness have not yet seen fit to reciprocate by advancing a general awareness of the role of hypnosis in the practice of mindfulness. Perhaps the reason why is because the well-known teachers and authors who have written the majority of major books on mindfulness to date lack serious credentials in either hypnosis research or practice. Thus, their ideas, recommendations, and reference lists are devoid of what should be widely acknowledged as directly relevant hypnosis findings and literature. In sharp contrast, Dr. Yapko is eminently qualified as an expert in hypnosis, suggestion, and the intricacies of psychotherapy. As the author of this groundbreaking and comprehensive volume, he offers us a fresh and in-depth perspective to acknowledge and expand the richness of the domain of mindfulness by helping to uncover its hidden roots in the power of suggestion.

Dr. Yapko's decades of experience in clinical practice and intensive teaching are well grounded in current science and shine through on every page. Relevant and current references are liberally cited throughout, yet his steady flow of practical ideas is refreshingly clear and easy to follow. His detailed understanding of the impact of suggestions on experiential processes such as mindfulness and hypnosis assures that you will be intrigued, as I was, to learn to recognize the many ways focused attention can be structured to be both clinically purposeful and spiritually satisfying. This book not only has intellect, it also has lots of heart and soul.

The linguistic, neurophysiological, and social psychological overlaps among guided mindful meditations and clinical hypnosis are highlighted throughout the book. Both are experiential and expansive processes that empower people to live better lives. And, as no other volume on mindfulness would seemingly dare to suggest, it will become clear that therapists using guided mindful meditation approaches in their treatments would benefit greatly from studying the intricacies of clinical hypnosis. He powerfully and persuasively makes the point that an in-depth knowledge of the dynamics of suggestion can only improve clinical outcomes no matter what form of treatment one happens to employ.

Dr. Yapko's ability to explain the relevance of hypnosis to a mindfulness practice is a tour-de-force. With this book, he takes all of us a step further along the path to an enlightenment that clinicians and clients alike can embrace.

Arreed Franz Barabasz, EdD, PhD, ABPP
Diplomat, American Board of Professional Psychology
Professor and Director, Attentional Processes/Hypnosis Laboratory
Washington State University, Pullman, Washington
Certified A.C.E., Society for Clinical and Experimental Hypnosis
Fellow, APA, SCEH, APS
Author (with J.G. Watkins) of *Hypnotherapeutic Techniques, 2E* and four other books

Introduction

In recent years, a form of meditation originating in Buddhist philosophy and practice called mindfulness meditation, or simply mindfulness, has attained widespread acceptance within the health care community, especially among psychotherapists and behavioral medicine specialists. In a relatively short period of time, mindfulness has become the topic of scores of books and hundreds of articles in both scientific journals and the popular press, and is now routinely addressed in clinically oriented conferences and workshops. Mindfulness has become integrated into many clinicians' private practices and a stable component of hospital and university-based treatment programs for stress reduction, pain management, anxiety management, and a host of other difficulties. Clinicians are now routinely encouraging their clients to focus and be aware, open, and accepting, and thereby derive benefit from the mindfulness experience.

How has mindfulness, a treatment tool that might easily have been dismissed as esoteric only a few short years ago, become so widely accepted and applied? One obvious answer: Because it works. The empirical foundation documenting the therapeutic merits of mindfulness is substantial and growing. The benefits of incorporating mindfulness into one's treatments are numerous and are mentioned throughout this book. This is not a book about documenting the therapeutic merits of mindfulness, however. Plenty of other books and articles have already done that and many more are sure to follow. Rather, the focus here is on the structure of guided mindfulness meditation (GMM) and especially the role of suggestion in these processes. Specifically, one of the primary questions I address in these pages is this: When a psychotherapist conducts GMMs for some clinical purpose, how does mindfulness work?

The word *mindfulness* can have different meanings: A system of thought, a vehicle for self-exploration, a path to enlightenment, a means of living. Mindfulness is rooted in ancient spiritual traditions, having originated more than 2,500 years ago in the teachings of the Buddha. It is rich with insight, profound in all it encompasses, inspiring in all it teaches. This book has one simple premise, but with profound implications, that is considered throughout: *Mindfulness is significantly altered in both intent and method when it is separated from its spiritual origins and applied in clinical contexts such as psychotherapy and behavioral medicine.* The shift from a spiritual to clinical framework requires a consideration of what mindfulness methods are intended to do and how they intend to do it. More specifically, when a clinician conducts GMM and then encourages the client to carry on practicing the core elements of that process, what personal, interpersonal, and contextual factors influence the degree of benefit derived by the client?

In posing the question above about how guided meditations work, other questions arise that are every bit as compelling: Does GMM contain structural elements that can be identified and amplified, and thereby employed more efficiently? How do we determine who is most and least likely to benefit from such methods? Can GMM be improved by adapting it to the needs of specific individuals rather than employing scripted one-size-fits-all approaches? How does mindfulness relate to clinical hypnosis, another experiential method used just as successfully in psychotherapy and behavioral medicine and also built on one's capacity for focus and absorption? These are just some of the questions that gave rise to this book.

Mindfulness Is More Than a Single Approach

Mindfulness is actually a generic term encompassing a wide array of methods that collectively share some common characteristics: Mindfulness emphasizes the importance of establishing a greater focus on being in the present moment rather than rehashing the unchangeable past or anticipating a future that may never happen. Mindfulness emphasizes attaining a higher level of acceptance for the conditions of one's life rather than focusing on dissatisfaction and continually trying to change what may well be unchangeable conditions. Mindfulness further emphasizes the importance of being able to observe without judging, especially one's own thoughts, as a means of preventing undue self-criticism and the associated anxiety and depression that often accompany frequent negative judgments about the self. I like mindfulness expert and author Dan Siegel's simple but nuanced definition of mindfulness: "Being mindful, having mindful awareness, is often defined as a way of intentionally paying attention to the present moment without being swept up by judgments.... Mindful awareness is simply a way of cultivating what we have defined as the integration of consciousness" (2010b, p. 83).

Meditations can take many different forms: Lama Surya Das, an acclaimed author and speaker and one of the foremost American lamas in the Buddhist tradition, stated that traditionally, "Buddhist meditations are generally divided into two kinds: shamatha and vipassana (generally translated as concentration and insight). Mindfulness pertains to either, both, and most interestingly is utilized in the third form of meditation known (by Tibetan masters, at least) as the union of shamatha and vipassana.... Mindfulness is crucial to both shamatha and vipassana" (personal communication, December 31, 2010). Jack Kornfield, a psychologist, author, and one of the leading Buddhist teachers in America, said, "There are many good forms of meditation practice. A good meditation practice is any one that develops awareness or mindfulness of our body and our senses, of our mind and heart. It does not really matter which kind you choose" (2008, p. 2). As for the number of possible meditations, Jack Kornfield estimated there were over 80,000 (according to psychologist and Buddhism expert Jon Carlson, personal communication, January 6, 2011). Some people prefer to simply use the term *meditation* for these approaches, while others prefer *mindfulness*. They are not exactly synonymous terms, but in many quarters have become so as the techniques and terminology grow in popular usage.

Solo Practice versus Guided Mindfulness Meditations

As mindfulness becomes integrated into clinicians' practices, mindfulness as a therapeutic (and, for some, spiritual as well) approach often involves the use of structured, purposeful meditation exercises. Some of these exercises are guided, perhaps by a clinician or possibly with the aid of an audio CD, MP3 download, or DVD, while others are meditations meant to be practiced alone, carried out in the privacy of one's own inner experience. When meditating alone, can the factors shaping one's subjective experience possibly be the same as when someone else is serving as a guide for the experience? There are clearly differences between experiences stimulated by internal, intrapersonal processes and those facilitated by someone or something external.

As a clinician, I am interested in how the presence of a guide influences what happens in the course of a GMM in the therapeutic context. These are interpersonal experiential processes, structured methods one actively carries out to transform the client's experience in, hopefully, helpful directions. These typically, but not always, begin with instructions to close the eyes and focus on the breath as a means to relax and develop focus. The exercises then proceed to guide the client's attention in whatever direction will facilitate the goals of the session (e.g., noticing whatever spontaneously enters awareness without judgment, being more aware of current sensations in the body, slowing down one's eating to take time to notice the taste of food, distancing from one's thoughts to reduce emotional reactivity to them, attaining forgiveness, cultivating happiness, and so forth). The key questions arise: How does focus, a process of selective attention, particularly when developed in response to the words of a guide through *guided* mindfulness meditation (GMM), give rise to any significant therapeutic benefit? *What role do the suggestions of the guide play in catalyzing potentially transformative experiences?* Furthermore, how might the use of these experiential processes enhance the quality of the relationship between clinician and client?

Suggestion, Interpersonal Influence, and Guided Mindfulness Meditation

This book is about the *interpersonal* dynamics of the clinical use of GMM. GMMs are typically verbal, even though the experiences they generate in people are beyond verbal levels. Talking about awareness obviously is not the same as being aware. When a clinician serves as a guide for meditative experiences, how do his or her words offered in the context of a therapeutic relationship affect the quality of the client's experience? To answer this question in a multidimensional fashion, it makes great sense to consider the salient findings from the field that has studied the phenomenon of suggestive communication to the greatest extent, namely clinical hypnosis. Clinical hypnosis has studied suggestion structures, suggestion styles, human suggestibility, the dynamics of social influence, individual differences in responsiveness, neurological substrates of attention, and a wide variety of other phenomena that all affect how an individual will respond to GMM.

As a clinical psychologist with more than 30 years of direct clinical experience treating individuals, couples, and families, I have a deep and abiding interest in the process of change. It is probably fair to say that every clinician shares that interest. What may be more unique to me, though, is my interest in the process of experiential learning, which I have explored in my clinical practice as well as in the many other books I have authored. More specifically, I have been interested in the phenomenon of clinical hypnosis and its profound capacity for enhancing therapeutic effectiveness. In this book, I hope to show the relevance of hypnosis to the effective utilization of GMM.

Clinical Hypnosis Is More Than a Single Approach

In the same way that there are different forms of meditation, there are also different forms of clinical hypnosis. One form is highly directive and another is highly permissive. One form involves the narrowing of attention to a specific stimulus (e.g., perhaps an idea or image) and another is expansive and parallels the mindfulness concept of an open awareness. Self-hypnosis is practiced as a solo exercise, and clinical hypnosis is typically structured as a guided experience. Hypnosis necessarily involves focus, as does meditation, and, like meditation, is largely defined by the *direction* and *quality* of the focus.

People often react negatively to the word *hypnosis* but virtually never react negatively to a description of the *process* of hypnosis. They say things such as, "Hypnosis? No way am I gonna do that! I'm not going to let you control my mind and make me do weird stuff that I don't even know I'm doing!" It would be a fair equivalent if someone said, when you suggested mindfulness as a component of treatment, "Mindfulness? No way am I gonna do that! I don't want to be a Buddhist and I refuse to engage in any kind of weird mystical stuff like that." In fact, some people do react that way, purely out of fear and misunderstanding.

However, the reaction is typically positive when you describe the experiential process to the same person who reacts negatively to the words *hypnosis* and *mindfulness*. The experiential process could be introduced as follows:

You've been so wrapped up in feeling bad, you've been so focused on all those things that are so hurtful to you, wouldn't it be valuable to be able to *start to focus* on other things that can help you feel better? So, to help you *shift your focus* and *get absorbed in a different way of experiencing yourself*, why not close your eyes, take in some deep, relaxing breaths, and . . . [the session unfolds].

The person will likely react to such an invitation with not only acceptance but willing participation. The process of focusing and the benefits to be derived from learning not only to develop focus but how to be more aware in a meaningful way are the foundation of experiential learning. That is true of GMM, clinical hypnosis, or any of the many other related experiential approaches (such as guided imagery, guided fantasy, and visualization).

Focus on the Process, Not the Label

Having studied and written extensively about hypnosis my entire professional life, including a widely used textbook called *Trancework: An Introduction to the Practice of Clinical Hypnosis* (currently in its third edition), I have been more than a little surprised at how hypnosis continues to be misunderstood and judged negatively on the basis of misinformation and simple prejudice. I suppose I should not be, though, given that I had to overcome the same prejudices in myself. Here's how that happened.

I was only an undergraduate at the time, but I remember quite vividly watching a remarkable demonstration in a clinical training session I was attending. Based on what I erroneously believed about the phenomenon to be demonstrated, I anticipated something would happen that would be both scary and fascinating. Scary, because I had heard so many times, mostly from television, movies, and other "reliable" sources, that people were not themselves during such experiences. Instead, they were "out of control" and passive subjects compliant to the will of others. Fascinating, because I had never seen people behave in such ways and, as a student new to the subject of psychology, I thought there would be much to learn from this unique display.

The therapist-instructor spoke quietly to the woman, his partner in this endeavor, and all of us in attendance had to strain to hear at times. He encouraged her to close her eyes, focus, breathe, and listen. His verbalizations were all gentle, soothing, and supportive. I waited for the scary parts, the "mind control" parts, but they never came. Instead, he offered calming images on which she could focus her attention, and eventually offered her images that were clearly attempts to divert her attention from the severe leg pain she had presented as the reason for her request for help. He suggested accepting rather than fighting her pain, a suggestion that seemed at odds with the goal of the session to my untrained point of view. He described the "troublesome sensations" she had been aware of as beginning to flow down her leg and drain out of her toes onto the floor. I thought this a peculiar image, and silently wondered what she thought about such images. I was fascinated when she replied to this very query the instructor posed that she "didn't think about" the images. Rather, she said she experienced them, and not only did she experience them, but "they provided full relief from the pain" that had been her constant companion for months.

I was perplexed and deeply curious about what I had witnessed and the woman's report of pain relief. She felt *empowered*, not controlled. She felt she was an active participant in responding to the instructor, not merely a passive receptacle for his words. The changes in her mood and outlook before and after the session were obvious and quite remarkable, especially given how little time it had taken to achieve them. It was beyond my grasp to understand what had just taken place before my eyes. I thought it must be my newness to the psychotherapy field, and felt better when highly experienced clinicians in attendance expressed the same incredulity. The common denominator we shared was a lack of understanding of the phenomenon of clinical hypnosis.

I realized in that moment that virtually everything I had heard about hypnosis was wrong. I also realized there was something so powerful in what I had just seen that I could not ignore it. I wanted to know how becoming focused and internally absorbed brought hidden talents, such as the ability to transform physical sensations, into the realm of the possible. I wanted to know how words could have so profound and positive an effect on someone not only psychologically, but physically as well. More than that, I wanted to be someone who would be able to have that kind of distinct and profound therapeutic effect.

Expanding the Focus

Jumping ahead more than three decades since observing that powerful demonstration, my preoccupation with the potential for human beings to focus their minds and achieve remarkable, self-enhancing changes is still as strong as ever. To my delight, a new domain of inquiry has now presented itself— mindfulness. I am still an intensely curious student of psychotherapy and behavioral medicine, and I strive to deepen what I know and learn more about what I do not know. So, with an open mind, what some mindfulness experts call a "beginner's mind," and a sharp desire to add to my range and depth as a clinician, I began my study of mindfulness as it is commonly applied in clinical practice.

As I began to immerse myself in the literature and experiences of this "new" phenomenon called mindfulness, particularly the methods of GMM, I found myself in a wonderfully familiar environment. I needed no convincing of the therapeutic value of focusing, for I had already become convinced during that first demonstration more than 30 years before; I have stayed convinced through countless such demonstrations of my own over the course of my professional lifetime. I was also already clear that so much of what happens in successful psychotherapy results from catalyzing a focus in people that leads them to evolve a change of focus. After all, so much of what shapes peoples' problems is when they focus on aspects of experience that work against them in one way or another. Focus is not what helps or hurts—it is the quality and direction of the focus that makes the difference in what and how we feel.

I became especially interested in the language of mindfulness and the process of creating and delivering GMMs meant to catalyze therapeutic gains. From my lifetime study of the intricacies of interpersonal influence, the power of language, the nature of conscious and unconscious information processing, the art of focusing in general and selective perception in particular, the science of attentional mechanisms in mind and brain, and their therapeutic implications, I bring a different description and explanation to the phenomenon of mindfulness. I offer what I hope will be a broader and deeper view of GMM to the subject, with the explicit goal of making such processes as well understood and creatively applied as their closest living relative, clinical hypnosis.

Are Mindfulness and Hypnosis the Same?

Are hypnosis and mindfulness the same? No, they are not identical. They differ in philosophical foundations and stated intentions. Despite these abstract differences, they do share a common practical foundation, common methodology, and common therapeutic orientation. I articulate these in later chapters. It helps to know, though, that the field of hypnosis has already paid a great deal of attention to many of the same phenomena that mindfulness practitioners and researchers are starting to pay attention to. These include the clinical merits of encouraging a therapeutic focus, the ways brains change when people become absorbed in such practices, the power of accepting what is inevitable in people's experience, and the ways a positive relationship with a clinician, an attunement, can provide a climate for meaningful change. Change is the goal of therapy. My intention is to draw your attention to the *structure* and *suggestive nature* of GMM, well explained by the insights gleaned through more than 75 years of serious scientific investigation into the structural elements of hypnosis.

Mindfulness practitioners are beginning to explore serious questions including: When is such an approach indicated and contraindicated? How and why do people vary in their capacities to focus? How can one's approach be better customized to fit with individual client needs? How does repeated practice of such techniques benefit the client? How does the suggestion that the method will have therapeutic impact affect the client's results? These and many, many more salient questions are addressed in this book, for the language and procedures of GMM inevitably contain the suggestions (i.e., verbal patterns) and parallel the goals (such as anxiety reduction or pain relief) already well described in the literature of clinical hypnosis.

I think it is important to raise and address an important issue: Am I seeing hypnosis where it does not exist because of my extensive experience with and commitment to hypnosis? The danger of seeing only what one expects to see is real, and the concern that I might impose a hypnotic framework on something that isn't hypnosis at all is legitimate. I want to go beyond the labels *hypnosis* or *mindfulness* to explore the processes employed and the actual experience of the person beyond the labels or philosophy typically used to represent them. In doing so, a better understanding of their foundational elements without the labels reduces the chances of excessive bias. That is the challenge for me in writing this book.

Mindfulness Good, Hypnosis Bad?

It is especially curious to me that mindfulness has already achieved a level of acceptance in the professional community that advocates of clinical hypnosis can only envy and aspire to achieve. Undeserved as it is, the reputation of hypnosis is checkered, not because of any serious clinical liabilities associated with its use, but rather because of its misapplication and the misconceptions that inevitably follow. Hypnosis is found in appalling nightclub routines, and it is regularly incorporated into television and movie scripts as a mechanism causing antisocial behavior. So myths abound that hypnosis means giving up control to someone evil or is the "devil's work" and is dangerous. How incredibly unfortunate for all those who would benefit from its sensible use. A long time ago, as I disclosed earlier, I held many of the same negative stereotypes about hypnosis.

Mindfulness has not faced any of these misperceptions. It is widely considered an entirely benign process that has its gentle roots in Buddhism, a non-threatening philosophy and expansive mind-set that most people seem to find agreeable and even exotic. Unlike clinical hypnosis, which needs a lot of defensive explaining to counter deep prejudices, mindfulness is typically greeted with open arms. Mindfulness practitioners never have to cope with the fears and doubts clients raise about mindfulness until someone starts advertising "hip mindfulness shows" in Las Vegas or television and movie writers start blaming mindfulness for the latest big bank heist.

Prejudices aside, clinical hypnosis and mindfulness share core values and practices. Each has the potential to inform the other in ways that can serve to enhance their effective use in clinical practice. In this book, I focus on both fields to underscore this main point: The more deeply one understands the structure of these overlapping experiential methods, the more effectively one can apply them across individuals. The straightforward goal is to better serve the people we strive to help.

Michael D. Yapko, PhD
www.yapko.com

CHAPTER 1

The Power of Focus

The most beautiful and profound emotion we can experience is the sensation of the mystical. It is the power of all true science.

Albert Einstein

The therapist gently invited the client, grimacing in obvious pain, to close her eyes and focus on just the natural rhythm of her breathing. Though she found it difficult at first to focus on anything but the pain, she soon found herself responding to the guidance of the therapist as she was encouraged to simply be aware of the sensations in her body without judging, interpreting, or anticipating them. The therapist encouraged her to notice and accept the sensations without feeling any need to either react to or change them. The therapist was silent for relatively long periods between occasional comments, gently suggesting relaxed breathing and enjoying a comfortable distance from any unpleasant sensations, just observing them with a sense of detachment as if they were interesting artifacts behind glass in a museum display case. When the therapist eventually invited the client to open her eyes again, it took her a few moments to do so and then a soft smile appeared as she said, "I feel much better."

The therapist smiled and said, "Now let's try something else that can help," and once again encouraged the client to close her eyes and focus on her breathing. This second time she seemed to relax more quickly. She was then encouraged to imagine floating weightlessly in a swimming pool, a favorite place of hers to unwind. The therapist continued to talk in a deliberately slow and rhythmic way about the many pleasant sensations of floating, feeling calm and soothed, "as if the water is gently massaging away any cares or worries or uncomfortable sensations and replacing them completely with wonderful feelings of comfort." Surprisingly quickly, the patient's blood pressure lowered, her breathing slowed, her grimace disappeared, and her body's muscle tone visibly relaxed.

When she opened her eyes a short while later, the therapist asked her to rate her current level of pain on a scale of 1–10. The client said, "2." Before the two focusing sessions, she had rated her pain level an "8"—a great improvement. But what happened?

Instead of simply empathizing with the patient, or immediately suggesting a pain medication, or exploring the "deeper meaning" of the pain, the therapist above did something far more valuable: she created an opportunity for her client to "go inside" and find, then mobilize, some of her own inner resources. She was able to do this in a way that substantially reduced her suffering and simultaneously empowered her. Now, that's good therapy!

I have long been fascinated by the capacities of the mind to transform subjective experience in ways that defy logic or even scientific measurement. Over the years, I have witnessed and even facilitated extraordinary experiences with people that left me shaking my head in wonder as I asked the same question over and over again: How did they do that? The current emphasis for many clinicians trying to answer this question is on the new wave of neuroscientific and genetic inquiries made possible by state-of-the-art brain scanning and gene mapping technologies. Through these technologies we have discovered that brains grow. New neurons form in a process called *neurogenesis*. Neurons change their growth and firing patterns with new experiences in an adaptive process called *neuroplasticity*. We have further learned through the study of epigenetics that genes are not destiny and that life experiences modify *whether* and *how* genes express themselves.

The capacities for people to transform their sensory awareness and physiological and emotional states, as well as their reactions to their life experiences, is currently being explored in entirely new ways that are both exciting and liberating. The new biological sciences encourage us to revise some of our most enduring beliefs about the nature of the relationship between brain and mind, and even mind and body. It is especially compelling to go from merely suspecting to actually proving that life experience changes brains in measurable ways. Instead of being victims of an unalterable genetic destiny or living out some unconscious mental script we must inevitably and blindly adhere to, we have a chance to reclaim greater control over our lives than most of us had dared to suppose.

This is an empowering realization, a fresh call to be active in redefining who we are and what we are capable of as human beings. However, before our appraisals become too lofty, the truth of the matter is, we have the same brains now as we did before we localized and measured neurogenesis. We just see them differently. We have the same genes we have always had, only now that we know they do not fully control all that we do, we can view them differently. Do our new scientific understandings change who we are and have always been? Perhaps, depending on how much redefining of human potential they lead us to do. We each have an established view of people and their problems that makes helping them easier—or inadvertently makes it more difficult.

The Malleability of Mind and Brain

When people close their eyes and focus, something extraordinary happens to both the brain and the mind. The rigid boundaries of perception that have held the person in place begin to soften. "Reality" becomes less real and more negotiable. People discover through direct subjective experience that their perceptions—of time, space, the body, the meanings ascribed to life experiences, self-awareness, and so on—are malleable. What the neuroscience shows us is that perceptions of the mind also have consequences in the brain. This new finding has actually been expected for a long time by many experts, but was awaiting the development of the technology that could prove it true.

Consider this fascinating PET (positron emission tomography) scan study on hypnosis conducted at Harvard University by Stephen Kosslyn and his associates (Kosslyn, Thompson, Costantini-Ferrando, Alpert, & Spiegel., 2000). The study was designed to find out whether hypnosis could be used to modulate color perception. Research subjects chosen for their high hypnotizability were shown a series of geometric patterns, some involving colors and some only shades of gray, while in usual (so-called waking) and hypnotized conditions.

Color stimuli were shown to be processed separately from the gray stimuli in the brain. Researchers suggested that the subjects visually study each image they were shown, whether color or black and white, while the PET scan measured brain activity. When subjects were hypnotized and given suggestions to see actual color shapes as only gray, a suggestion for a visual hallucination in hypnotic terms, the color-processing areas of the brain were less active. Likewise, when suggestions were given to see a gray stimulus as colorful, the color-processing areas were more active in both hemispheres, just as they would be when genuinely exposed to a color stimulus. When subjects were not in hypnosis and were told to simply visualize the colors, only the right hemisphere became active. *The brains of hypnotized individuals responded to the suggested experiences rather than the actual stimuli in measurable ways.* Can the brain be altered through suggestions given to people in states of focused attention? Apparently so. This, and many other studies just like it, demonstrate that suggestions can profoundly influence people's subjective experiences in objectively measurable ways. People can even respond to suggestions they are given while being told they are not being given suggestions.

Why and how does this malleability of perception occur that makes experiential processes that amplify the subjective, such as mindfulness and hypnosis, so valuable as therapeutic tools? Furthermore, how does a deeper understanding of these experiential processes create new therapeutic options that may make treatment both easier and more effective? Both guided mindfulness meditation (GMM) and clinical hypnosis strive to help people by enlisting more of their own resources in the therapeutic endeavor. As soon as the client is encouraged to focus and discover and mobilize internal resources either forgotten or never known, great possibilities emerge. Hidden, untapped resources surface that can happily surprise both therapist and client. What we explore in these pages is how a knowledgeable and skilled therapist can actively create an environment that makes such greater self-awareness and self-efficacy in the client possible.

Objective Support for Subjective Experience

What if we go back to a time before these neuroscientific breakthroughs and ask how it is that some people already live their lives confidently knowing they can actively transform their own subjective experience? When Buddhist monks of today or from hundreds or even thousands of years ago were meditating and living extraordinary lives, they sensed a powerful ability to transform their experience in doing so. When Scottish surgeon James Esdaile, in the mid-nineteenth century, before the development of chemical anesthesia, performed major surgeries (including amputations) on patients in hypnosis and had a mortality rate only *one tenth* that of other surgeons, he sensed and dramatically demonstrated what a focused mind could achieve despite having no knowledge of the neuroscience of his methods. When the therapist in the vignette at the beginning of this chapter encouraged the client to observe sensations in her body without interpreting or judging them, she cocreated a context of empowering self-discovery for her client. She did it without the benefit of a brain scan to prove it. My point is not to minimize the value of the neuroscience; my point is that the neuroscience available now is being used to justify methods like hypnosis and meditation that have had obvious merit all along. Is their current popularity due only to their receiving empirical support? If so, what does this say about how we regard such experiences?

Rethinking Treatment

Therapy, indeed the entire field of health care, is at a crossroads, facing important decisions about the direction it will take in defining the roles of clinicians and patients. The traditional medical model of diagnosing and treating a pathology, an isolated presumed dysfunction of some sort in the body or mind, has a diminishing level of acceptance in many areas of health care, and for good reason. Too many of the conditions health professionals are asked to treat are not purely biological in their origins, nor are they independent of other contributing factors, such as mood states, diet, habit patterns, and social connections, to name just a few.

One of the clearest signs of the growing backlash against the reductionism of medicalizing people's problems is the parade of books and articles openly criticizing antidepressant medications, which are among the most popularly prescribed medications in the United States. *Anatomy of an Epidemic* (Robert Whitaker, 2010), *The Emperor's New Drugs* (Irving Kirsch, 2010), *Let Them Eat Prozac* (David Healy, 2004), *Comfortably Numb* (Charles Barber, 2009), and my own book, *Depression Is Contagious* (Yapko, 2009) are just a few of the many well-researched books that cite compelling scientific evidence that common problems people face, such as anxiety and depression, are *not* simply about hypothetical biochemical imbalances in the brain. Some experts go even further and argue that medicalizing these problems has increased, rather than decreased, their prevalence. Because we have the drug hammer, everything begins to look like a nail.

As more clinicians have become disillusioned with drug treatments that don't even come close to living up to their advertising hype, many of them have begun to explore what else they can do to help people. Therapists have grown bolder in their assertions that although a specific form of treatment may be empirically supported when an insurance company dictates they use it for a particular client, it may not be the best choice. The emphasis on the science of psychotherapy continues, to be sure, but the value of psychotherapy as art is being appreciated again.

Many therapists have been looking for, and only lately finding, an orientation to treatment that is more multidimensional, effective, and empowering than prescribing drugs or learning to be more logical. A remarkable shift has taken place as the approach called mindful meditation, or mindfulness, has grown in popularity.

Mindfulness encourages in us what some in the Buddhist tradition call a beginner's mind. A beginner's mind is an open mind, curious and observant without burdensome and restrictive filters of expectation and prejudice. Can we facilitate an experiential process with someone who has a beginner's mind? Can we explore what may be possible for the client to experience without having a preconceived notion of what the right response is?

Approaching clinical practice in general, and experiential approaches such as hypnosis and mindfulness in particular, with a beginner's mind is no easy task. Each of us has evolved perspectives, opinions, and biases based on our life experiences, whether directly or only indirectly. Complicating the holding of a beginner's mind even more, though, is the quality of clinical training that suggests, or even demands, that you develop an allegiance to a specific form of treatment and its philosophical underpinnings. The field of psychotherapy is deeply divided within itself, as different theorists and practitioners take swipes at each other over whose approach is better. Most psychotherapists describe themselves as eclectic, but being eclectic does not preclude being biased.

For clinicians who have had enough of these ongoing, tiresome philosophical and empirically based duels, mindfulness has provided a credible and positive way to walk off the therapy battlefield. Mindfulness suggests a gentle way of encouraging each person to find his or her own equilibrium in living life with greater awareness, self-respect, and a deeper sense of possessing an endless wellspring of internal strengths to be discovered and cultivated.

The field of clinical hypnosis has already discovered that people are capable of much more than they consciously realize. To practice hypnosis in a clinical context is to encourage a quiet, gentle focus that creates an opportunity to explore oneself and discover hidden talents, such as the ability to transform an image into a deliberate physical response (e.g., an anesthetized body part). Hypnosis, depending on how it is structured, can be an experience of greater sensory awareness, structurally identical to that of mindfulness exercises. Hypnosis can also take the methods of mindfulness a step further. For example, subjectively distancing oneself from physical pain as a means of accepting it and reducing its negative effects (such as catastrophizing or negatively interpreting its symbolic meaning) is a valuable pain management strategy described in the mindfulness literature (Kabat-Zinn, Lipworth, & Burney, 1985; R. Siegel, 2010). Would this approach be enough to allow someone to undergo surgery without chemical anesthesia? Probably not. Yet, hypnosis as a focusing tool does allow this kind of remarkable phenomenon to occur; hypnosis as the sole or primary anesthetic in major surgical procedures is a well-documented phenomenon. This is, arguably, the most dramatic application of hypnosis. Pain management is also the most empirically supported application of hypnosis (Elkins, Jensen, & Patterson, 2007; Patterson, 2010; Patterson, Jensen, & Montgomery, 2010).

Both mindfulness and hypnosis share a highly optimistic appraisal of people as being resourceful, and both actively encourage people to discover and use their resources in self-enhancing ways. Both make use of procedures that encourage focusing and the development of a selective attention, although often on different focal points. Many more similarities, and some differences too, will be pointed out as we explore the insights that the field of hypnosis offers us into the merits of mindfulness.

Defining What Cannot Be Defined

Before going any further in talking about mindfulness and hypnosis as experiential processes, it may be helpful to offer some inevitably flawed definitions of each. As you will no doubt notice, the definitions I will provide are not really definitions at all, at least not by offering any precise meaning. Rather, they tend to describe characteristics of the experience. This is to be expected, I believe, rather than criticized, a point I made when responding by invitation, along with some others, to comment on the definition of hypnosis offered by the American Psychological Association's Division 30 Society of Psychological Hypnosis (Yapko, 2005/2006). After all, how do you define such highly subjective experiences? If we describe what is going on in the brain from a purely neuroscientific point of view, only observing brain waves or blood flow to different regions of the brain, or if we examine other physiological measures, such as heart rate or blood pressure, we still have no idea what the person is actually subjectively experiencing. If we intrude on the experience and ask the person to describe what is happening for him or her, transforming internal experience into a verbal narrative necessarily alters the experience to some unknown degree. If we wait until it is all over to ask what happened, then we are relying on the client's memory for experiences that may include significant levels of unconscious experience or that may have slipped from conscious awareness into unconscious processing or even disappeared altogether.

So, with the inevitable limitations of trying to define subjective experiences in mind, here are definitions of mindfulness that have previously been offered by a few leading advocates:

> Mindfulness is paying attention, on purpose, in the present moment, as if your life depended on it, non-judgmentally. (Kabat-Zinn, 2006)

> Being mindful simply means having good control over your attention: you can place your attention wherever you want and it stays there; when you want to shift it to something else, you can. (Hanson & Mendius, 2009, p. 177)

The following definition is more experiential:

> Breathe.
> Breathe again.

Smile.

Relax.

Arrive

Where you are.

Be natural

Open to effortlessness,

To being

Rather than doing.

Drop everything.

Let go.

Enjoy for a moment

This marvelous joy of meditation.

(Das, 1997, pp. 21–22)

Mindfulness meditations can take more than one form. Interestingly, psychologist Marsha Linehan, who has had a great impact on the field of psychotherapy by integrating mindfulness into her dialectical behavior therapy (DBT) model of treatment for borderline personality disorder, makes a distinction between what she calls "two versions of mindfulness." She thinks of one version as a "spiritual mindfulness" and the other as a "nonspiritual mindfulness" (L. Zeig, 2010). Both, though, involve "the notion of acceptance and change together," and she stresses heavily the importance of being nonjudgmental as the core of the compassion that mindfulness engenders (2010, p. 23). Linehan, in stating, "the role of the therapist is not [to] promulgate spirituality," is clearly an advocate for teaching mindfulness skills in the therapy context, where the goal is to develop a more "effective way of transacting with yourself and the environment" (2010, p. 24).

It may not necessarily be philosophically correct in the *spiritual* realm of mindfulness, but it is *clinically* relevant that mindfulness skills are brought into the therapy relationship and employed as a vehicle for attaining improvement. In fact, they have been integrated into DBT, cognitive-behavioral therapy (CBT), and other active, goal-oriented approaches to treatment. In this sense, these skills feature methods with *structure* and *direction*, overlapping exactly the methods of hypnosis. Hypnosis is undeniably—and unapologetically—a goal-oriented approach to treatment. A hypnosis session with a client in the psychotherapy context is always conducted for a reason and with a goal in mind, however well or poorly defined that goal might be. The art and science of clinical hypnosis, then, is how to provide experiential learning that helps facilitate reaching a goal. Like mindfulness, the client is instructed in the purpose of doing hypnosis and the underlying philosophy associated with its use. Depending on the needs of the client, the philosophy may be explained in detailed, scientific terms, or may be a general explanation of a gentle philosophy of spiritual or personal empowerment through better using inner resources, or may be a more abstract philosophy of "tapping into the wisdom of the unconscious."

Just as Marsha Linehan made a distinction between spiritual and nonspiritual mindfulness, hypnosis practitioners also distinguish between different types of hypnosis. My friend and mentor, Jay Haley, was one of the early pioneers of family and strategic therapies and is widely regarded as one of the most highly influential therapists of the 20th century. He was also a student of Zen Buddhism.

> "Haley said, "I tend to think of three different hypnoses: 1) the personal hypnosis, where you go through a yoga experience or meditation experience, or whatever; 2) research hypnosis, where you're trying to find the limits of influence of hypnosis in various ways—in terms of deafness, color-blindness, or whatever; and, 3) clinical hypnosis, where you're trying to change someone—and I don't think that has anything to do with the other two hypnoses.... It's so different changing someone; the person's motivation is different, the responses are different." (in Yapko, 2003, p. 530)

I would agree with Haley and reiterate that his point is the basis for this book: *Mindfulness applied in a clinical context for the purpose of changing someone is quite different than mindfulness for spiritual enlightenment.* These differences have not yet been well considered, in my view. As a direct consequence, the guided meditations that mindfulness practitioners provide are structured and delivered in ways that overlap hypnosis. The popular mythology is that mindfulness imposes nothing and simply elicits an "awakening." In contrast, the outdated, stereotypical, and entirely incorrect view of hypnosis, apparent in many of the mindfulness experts I interviewed, is that you are imposing your will on the client by actively suggesting, even demanding, he or she respond in some compliant way. Hypnosis is thus erroneously viewed as a means of usurping the will of the client, leading him or her away from self-awareness and greater self-acceptance.

So, what is hypnosis? Is it telling people what to do, what to think, or what to feel? No. Are there some people who attempt to use hypnosis in such ways? Yes, but they are not the mainstream of clinical hypnosis practitioners any more than the people who run weekend workshops promising instant enlightenment are mainstream Buddhist teachers. To the contrary, what the study of clinical hypnosis provides is insight into individual differences and how these relate to the formation of subjective realities. Hypnosis can be done on one's own (self-hypnosis) or with another person (the clinician or hypnotherapist). In this book, I focus on mindfulness and hypnosis as *interpersonal* processes, when a clinician and client interact. Specifically, I focus on the language and intent of both guided meditations and hypnosis.

The following are some definitions or descriptions of hypnosis by some of the experts in the field:

> Hypnosis is a procedure during which a health professional or researcher suggests that a client, patient or subject experience changes in sensations, perceptions, thoughts, or behavior. The hypnotic context is generally established by an induction procedure. Although there are many different hypnotic inductions, most include suggestions for relaxation, calmness, and well-being. (American Psychological Association, Division of Psychological Hypnosis, 1985)

Hypnosis is the ability to "represent suggested events and states imaginatively and enactively in such a manner that they are experienced as real" (Tellegen, 1978/1979, p. 220).

"Hypnosis typically involves an introduction to the procedure during which the subject is told that suggestions for imaginative experiences will be presented. The hypnotic induction is an extended initial suggestion for using one's imagination, and may contain further elaborations of the introduction. A hypnotic procedure is used to encourage and evaluate responses to suggestions. When using hypnosis, one person (the subject) is guided by another (the hypnotist) to respond to suggestions for changes in subjective experience, alterations in perception, sensation, emotion, thought or behavior"(Green, Barabasz, Barrett, & Montgomery, 2005, p. 263). This is the formal definition adopted by Division 30 of the American Psychological Association, now called the Society of Psychological Hypnosis.

Finally, although I am no more successful in defining hypnosis than anyone else before me who has attempted to do so, here is my own definition: Hypnosis applied in clinical interaction employs suggestions provided by the clinician to facilitate the client proactively and collaboratively developing a state of experiential absorption. When so engaged, the client typically experiences a dissociation allowing him or her to respond to suggestions and interventions on multiple levels of awareness, thereby more fully utilizing resources in a goal-directed fashion. The practice of hypnosis involves the core skills of using words and gestures in particular ways to achieve specific therapeutic outcomes, acknowledging and utilizing the many and complex personal, interpersonal, and contextual factors that combine in varying degrees to influence client responsiveness.

Contexts for Focusing

It quickly becomes apparent to almost anyone who engages people in these kinds of deep, experiential processes that they typically discover positive resources in themselves they didn't know, or perhaps once knew but forgot, they had. These resources can be used in so many different ways: to help with issues such as pain and habit control, improve academic performance, and improve employee performance.

The expanded application of hypnosis and mindfulness beyond psychotherapy and behavioral medicine has an associated hazard. Since hypnosis and mindfulness can go in an almost unlimited number of directions, they can expand to the point of becoming so diffuse they lose their original focus and intent. Thus, hypnosis ends up in nightclubs, and mindfulness becomes a "hook" for developing better money management skills (Mellan, 2010). Mindfulness and hypnosis can be applied (some might even say misapplied) in some unusual contexts. An unfortunate consequence is that misconceptions may arise from such applications. Nevertheless, what makes clinical hypnosis and GMM equally therapeutically valuable and inextricably entwined with each other is their experiential nature and the empowerment that comes directly from such experiences. In this frenzied, frenetic, work-ever-harder world, taking time to stop and focus can literally be lifesaving.

Mindfulness, Hypnosis, and Clinical Efficacy

One of the challenges in the therapy world today is that treatments rooted in common sense still need to prove themselves. I loved the comment from Andrew Weil, MD, about the therapeutic benefits of mindful breathing during his keynote speech at the Evolution of Psychotherapy conference sponsored by the Milton H. Erickson Foundation in 2009. He poked fun at the empiricists wanting evidence of its merits when he said that we really don't need to wait for the supportive studies "because the risks associated with breathing are so low!"

I can appreciate the standard argument that skeptically asks, "Whose common sense are we to trust when common sense isn't very common and is too often proved wrong?" The specific irony of mindfulness, though, is that it is an approach that largely emphasizes being, not doing. As proponents of mindfulness consistently advocate, mindfulness isn't about doing something or striving to achieve something. Rather, it is about cultivating awareness through stillness, an openness to just being present without having to do anything.

But, in a therapy world driven by the need to prove itself, certainly to others if not to itself, where data can provide us with empirically supported treatments, we need to prove that just being actually *does* something. Likewise, in the domain of hypnosis, where people sit quietly and allow their focus to engage with new possibilities either suggested or catalyzed by the therapist, there is a quality of just being with the possibilities that makes doing something seem unnecessary. Indeed, it is the *automaticity* of hypnotic responses, that is, the reflexive nature of forming meaningful responses, that makes hypnosis so intriguing. People who learn to meditate have a parallel experience when they discover the effortlessness of relaxing when they focus on their breathing, or the comfort they develop in automatically detaching from the need to interpret or judge their experiences, thereby diminishing problems of perfectionism or self-criticism.

The therapeutic merits of these experiential processes have been well considered and carefully examined. Let's consider mindfulness first.

There has been a huge increase in the number of psychological and medical reports on the efficacy of mindfulness across different clinical populations in the last few years. More than 600 such reports have been published just since 1990 (for a review of trends and applications of mindfulness, see Brown, Ryan, & Creswell, 2007). Mindfulness and techniques based on mindfulness strategies have been effectively incorporated into programs for stress reduction and treating anxiety (Kabat-Zinn, Massion, Kristeller, & Peterson, 1992), depression and depression relapse prevention (Ma & Teasdale, 2004; Segal et al., 2010; Teasdale et al., 2000; Williams, Teasdale, Segal, & Kabat-Zinn, 2007), enhancing immune system function (Solberg, Halvorsen, Sundgot-Borgen, Ingjer, & Holen,

1995), enhancing parenting skills (Placone, 2011), dermatological healing (Kabat-Zinn et al., 1998), borderline personality disorder (Linehan, 1993; Mc-Quillan et al., 2005), alcohol abuse (Bowen et al., 2006), addictions (Marlatt, 2002), dealing with chronic illness (Bonadonna, 2003), coping with cancer (Tacón, 2003), and managing pain (Kabat-Zinn et al., 1985), as well as other disabling conditions.

Likewise, clinical hypnosis has been successfully applied across a wide variety of clinical populations suffering from disorders such as anxiety (Mellinger, 2010), depression and depression relapse prevention (Alladin, 2006, 2010; Yapko, 1992, 2001a, 2006), post-traumatic stress disorder (Spiegel, 2010), anorexia nervosa (Nash & Baker, 2010), pain (Patterson, 2010; Patterson et al., 2010), habit control (Green, 2010; Lynn & Kirsch, 2006), irritable bowel syndrome (Palsson, Turner, Johnson, Burnett, & Whitehead, 2002), headache and migraine (Hammond, 2007), asthma (Brown, 2007), sleep disorders (Graci & Hardie, 2007), cancer (Néron & Stephenson, 2007), psychosomatic disorders (Flammer & Alladin, 2007), and many other medical and psychological conditions.

The evidence for the merits of both approaches in a wide variety of clinical applications is quite formidable. As many parallels as there are in their methods, though, how each might help inform the other is only beginning to be explored (Harrer, 2009; Holroyd, 2003; Lynn, Das, Hallquist, & Williams, 2006; Lynn, Barnes, Deming, & Accardi, 2010; Otani, 2003; Williams, Hallquist, Barnes, Cole, & Lynn, 2010). There are compelling reasons to integrate mindfulness with hypnosis, but because key writings on the subject only appear in hypnosis specialty journals or texts, the odds do not seem to favor advocates of mindfulness ever seeing them. I hope clinicians who have embraced mindfulness discover that mindfulness approaches are more strongly related to patterns and dynamics of hypnosis than they may have realized. Learning about them will provide a stronger foundation for their skilled integration. Mindfulness works; hypnosis works; and it is the task of clinicians to ask the penetrating questions about how they work, for whom, and under what conditions.

Content, Process, and the Power of Focus

One of the important distinctions to make at the outset is the distinction between the content and the process associated with any approach. Content is revealed by *what* the person focuses upon. The process is the structure through which the technique carries out its intention. They are inseparable, two sides of the same coin. Likewise, they are inseparable from the context in which the approach is utilized. It is a fundamental principle across therapies that unless the context fully supports its use, a technique does not matter much. All therapists learn this the hard way when they try a technique they learned and it falls flat. The power to get better, or to become enlightened, or to integrate levels of consciousness is not in the technique. That is why it is so important to examine where and when a technique is introduced to the client, the way it is introduced, what it promises, how it is delivered, and how it is absorbed by the client. These are factors we will explore as we consider methods of GMM and hypnosis.

When someone is encouraged to focus on his breathing, as the basis for building a deeper experience of absorption, the content of the approach is the breath. The client becomes aware of the sensory details associated with breathing, such as the rate of inhaling and exhaling, the volume of air taken in and released, the location of the breath (whether at the nostrils or in the chest or diaphragm), the temperature of the breath, and so forth. These sensory details can easily occupy the person's awareness as it flitters from one sensory experience to another, all a part of being in the moment.

At the process level, though, the person is encouraged to focus attention on an internal experience. The content is what is focused on, which naturally varies from technique to technique: One can focus internally on the taste and texture of food in one's mouth if one wants to learn to eat mindfully; one can focus internally on emotions that surface in response to different images or thoughts that pass through awareness if one wants to become more emotionally present; or one can focus internally on sensations changing in location or intensity if one strives to better manage pain mindfully. What you focus on is vital, for it is unquestionably true that what you focus on defines the quality of your experience.

Consider how direction and intensity of focus shape experience. How often is it the case that what clients focus on actually works against them? The examples are as endless as the problems that drive people into therapy: Someone focuses on feelings of helplessness and thereby misses opportunities to take steps to help himself. Someone else focuses on how terribly risky it feels to meet someone new and try to engage her in light conversation and thereby suffers the despair of a self-imposed loneliness. Someone else focuses on the "feeling in the moment" and does reckless, impulsive things she and others later regret. What you focus on and what you are aware of matter.

Are Focus and Awareness Good for You?

From the above discussion, it is evident that focus is not innately a good thing. What makes focus potentially a very good thing is that it allows engaging with something that serves to enhance experience. The process has to be both conceptually and pragmatically sound, and the content has to be consistent with and serve the aims of the process. It is not that focus itself is hazardous; rather it is the direction and intensity of focus that can work either for or against someone.

One of the most valuable principles I learned early in my therapy career has been affirmed over and over again through the years: Anything that has the potential to help people inevitably has the potential to hurt them as well. Whether it is medication, surgery, cognitive therapy, psychoanalysis, imagery, hypnosis, or mindfulness, the potential exists for untoward effects. Iatrogenesis, that is, people getting worse as a result of treatment, is always a possibility.

Ronald Siegel (2010), author of *The Mindfulness Solution*, candidly described how some clients react poorly to mindfulness exercises. He described a person who, instructed by the therapist to focus on silence, suffered a panic attack only 3 minutes into the process. Similarly, there are individuals with a history of trauma who, when encouraged to close their eyes and go inside, practically bolt out of the chair. As soon as quiet or an internal focus is suggested, some people immediately return to and get overwhelmed by their source of distress, such as a traumatic episode. As clinicians we can help people stay with and work through such reactions, and they can become therapeutically valuable. In fact, many therapists work in just this way. However, these reactions are often preventable. I would suggest that the less therapists are bound to specific techniques and the more they understand the process and content of their techniques, the better they can tailor their approaches to the unique needs of the individuals they treat.

I have seen too little consideration of the structure of the methods of mindfulness, unlike the methods of hypnosis, which have been picked apart mercilessly in a legitimate effort to understand how hypnosis works. So much of the mindfulness literature repeats the same positive and inspiring general philosophical principles that reveal far too little about what actually makes mindfulness tick. And someone who wants to find out more may be accused of "not getting it." I have faced this criticism and expect to face more of it in the future. I think I *do* get it just fine, actually. I just get it from a different point of view. Here is some of what I think I understand: Human beings get into frames of mind that regulate their physiology, belief system, and behavior. One person prays and feels the love of Jesus, while another meditates and feels the Buddha within, while another takes a walk through the forest and feels the presence of the Earth Spirit.

These are all content differences, how our beliefs shapes our lives from our neurophysiology to our emotions. The fact that humans feel a need to believe is what is interesting. One belief system may seem more noble than another, or more spiritually advanced, but this is based on subjective reactions that divide people. I admire the Dalai Lama for saying, "Whether one believes in a religion or not, and whether one believes in rebirth or not, there isn't anyone who doesn't appreciate kindness and compassion" (1998, p. 69). Mindfulness and hypnosis are two approaches among many that can be structured to promote kindness and compassion.

Changing Beliefs: An Example of an Extremely Radical Acceptance

How quickly people can change their beliefs and lives in dramatic ways with a new piece of information or a new experience! Here's an amazing story to illustrate: Two Polish people, Pawel and Ola, were the subject of a CNN documentary (CNN International, 2010). The two met at school as early adolescents and, despite their young age, fell in love. They married at age 18. Ola joined Pawel's world, the world of violent neo-Nazi skinheads. The two committed terrible acts of violence and abuse against Jews.

As CNN stated, "In the Communist era, many families did not tell their children about their Jewish heritage fearing retribution." Ola's mother had mentioned to her at age 13 something about her having Jewish roots but, she said, "It went over my head." Years later, with the faint memory somewhere in the back of her mind, she went to the Jewish Historical Institute to look up family records and found out what she most dreaded: she was Jewish. She feared telling Pawel, but did so, creating doubts in his mind about his own heritage. Remarkably, in looking up his family history, he discovered that he was Jewish, too! As a skinhead, he said he was sure "Jews were the biggest plague and the worst evil of this world." Now, both 33, Pawel and Ola have not only embraced their Jewish identity but have become Orthodox Jews active in their local synagogue. What does this say about the capacity for change? The power of hidden identity? The ability to redirect the zeal of a neo-Nazi into a complete commitment to Judaism? Same process, different content. (It is a bit melodramatic, I admit, but what if mindfulness looked up its history and found hypnosis lurking in its background?)

Philosophers, religious experts, and psychologists have studied how changes in viewpoint occur. Hypnosis holds a special fascination for many because it can demonstrate how beliefs can change relatively quickly in response to beneficial suggestive procedures. Studying the intricacies of hypnosis has also taught us that every method is potentially valuable somewhere with someone, but not everywhere with everyone. In fact, many variables determine how appropriate or effective a particular intervention will be, ranging from its conceptual and linguistic structures to the person's expectations to the person's capacities for focus, frustration tolerance, and dissociation, as well as other variables we'll explore later. Knowing the factors that can contribute to a method's success increases the likelihood of applying that method successfully.

Focus Amplifies Experience . . . Perhaps Superstitiously

The very first principle you learn when you study hypnosis is this: What you focus on, you amplify. If I ask you to be aware of the sensations right now in your right hand, such as its temperature, the pressure or weight of anything you might be holding, or whatever else you might become aware of related to that hand, you can focus your attention increasingly on that hand and really become aware of it, and while you do so, you have no awareness of your left foot—until I draw your attention to it.

The salient question for any clinician is this: What do you want to focus your client's attention on, and why? It seems like an obvious question for an aware therapist to ask, but is it? When someone has been trained in a particular modality or adopts a particular orientation in psychotherapy, it becomes reflexive to orient the client toward the therapist's preferred focus. Cognitive therapists typically focus on cognition; family therapists usually focus on families; and psychiatrists generally focus on neurochemistry. Are other styles of intervention considered, or do therapists mechanically do the kind of therapy they do? When someone trains to become a trauma specialist and the training mandates focusing on the trauma, reliving the trauma, desensitizing the trauma, and so on, therapists learn the process and use it. When things go well and the client seems to benefit, the value of the process is reaffirmed. But, when things go wrong and the client doesn't benefit, is it the approach that becomes suspect or is it the client? Therapists can easily attribute the lack of success to an unmotivated client, a too severely pathological client, a client with too many secondary gain issues, and so forth. When a therapist adopts a specific modality, it requires an allegiance that may or may not serve the client well.

Why point this out now? If we are going to focus people on developing a mindful orientation—and I think we should—we need to be explicit about the nature of the process of mindfulness, providing a greater insight into its methods so we do not foster rigidity in either ourselves or our clients. For example, we need to be clear that if and when we ring a Tibetan meditation bell to encourage "a sense of arriving" or to signal the start (or end) of a meditative period, the bell is meant to be an associative cue that signals something is expected of the client or student. Thus, the bell is only content. You could just as easily substitute a finger snap, a Led Zeppelin riff, or any other auditory stimulus that the client accepts as a valid signal for shifting and engaging attention. It's not the bell that is significant; rather, what is significant is that a signal suggests to the listener that something important is about to occur. The signal further suggests that he or she pay attention in the manner of the others present or in the manner modeled by the therapist as the right way to respond. The bell offers what is called, in hypnotic terms, an implied directive, an indirect suggestion about how to respond appropriately. In this respect, mindfulness is like every other intervention: a client has to be instructed in the concepts, terminology, rituals, and methods of a particular therapy. Whether it's the willingness to lie down on a couch with the analyst sitting behind you while you describe your dreams or whether it's keeping a daily thought record and catching your cognitive distortions, therapy is a process of absorbing the client in the rules and rituals of a perspective that is expected to help. The more invested someone is in following those rules and rituals, the more likely he or she is to benefit from them: There is evidence that the more demands you make on the client, the better the client's results (Kirsch, 2010).

The Content Can Help You Wonder About the Process

Here's another example of content and process and wondering what works: The "eating meditation" is a common mindfulness meditation strategy used to encourage sensory awareness, especially by those teaching mindful eating (Hanh & Cheung, 2010; Kabat-Zinn, 2002). In this exercise, an individual is given a raisin or an apple to meditate upon, using it to develop a greater awareness of the many sensations one might notice with a food stimulus. Focusing on the content associated with a raisin or apple, one can notice such variables as its texture, smell, and taste. To focus on a raisin is an excellent exercise in striving to maintain a narrow yet comprehensive focus on a specific stimulus for some prescribed length of time. But the raisin is mere content. It wouldn't matter if you used a raisin, an asparagus spear, or a piece of saltwater taffy. Just focusing on the various sensations associated with keeping something edible in your mouth without simply chewing and swallowing it as quickly as usual will have a noticeable and probably therapeutic effect. Is it the increased sensory awareness that is therapeutic, or the interruption of a usual behavioral sequence? Is it meditating on the raisin that is therapeutic in and of itself, or is it the empowering realization in response to the suggestion that one's eating behavior can change followed by a direct experience of deliberately and proactively changing it?

There is a parallel in the world of hypnosis. In the older, traditional practice of hypnosis, many practitioners paid a great deal of attention to the hypnotic induction, the procedure meant to guide someone into the hypnotic experience. They used gadgets to perform the induction, such as the iconic swinging watch or the "hypnodisc," a spiral optical illusion that creates a sense of being drawn in. People mistakenly thought there was something about the swinging watch that induced hypnosis, but the watch is merely a content prop. It would not matter if you dangled a watch in front of the person's face or a picture of Albert Einstein or a toddler's sloppy drawing of a tree. As long as the procedure has face validity, that is, it is accepted as a plausible procedure by the client, then the experiential process can successfully get underway. As research in the domain of hypnosis has already suggested, what makes an induction effective is the client believing it is effective. That is why the number of different types of inductions is virtually unlimited, and they all have the potential to work well with someone.

In the same way a food awareness exercise can be understood from a perspective that emphasizes impulse control, frustration tolerance, a sense of empowerment, and other such personally enhancing factors, hypnotic processes can also be understood in terms of what resources they encourage. In previous books (Yapko, 1992, 2001a, 2003), I have detailed hypnotic processes for building positive expectancy, facilitating flexibility, thinking preventively, and many other core components of psychotherapy. I have made this point many times and in many ways: *Hypnosis cures nothing.* What has the potential to be therapeutic is not the experience of hypnosis. Rather, it is what happens *during* hypnosis that has the potential to establish new subjective associations, new awareness, and new skills, as well as connecting people with dormant personal resources.

Similarly, it is not mindfulness that is therapeutic; rather, it is what happens during mindfulness that has potential therapeutic value. The new, helpful associations made during mindful experiences are what matter. Is mindfulness still valuable if it is separated from Buddhist philosophy and embedded in clinical work? Of course. Is mindfulness still valuable if it is integrated into, say, a cognitive therapy program where people learn to develop a sense of control over the rate, direction, and quality of their thoughts? Of course. Mindfulness-based cognitive therapy (Segal, Williams, & Teasdale, 2002) is already an established approach training patients to "disengage from dysphoria-activated depressogenic thinking" (Teasdale et al., 2000, p. 615).

Realizing GMM has structural components (e.g., suggestions, expectations) that make it effective strips away the necessity of conducting the traditional rituals of the procedure and allows us instead to distill the essence of the approach into something more malleable. The distillation process is complicated and inevitably involves some degree of interpretation, giving rise to an array of differing viewpoints. That is as it should be. Many of these viewpoints can be examined in the research context as different methods are broken into component parts and studied for their relative contribution to the overall result. One of the most compelling studies in recent years did exactly this with CBT. Neil Jacobson and his colleagues (1996) conducted a study of the effective ingredients of CBT for depression. They separated changes in cognition from changes in behavior, analyzed them, and argued convincingly that what made CBT effective was *not* specific cognitive changes, as was generally assumed. In fact, the analysis showed that the cognitive component added little to the overall treatment of depression. Rather, they concluded that it was the activation of purposeful and goal-oriented behavior. Subsequent research has shown that therapeutic change is likely to be greater in those therapies that employ homework (such as practicing mindfulness or self-hypnosis) than in those that do not (Burns & Spangler, 2000; Detweiler-Bedell & Whisman, 2005).

The unanswered questions about the components of mindfulness make it difficult to identify the core ingredients of its effectiveness. How important is the preliminary explanation about the Buddhist origins of mindfulness before conducting GMM? How important is the use of specific language that encourages acceptance and even forgiveness to someone in a meditative state? How important is the timing of suggestions during the meditative experience? As we learn more about what meditating brains look like, and as we learn more about the language of GMM and the shifts in subjective phenomenology it elicits, we will evolve much greater insight into what makes these methods valuable.

Marsha Linehan may well be correct that the benefit of mindfulness is exposure. She said, "The non-spiritual mindfulness works for a number of reasons: it is exposure to your Self, your thoughts, feelings, etc. You learn to be less reactive to what's going on. . . . Mindfulness in that sense leads to more effective behavior" (L. Zeig, 2010, p. 24). When so many different pathways are available to attain "exposure to your Self," then why use mindfulness? More to the point, how does such exposure lead to less reactivity and more effective behavior? Is it through a neural rewiring? A belief that the procedure will work? A desire to please the therapist? Acquisition of specific skills? Some combination of these and perhaps other factors as well?

The same kinds of questions have been asked of hypnosis and addressed in the literature for many decades. In the same way that there are mindfulness scripts that provide specific wording for therapists to employ (as in Chapter 3), there are hypnosis scripts by the thousands. There are scripts addressing common problems such as smoking, and uncommon ones such as attaining enlightenment. Too many practitioners have been remarkably literal, telling their clients to close their eyes and then surreptitiously reaching into a drawer to pull out a script to read. Such a practice presupposes that the "magic" is in the incantation: say these words in this sequence and presto!, your client will be transformed. Highly experienced practitioners of hypnosis still argue for and against the use of such scripts. I argue against them.

Is the power of hypnosis in the words? If the same words are spoken to 10 different clients, will they all react in the same way? Of course not. Telling 10 different people the same thing as if they are all the same simply because they all happen to share the same problem misses the chance to respond to the uniqueness of each person. This speaks to the main reason why getting to the essence of an approach is so important: We can vary the content according to individual needs when we understand the essential process. If you are my new depressed client and I want to tell you that your hopelessness is unrealistic, how can I phrase it in a way that you will actually hear? I cannot make you hear it, to be sure, but I can certainly strive to adapt my message to your self-image, view of the world, information processing style, and many other such factors I will explore later to increase the likelihood that you will be able to absorb my message.

This is what the study of hypnosis is about. The purpose of hypnosis is to create a context in which the client can become absorbed and explore new awareness and new possibilities for transforming his or her experience, usually without judgment but always with a direction. Isn't this immediately relevant to the effective use of mindfulness? In mindfulness, we strive to create a context in which the person can become sufficiently engaged in the process of developing awareness to achieve a comfort with his or her deeper self, accomplished through a variety of mechanisms that involve exposure, acceptance, detachment, and so on. When we examine the roles of context, the therapeutic alliance, expectations, how and when meditative processes are introduced, and the language used, we enter the domain of hypnotic inquiry. Hypnosis has extensively studied many of the phenomena associated with therapeutic influence, which are the subject matter of this book as I explore their relevance to the wonderful practice of mindfulness.

CHAPTER 2

Suggestion: The Catalyst of Experiential Methods

The influence of hypnosis upon all forms of therapy has not been fully appreciated. It can be argued that most therapeutic approaches have their origins in that art. . . . Out of hypnotic training comes skill in observing people and the complex ways they communicate, skill in motivating people to follow directives, and skill in using one's own words, intonations, and body movements to influence other people. Also out of hypnosis come a conception of people as changeable, an appreciation of the malleability of space and time, and specific ideas about how to direct people to become more autonomous.

Jay Haley in *Uncommon Therapy* (1973/1986, p. 19)

Every clinician has had the experience of applying a specific technique to a client, presumably with some forethought about its relevance and purpose, only to have the technique fall flat. A key lesson from such disappointing outcomes is that however valuable the technique might be, the power to effect therapeutic change is not found in the technique alone. GMM and clinical hypnosis may be great approaches, but not to a disinterested client. The power of the technique exists in the complex relationship between the technique and the context in which it is applied.

Suggesting a Technique in Context

The context encompasses a broad array of variables that will influence what happens, including how and when the technique is introduced, how noisy or quiet the environment is, the motivation of the client to participate, the client's previous history with such methods, whether the client is alone or part of a group, the client's expectations regarding treatment in general and any one technique in particular, the client's beliefs, the way the therapy relationship is defined, how strong the therapeutic alliance is, and many other personal, interpersonal, and contextual factors. In delivering a therapeutic message to a client, the clinician has to find a way to structure the message that increases the chances the client will be able to absorb it. Offering possibilities is the suggestive core of any—and *every*—approach to treatment. Science may validate approaches, but the artistry of therapy is in the delivery—the specific words, phrases, and gestures you employ—with a specific client. To be clear, I am addressing interpersonal applications (i.e., GMM and clinical hypnosis sessions conducted by a therapist). There are points relevant to intrapersonal applications (personal meditations and self-hypnosis) as well, but the primary focus here is on what happens when a therapist suggests possibilities to a client in the course of clinical interaction.

GMM and clinical hypnosis are *highly* suggestive experiential procedures. Any practitioner who employs these methods naturally suggests that the client develop a certain quality of experience, such as focus, relaxation, acceptance, or compassion. The clinician offers both information and perspective to the client that will inevitably serve to either enhance or diminish the client's ability to respond meaningfully. The information and perspective are typically entirely positive in their intent: They are meant to foster growth on many different levels, and they are meant to reaffirm the power of the individual to live life more fully and satisfyingly. How does suggestion play a role in these endeavors? What determines the likelihood of someone responding in the desired direction or, more ominously, in an antitherapeutic (iatrogenic) direction? In this chapter, I explore the nature of suggestion and the phenomenon of human suggestibility as they relate to the skilled practice of GMM and clinical hypnosis.

The phrase "the power of suggestion" has been used in a wide variety of contexts ranging from commercial product advertising to hypnotically based psychotherapy. Whereas most people seem to have a general, intuitive sense of what the power of suggestion might be like, the more subtle aspects of suggestion often go unappreciated and even unrecognized in the course of treatment by many health professionals. The power of suggestion is especially likely to be underestimated by those who have not studied this phenomenon in depth, which can lead them to form erroneous explanations regarding therapeutic outcomes. Likewise, therapists may incorrectly think of hypnosis as somehow separate from other more ordinary interactions:

> Most people, including many clinically trained professionals, think of hypnosis as a special situation unlike other situations in life. People untrained in hypnosis think of it as a procedure in which a hypnotist says "Relax" and the subject goes to "sleep," and then suggestions are given to him. Or a subject is asked to look at a light or an object and is told that his eyelids will get heavy and he will go to sleep. The naïve person thinks that unless such a ritual is followed, there is no hypnosis. . . . As the word "hypnosis" is used here, it does not apply to a ritual but to a type of communication between people. (Haley, 1973/1986, pp. 19–20)

Suggestion Can Be Misapplied

Let me give you a powerful example of the phenomenon of suggestibility and its potential untoward effects. I am deliberately starting with an example that does not flatter the therapy field for a reason: suggestion is indeed powerful, but it is not innately benevolent. Someone can have positive intentions yet catalyze negative outcomes through the misapplication of suggestion. If we are to apply clinical hypnosis and GMM in truly therapeutic ways, we must openly acknowledge our suggestive role in the process and accept—and strive to eliminate—the potential for misapplication. Mindfulness does not escape this truth any more than hypnosis does. The goal is to use suggestion skillfully without a strong commitment to a particular theory or philosophy that may or may not be helpful to an individual.

An example of the misguided use of suggestion concerns what many came to call the "memory wars," which began noisily in the mid-1980s and reached a deafening crescendo in the mid-1990s. As therapists became more sensitive to the issue of childhood sexual abuse, a phenomenon that had historically and incorrectly been considered rare, the theory took hold that repressed memories of abuse were the likely basis for a wide variety of presenting problems. Seemingly credible experts suggested that people tend to dissociate when traumatized and that dissociation would fuel repression of the abuse as a coping mechanism, thus leaving the victim with no conscious recollection of any abuse having taken place. The only evidence would be unexplained symptoms that the savvy therapist would identify as signs of repressed memories and, therefore, evidence of abuse that had been buried. Therapy, as the logic went, would need to recover these repressed memories (i.e., bring them into conscious awareness) and work through them (Yapko, 1994).

So therapists used a variety of highly suggestive methods (such as hypnosis, guided imagery, visualization, and unreliable symptom checklists) to uncover repressed memories as a means of promoting resolution of the presenting symptoms. Though their intentions were presumably benevolent, the effect was to lead literally thousands of people to believe they were abused when no such abuse had actually taken place. Too many therapists had absolutely no idea that by digging for memories of abuse, they could, through suggestion, *create* them. They mistakenly thought they were simply uncovering what was hidden, not suggesting anything of consequence. Thus, when framed dogmatically by ignorant clinician-believers as "hidden truth," the extraordinary stories of sexual abuse that seemed to come from somewhere deep inside themselves led many trusting and vulnerable individuals to believe they were abused, had participated in ritualistic murders as part of a satanic cult, and much more. Suggested memories were *experienced* as true because the memories were vividly detailed, emotionally powerful, and plausibly explained symptoms not as easily explainable in another way. Families were splintered in the wake of horrific allegations, and individual lives were torn apart as people came to adopt a new self-definition as abuse survivors.

The fact that people got worse as a result of such treatment finally led to the explosion of research that made it apparent even to those invested in such approaches that people could be gently and gradually convinced through suggestion to have richly detailed and highly emotional memories for things that never happened. Judging by the sharp drop in lawsuits filed on the basis of repressed memories, it seems most therapists have learned to treat these delicate issues with greater objectivity and a more sensible caution.

Suggestion is, indeed, powerful. It holds the potential to transform peoples' lives for better—or worse. By studying the dynamics of suggestion, the primary research domain of clinical hypnosis, we have the opportunity to better understand how the language we use affects people, potentially catalyzing remarkable results such as relief from anxiety, depression, or pain. We can develop the means to better understand how the philosophy of an approach gets translated into the specific language a practitioner uses when applying its methods. By evolving the artistry of suggestion, addressing the personal, interpersonal, and contextual dimensions that affect a technique's chances for success, techniques can be better fitted to individuals and thereby increase their chances for success. We want to avoid our clients becoming more mindful—of failing.

Defining Suggestion and the Therapeutic Relationship

A suggestion can be defined as any communication device that is intended—directly or indirectly—to influence a specific outcome or response. For example, consider the open-ended suggestion to "experience fully whatever comes up," a specific type of suggestion called a presupposition because it presupposes something will come up. If I tell you, "Other clients I've treated with the same symptoms as yours all benefited greatly from practicing mindfulness," I am using indirect suggestion. The things we routinely say to each other in our interactions ("We saw this great movie" or "That restaurant was great") are suggestive.

Thus suggestion is virtually inevitable in most human interactions but is especially prominent in the context of psychotherapy. Every form of psychotherapy, even if it is nonverbal, is necessarily suggestive. As soon as a relationship is defined as therapeutic, with one person in the role of clinician and the other in the role of client or patient, there is a suggestion that this relationship has a purpose, namely to be of help to the client. The suggestion is usually explicit, but in some approaches may only be implied, that "this approach to treatment will help you."

Suggestions can be interpersonal, as in psychotherapy, where influence is an obvious goal. Suggestions can also be intrapersonal, focusing oneself on whatever is deemed likely to be helpful. Whether it is structured as a quiet meditation focusing on self-suggesting a sense of stillness for the purpose of self-calming or greater self-acceptance, or structured as a focused internal dialogue about changing one's reactions to some troublesome situation, the suggestions are clearly intended to help empower the self. Such suggestions are in line with what is commonly referred to in the literature as emotional self-regulation. For approaches that incorporate mindfulness into their treatment plans, such as acceptance and commitment therapy, dialectical behavior therapy, cognitive control training, and mindfulness-based cognitive therapy, the mindfulness exercises are a vehicle for evolving skills that make emotional self-regulation possible.

In Chapter 1, I described the merits of focusing and suggested directly that the process of focusing was more important than the content. Whether a therapeutic approach encourages no thoughts or deep thoughts, a quiet mind or a mind full of great possibilities, a focus on breathing or a focus on the vivid memory of a favorite place, the benefit across these varied experiential approaches is remarkably similar. The content may differ from approach to approach, but the process of suggesting absorption and faith in some methodology does not. The barely disguised suggestion is, "Believe and you will be healed [improved, better, happier, more attuned, enlightened, etc.]." When a client turns a belief in the healing potential of a treatment into an actual healing response, we see the powers of suggestion and expectancy at work, the foundation of the well-known placebo response. When it works in the reverse direction, that is, negative suggestions and expectancy that leads to a worsening of some condition, we see the nocebo response.

I think I learned this important lesson about the power of suggestion the hard way, as many clinicians do. I have had the good fortune in my life, especially in the earlier days of my training, to study psychotherapy methods with many of the best theorists and clinicians who ever walked this earth, famous therapy pioneers whose names are instantly recognizable to serious students of therapy. In awe, intimidated by their prestige and reputations, I strived to be a good student and learn well the intricacies of their approaches. At first, though, doing so posed a serious challenge simply because of how far apart the experts were in what they thought the proper focus of therapy should be. One told me to focus on people's feelings and another told me to focus on their cognitions. One told me to focus on the body, another on the mind. One said the key to change is in the person's past, but another said the future holds the key.

Yet when I watched highly credible experts do therapeutic magic with their clients, it became apparent that each approach was valuable despite having entirely different and even contradictory focal points. Each model worked, at least often enough to justify learning something about it. Each therapist could cite impressive recent data affirming its therapeutic efficacy. And each therapist initially offered the client the suggestion, "This approach works and so you can expect it to work for you." It became ever clearer to me that there are *many* right ways to do therapy. The therapeutic efficacy literature verifies this point. It also became clear to me that the more skillfully an approach employed the power of suggestion, the better it performed.

Human Suggestibility

Is suggestibility an individual personality trait that exists in stable form across different contexts? Or is it determined by additional factors beyond the person's capacity to respond to suggestion, such as the salience of a suggestion or the demeanor of the person who offers it?

My response to these important questions is *both*: Suggestibility in a general sense is relatively stable over time. But in a particular context, such as a clinical interaction, suggestibility is mediated by a variety of personal, social, and situational factors that can increase or decrease someone's responsiveness. The field of social psychology in particular offers many valuable insights into the dynamics of interpersonal influence that are immediately relevant to the clinical context in general and to the use of GMM and clinical hypnosis in particular. Social psychology evolved out of the recognition that people will do things when they are alone that they will not do if even one other person is around. An individual's behavior changes in the presence of another individual, often in systematic and predictable ways.

What is the role of suggestibility in GMM and hypnosis? It is an openness to accepting new ideas, a willingness to absorb new information or perspectives. Furthermore, it is a focused capacity to translate these ideas into suggested responses, what in hypnotic terms are called ideodynamic responses. These are unconscious responses on motoric, sensory, affective, and cognitive levels that arise as the individual attends to and processes the offered suggestions. Suggesting someone's breathing can slow down can easily translate into an actual physical slowing of respiration without conscious effort. Few people are completely noncritical in accepting information, so there is an important difference between suggestibility and gullibility. Let's briefly consider key aspects of social influence as they relate to utilizing GMM and clinical hypnosis in therapy.

Uncertainty Elevates Suggestibility

Both social psychology and common sense have taught us that when we experience uncertainty, other people become very important to us as sources of information. When we are not sure what to do or how to regard something that has happened, we are likely to adopt the perspectives of others who seem to have a higher level of certainty. This is why we turn to experts for advice to help us reduce our own anxious uncertainty. It is why we turn to friends, for example, to observe their reactions when we are not sure if something is funny. This principle is a robust finding in social psychological research.

Increased conformity in the face of uncertainty is immediately relevant to the clinical context regardless of what method a clinician employs. However, in more abstract, subjective realms of human experience, especially mindfulness and hypnosis, ambiguity is even greater. Clients exposed to GMM and clinical hypnosis routinely wonder, "Is this it? Am I in hypnosis now? Am I meditating correctly? Is this what it's supposed to feel like?" If you choose to answer directly by saying, "Yes, that was it," and give specific indicators by saying something such as, "Did you notice the changes in your breathing? And the changes in your musculature? And how relaxed you felt?" then quite probably the client will adopt your apparently expert perspective on the ambiguous interaction as if it were his or her own. The need for certainty and the need to have a perceptual frame into which the experience can be integrated may motivate the person to simply accept your explanation of the ambiguous hypnotic or meditative experience.

Clinician Power

The person seeking help has already accepted (or at least acknowledged) his own ignorance and powerlessness about the problem, and with a strong sense of hope, the therapist is looked to as the person who can make the hurt go away. In the face of uncertainty about what to do, the clinician is turned to for expert guidance.

When someone comes for help to deal with a distressing problem, that person is making an investment in the clinician as a person of authority and, hopefully, a source of relief. Where does the power of a clinician come from? The status of the therapist or the supporting institution is one key factor, and his or her perceived expertness is another. Probably the greatest source of power, however, is the social role of the therapist; the relationship between a clinician and a client is generally not one of equals (Spinelli, 1994; Szasz, 2010). The person coming in for help must divulge personal and sensitive information to someone about whom he or she knows very little—only his or her professional status and, for the more inquisitive, academic background and clinical training.

Social psychology suggests there are at least five different types of power: (1) coercive (derived from the ability to punish); (2) reward (derived from the ability to give benefits ranging from monetary to psychological); (3) legitimate (derived from position, including elected and selected positions); (4) expert (derived from greater knowledge in an area); and (5) referent power (derived from personal characteristics, such as likeability or charisma) (Aronson, Wilson, & Akert, 2009; Yapko, 2003). All five of these powers may be operational in almost any context to one degree or another, but they are especially prevalent in the therapeutic context, particularly when employing gentle, supportive, client-centered experiential methods that can lull the client into a higher level of vulnerability.

The power (i.e., potential for influence) of a clinician in the therapeutic relationship must be acknowledged. The capacity for influence in the principles and techniques of mindfulness and clinical hypnosis must lead each of us to consider the phenomenon of power in relationships if we are to use power sensitively for the benefit of the client. Therapists who deny their power to influence and see themselves as separate from the client's treatment process, as if higher awareness magically occurs without the therapist suggesting it, are at the highest risk for being oblivious to their impact on the client.

The Need for Acceptance

Recognizing and respecting the client's need for acceptance is an important factor to consider in addressing the issues of whether and to what degree the client conforms to the demands of clinical intervention. How far is your client willing to go to get your approval? No clinical context can fully avoid what are known as the demand characteristics of treatment, but an aware clinician can strive to foster less compliance and more internalization on the part of the client.

Expectations

The power of expectation has been demonstrated in numerous contexts and called by many names, and virtually all models of psychotherapy emphasize the value of positive expectations in enhancing treatment results. In the realm of psychotherapy, this has been known a long time.

Expectations can work either for or against attaining desired therapeutic outcomes, depending on their positive or negative quality. In clinical practice, people may seek you out because they have been referred by someone else you impressed, increasing the odds of your being able to impress them, too. Or someone has a positive expectation because of your affiliation with an institution he or she holds in high esteem, or because of your title and status, or for any of dozens of possible reasons. Unfortunately, people can also develop negative expectations for equally arbitrary reasons: They don't like your gender, your age, your walk, the institution you work for, the length of time they had to wait to see you, and on and on. Addressing the issue of expectations—both yours and the client's—makes good clinical sense.

Experiential responses are especially heavily influenced by the client's beliefs and expectations. Thus, for the client, a good hypnotic induction or mindfulness exercise is simply one that the client *believes* is good. It is subjectively understood and experienced (Kirsch, 1990). What it takes to build positive expectations for treatment in a person varies from individual to individual. Skillfully finding out what a person needs to build positive expectations can be a major catalyst to getting the therapeutic process going in a helpful direction.

Communication Style

Your style of communication is another significant factor shaping the quality of your client's suggestibility. By communication style, I refer to the manner in which you convey information and possibilities to your client. A clinician who wants to get a message across must consider what style of communication the client is most likely to respond to in the desired way. The structures and styles of suggestions are dealt with in great detail later in this chapter; suffice it to say here that there are many ways to package ideas, and no single style is going to be effective with everyone. The process of discovering what your client wants and how best to reach him or her is part of the process of building the therapeutic alliance, the relationship between you that serves as the foundation for the experiential techniques you may eventually introduce in your interventions.

Introducing Mindfulness and Suggestions of Therapeutic Benefit

How you introduce mindfulness and the merits of GMM will undoubtedly influence the client's response to the methods you employ. GMM is typically introduced as a method that is philosophically rooted in ancient Buddhist tradition as well as in religious and philosophical texts. The mindful therapist offers a rationale as to how and why these ancient traditions are immediately relevant, suggesting directly that there is an established link between the methods to be learned and the prospects for symptom improvement. The suggestion is typically clear and explicit in its promise of helpfulness. If the client accepts the suggestion, there is an agreement that the client will participate in the therapist's treatment plan involving mindful approaches. That does not ensure their success, of course, but it does increase the likelihood.

What does an introduction to mindfulness actually sound like? The following is an excerpt from a popular book, *The Mindful Way Through Depression*, which illustrates the skillful introduction of mindfulness to the reader:

> We offer a series of practices that you can incorporate into your daily life to free you from the mental habits that keep you mired in unhappiness. This program . . . brings together the latest understandings of modern science and forms of meditation that have been shown to be clinically effective. . . . These different ways of knowing the mind and the body can help you make a radical shift in your relationship to negative thoughts and feelings. (Williams et al., 2007, pp. 2–3)

When the mindful therapist is educating the client in the treatment philosophy and methods, he or she is building an expectation of treatment success if the client follows the plan. In the example above, the reader is told to expect a "radical shift" based on the "latest understandings of modern science." These are powerful statements for inspiring hopefulness to counter the hopelessness so typical of depression. This expectancy-building approach continues when the authors write, "our hope is that you will discover in this book and the accompanying CD something of potentially enormous value that can help you free yourself from the downward pull of low mood and bring a robust and genuine happiness into your life" (p. 3). What depressed person *wouldn't* want a "robust and genuine happiness"?

The reader is educated to help form the belief that the latest science validates the meditative experiences that will be applied for the purposes of "cultivating attitudes of patience, compassion for yourself, open-mindedness, and gentle persistence. These qualities can aid in freeing you from the 'gravitational pull' of depression" (p. 4). Again, who wouldn't want patience (right now, please!), compassion, open-mindedness, and persistence? And what therapist wouldn't want to learn an approach that promises to provide these benefits, especially one that has empirical support and is growing in popularity?

The suggested benefits add up as the authors write,

> The mindfulness practices taught in this book can help you take a wholly different approach to the endless cycles of mental strategizing ... help you disengage from this entire pattern ... help you let go both of past regrets and worries about the future. It increases mental flexibility ... helping us get back in touch with the full range of our inner and outer resources for learning, growing, and healing, resources we may not even believe we have. (Williams et al., 2007, p. 6)

Therapists across different treatment models may say similar things differently, but *all* provide a series of suggestions that will attempt to lead the client in the direction of cooperating and *expecting a benefit for doing so*. The therapist builds expectancy and thereby motivation to participate. Sometimes the suggestions are quite straightforward, like those above, or they may be a bit convoluted or even incongruent, as we will see later. What is more difficult to tease out is this: How much of the benefit of mindfulness comes from the positive hopes and expectations that accompany its use? This is a suggestive part of mindfulness that is well described in the hypnosis literature in particular, a domain of research that has examined the placebo effect in depth (Barabasz & Watkins, 2005; Benham, Woody, Wilson, & Nash, 2006).

The fact that any treatment model, mindfulness included, must educate the client in the foundations of the model is a given. Here, again, is an excerpt from *The Mindful Way Through Depression* that illustrates this process:

> Curiously enough, our individual lines of research and inquiry led us to examine the clinical use of meditative practices oriented toward cultivating a particular

form of awareness, known as *mindfulness*, which originated in the wisdom traditions of Asia. These practices, which have been part of Buddhist culture for millennia, had been honed and refined for use in a modern medical setting. (Williams et al., 2007, p. 5)

For many people, it would be difficult to flatly negate Buddhism or the ancient practices it teaches, even if their own beliefs differ markedly. How could an individual hope to sensibly counter the collective wisdom of an entire culture, especially one generally known for its spiritual sophistication? How could someone resist powerful methods that have been "honed and refined" by serious-minded clinicians and researchers for the clinical context? The power of such statements, whether verbal or in writing, is evident in the reduced likelihood that the client will reject them and increased likelihood of acceptance. The statements are so persuasive in their unshakeable foundation, so obviously true, how can a client legitimately refute them?

Building the Mindful Response Set Hypnotically

In hypnotic terms, this pattern of suggestion, designed to build higher levels of responsiveness in the client, is called "establishing a response set" (Lynn et al., 2006; Yapko, 2003). A response set is generally considered a core element of good hypnotic procedure. The goal in building a response set is to increase the client's receptivity to suggestions, using different types of suggestion structures such as those described later in this chapter.

The most commonly applied response set in the therapy context is commonly known as the "yes set" (Erickson, Rossi, & Rossi, 1976). It strives to increase client responsiveness, perhaps by offering a series of suggestions called truisms, suggestions that are so obviously true that the client readily agrees with them. Consider these statements:

1. The pace of most people's lives seems to get faster and faster, making it stressful at times to try to keep up.
2. People get caught up in having to do more and more each day just to catch up.
3. It would be valuable to spend less time doing and more time just being.
4. Taking the time to "just be" can allow us to increase our awareness of what we are experiencing right now.

5. Becoming more aware of what we're experiencing right at this moment can allow us to feel connected to something greater.

Did you find yourself silently agreeing with each statement as you read it (saying yes)? Did you notice that as you moved from one statement to the next, momentum began to build for more easily accepting each statement? Each yes increases the chances for another yes with the next statement; hence the term response set. By gradually absorbing the client in a mind-set that will increase the probability of the desired response, a foundation for meaningful interaction is established.

The inevitability of suggestion in GMM—indeed, in *any* approach—must be acknowledged. Consider the role of suggestion at various stages of mindful approaches to treatment: The foundational suggestions in introducing GMM, the suggestions for establishing its relevance for the client, suggesting specific benefits to be obtained, detailing methods to be employed and how they will serve the larger goals of treatment, introducing the specific methods and facilitating guided experience with them, debriefing those methods afterward, and finally reinforcing their potential for having a growing positive impact over time. Let's briefly consider the role of suggestion in hypnosis, and then examine the specific language of suggestion more carefully.

Introducing Hypnotic Approaches and the Suggestions of Benefit

In the same way that a clinician would introduce a GMM by giving it a name, a philosophical or theoretical foundation, an explicit purpose, a methodology, and an expectation, so would a practitioner of hypnosis introduce a clinical hypnosis session. Views and methods of hypnosis vary widely across practitioners, so how a practitioner thinks about the nature of hypnosis will determine to the greatest extent how he or she will apply it.

Are Hypnosis and GMMs Framed Correctly as Therapies?

Hypnosis is generally not considered a therapy, despite the common usage of the term hypnotherapy. Rather, hypnosis is considered a tool of treatment, a focused means for delivering ideas in therapy and facilitating experiential learning. Hypnosis may be applied to advance cognitive behavioral methods, psychodynamic approaches, or some other model of treatment. The fact that hypnosis can be used in an integrative manner with virtually any treatment modality is a testament to its flexibility and emphasis on the inevitable role of suggestion in the delivery of therapy. At the same time, because hypnosis is not a therapy in its own right, people typically ask the sensible but off-target question, "How does hypnosis compare to therapy X, say, for depression?" Instead, the on-target question is, "If we do therapy X without hypnosis, and we do therapy X with hypnosis, does the addition of hypnosis measurably enhance the treatment?" The efficacy research on hypnosis provides broad empirical support for a yes answer (Moore & Tasso, 2008; Lynn, Kirsch, Barabasz, Cardeña, & Patterson , 2000).

Mindfulness has a more coherent philosophical and spiritual base that has explicitly defined its foundational cornerstones of awareness, openness, acceptance, tolerance, and detachment. These underlying principles have been well articulated and have provided a spiritual base for countless people over the millennia. The concept of acceptance, what some Buddhism experts such as Tara Brach (2004) even call "radical acceptance," has been promoted in religious and philosophical texts as old as recorded time, as has the concept of detachment as a means of transcendence. Hypnosis does not use this language, but its underlying principles are identical. The fact that hypnosis has not been connected to a specific religion or philosophy has contributed to it being viewed as separate from rather than part of mainstream experience. Hypnosis has had to work especially hard to prove its relevance.

However, mindfulness is now being adapted to the psychotherapy and behavioral medicine contexts, changing its original spiritual intent to a therapeutic one. Consequently, it too is being compared to therapy X, and it too is being integrated into a wide variety of therapeutic regimens ranging from cognitive-behavioral to psychodynamic. The purity of mindfulness as a path to greater awareness is being diluted as its popularity continues to rise, just as hypnosis was decades ago. While the underlying philosophy of spiritual growth will inevitably lose some of its luster, the practicality and tangible benefits of incorporating such experiential approaches to empower people will, hopefully, grow stronger. The value of acquiring hypnotic skills to conduct GMM should be well recognized if these methods are to endure after the current wave of enthusiasm for all things called mindful inevitably begins to recede.

Introducing Hypnosis to the Client

Hypnosis is typically introduced to the client as a tool of treatment with a long history of efficacy in a wide variety of contexts. One might describe interesting facts about its colorful history or its current pivotal role in shaping neurological and medical scientific inquiry because of the insights it affords us regarding the relationships between mind and brain as well as mind and body. The hypnosis practitioner offers a rationale for how and why hypnosis-generated insights and hypnotic focusing methods are immediately relevant, suggesting a direct link between the hypnotic methods to be experienced and the likelihood of symptom improvement. The suggestion is typically unambiguous in its promise of helpfulness. If the client accepts the suggestion, it implies an agreement has been reached that the client will be an active participant in the therapist's treatment plan.

What might this suggestion for therapeutic improvement actually sound like? Here are two examples. The following is an excerpt from *Essentials of Clinical Hypnosis* by Steven Lynn and Irving Kirsch (2006, p. 34) introducing the client to hypnosis:

> There are two procedures that we can use to help you. . . . One of these is hypnosis . . . [which] involves focusing your attention inward, so that you can make full use of your imaginative abilities. . . . Many people find hypnosis particularly helpful, and there is evidence that it can increase the effectiveness of treatment.

Joseph Barber, PhD, offered the following suggestions for describing hypnosis to pain patients in his book, *Hypnosis and Suggestion in the Treatment of Pain*:

> You probably know that the relationship between mind and body is a powerful one. I can show you how to use the power of your imagination, for instance, to help you feel better. . . . Mental imagery can be very helpful in retraining your nervous system so that the nerves that carry the useless information about your pain will do so less and less in the future. . . . Your ability to become deeply absorbed by your imagination can be really helpful now. (Barber, 1996, p. 23)

Contrary to popular mythology, hypnosis serves to empower people. Hypnosis can be used to suggest whatever one cares to suggest (e.g., a full awareness of this moment, a decreased awareness of an unpleasant sensation) on whatever dimension of experience one cares to address (e.g., cognitive, physiological). The hypnosis suggestions can be scripted, just as mindfulness suggestions can be scripted, but both hypnosis and mindfulness are likely to be more powerful for the individual when they are more personal.

Let's turn our attention now to the various ways suggestions can be structured to promote experiential learning through GMM and clinical hypnosis.

The Specifics of Suggestive Language: Structures and Styles

This section focuses on some of the communication variables of hypnotic patterns, specifically the range of communication styles and structures that can be used to form hypnotic suggestions. Knowing these will be especially helpful when reading the next chapter, which identifies suggestion styles and structures found in GMM.

Suggestions are dynamic, not static, in their structure. They can range across a number of continua, sharing multiple, simultaneous traits. Your suggestions will fit into more than one category, and you will want to move up and down on a particular continuum as you offer a series of suggestions to a client. What are these continua? One continuum of suggestion has positive and negative poles. A second one ranges from direct to indirect. A third continuum includes process and content suggestions. And a fourth continuum has stylistic possibilities ranging from permissive to authoritarian suggestions. In a related but separate category are posthypnotic suggestions, an essential and well-considered part of any experiential clinical intervention. Let's consider each of these categories in turn.

Positive and Negative Suggestions

Positive Suggestions

Positive suggestions are by far the most common, simple, and useful type of suggestion structure. They are supportive and encouraging, and are phrased in such a way as to give the client the idea that he or she can experience or accomplish something desirable. The generic structure for a positive suggestion is, "You can do X." (You will come to recognize this as a permissive suggestion as well.) The following are examples of positive suggestions:

- You can feel more and more comfortable with each breath you take in. (Deepening)
- You can remember a time when you felt very proud of yourself. (Age regression)
- You are able to discover inner strengths you didn't realize you had. (Resource building)
- You can notice how good it feels to relax. (Deepening)
- You may notice a soothing feeling of warmth in your hands. (Sensory alteration)

Negative Suggestions

Negative suggestions employ a sort of reverse psychology approach when used skillfully. Negative suggestions may be used to obtain a response by suggesting the person *not* respond in the desired way. The generic structure for a negative suggestion is, "You cannot do X." If you tell clients what not to do, they still have to process and interpret what you say, and various subjective associations inevitably surface as they do so.

The following are examples of negative suggestions. Notice your internal experience as you read each of them.

- Do not think of your favorite color.
- Do not allow yourself to wonder what time it is.
- I would suggest that you not notice that sensation in your leg.
- You shouldn't be thinking about work right now.
- Please try not to notice the noises in the room.

Did you find yourself doing what was suggested that you not do? If so, why? Quite simply, to make meaning of the words, you have to link the words to the experiences they represent. If I ask you not to think of the taste of pizza, don't you have to first think of it before attempting to erase it from your mind?

You can offer negative suggestions that suggest what you want by skillfully suggesting against it: "Don't think about enjoying the experience of stillness just yet. . . . Don't let your mind grow quiet right away. . . . First notice the easy comfort of breathing."

Direct and Indirect Suggestions

Hypnotic communications can be structured in direct and indirect forms. Not only are they not mutually exclusive, but it is neither possible nor desirable to do an effective experiential process exclusively in one form or the other. Realistically, both styles will be evident in a given process at various times. Furthermore, each suggestion will vary in the degree of directness. Which style to use at a given moment depends on the suggestion's complexity, novelty, potential for raising the client's anxiety or defenses, and the degree of responsiveness of the client.

Direct Suggestions

Direct suggestions deal with the problem at hand or the specific response desired overtly and clearly. Direct suggestions provide specific directions as to how to respond. Consequently, they are not known for being subtle. The generic structure for a direct suggestion, shared with positive suggestions, is, "You can do X." The content of a direct suggestion can vary within this generic structure, depending on your specific word choice.

To initiate the mindfulness or hypnosis session, the clinician will typically suggest that the client close his or her eyes. A clinician who chooses a direct approach might offer any of the following direct suggestions:

- Close your eyes.
- Please close your eyes.
- You can close your eyes.
- Let your eyes close.
- I would like you to close your eyes now.

Each of these suggestions directly relates to closed eyes as a specific response. There is no mistaking what the clinician wants the client to do. The same direct suggestion structures, by changing their content (i.e., associated details) might be used to obtain virtually any desired response:

- You can detach from your thoughts and let them float by like clouds in the sky. (Cognitive dissociation)
- You can go back in your memory and remember when you went to your first school dance. (Age regression)
- Focus on your breathing, feeling how your chest rises and falls with each breath. (Sensory association)
- You will be able to make your hand pleasantly numb in the next few seconds. (Analgesia)
- Experience each minute as if it were an hour. (Time distortion)

The desired response in each of these examples is apparent because the suggestions directly ask for it. Nothing is hidden from the client. Each suggestion is intended to generate a specific response.

Indirect Suggestions

Indirect suggestions relate to the problem at hand or the specific desired response in a covert or, at least, less obvious way. They can be quite subtle and thereby escape full awareness and analysis. Such suggestions usually do not relate directly to the person's conscious experience. Because they are indirectly related, they require the client to interpret them in a proactive and idiosyncratic way to make meaning of them. Indirect suggestions can take numerous forms, including storytelling, analogies, jokes, puns, homework assignments, role modeling, and disguised and embedded suggestions. Any communication device that causes or requires clients to respond without directly telling or asking them to do so involves some degree of indirect suggestion. Zen stories and koans are also good examples.

The generic structure of an indirect suggestion is, "I knew someone who experienced X." By talking about someone else or some other situation, a meaningful response (e.g., developing an insight, modifying a perspective) is indirectly invited. Use of indirect suggestions can have the client wondering what you are talking about, or perhaps may simply occupy (amuse, entertain, fascinate) the person at a conscious level, while at the same time unconscious associations are generated that can pave the way for changes to take place.

Indirect suggestion is a focal point of study in the utilization approach to hypnosis, largely due to the many creative ways it was used by pioneering psychiatrist Milton H. Erickson, MD. Erickson's therapeutic effectiveness with hypnosis and indirect suggestions has inspired intensive analysis of his methods and helped establish an appreciation for the merits of indirect approaches.

When you read Erickson's fascinating and unusual cases, you will find that many of his ingenious hypnotic and strategic interventions were so indirect, they seemed to have absolutely no relationship to the presenting complaint. The indirect approach was developed as a means to bypass resistance or the self-imposed limitations of the client's perspective. If you suspect, on the basis of feedback from your client (perhaps by observing hesitation or ambivalence about participating), that you would be more likely to get closed eyes through indirect methods, then you might offer any of the following suggestions:

• A responsive client usually begins the hypnotic experience by closing his eyes.
• I wonder just how soon you'll allow your eyes to close.
• Many of my clients like to sit there with their eyes closed.
• Isn't it nice not to have to listen with your eyes open?
• Have you ever noticed how you can focus more easily when your eyes are closed?

Each of these examples seeks closed eyes as a specific response, but does not ask for it directly. As with closed eyes, indirect suggestions can be varied in content to obtain virtually any response:

• I was lying on the grass in the park, watching the clouds go by. One was shaped like self-doubt and as I watched it sail by my indecision went with it. (Cognitive dissociation)
• A close friend of mine has a daughter who went to her first school dance, and I don't know if you can remember yours, but it sure was an exciting time for her. (Age regression)
• I was watching a hawk riding the thermals, the hot air that rises and cools and falls as if the earth itself were breathing in and out at a slow and steady rate. (Sensory association)
• Can you imagine what it's like to have a barehanded snowball fight and have so much fun making and throwing snowballs you forget to notice you aren't even wearing gloves? (Analgesia)
• Meditators often say that time is so difficult to keep track of because a minute of deep absorption can seem like 5 or 10 minutes or sometimes even longer. (Time distortion)

In each of the above examples, someone else's experience seems to be the focal point, rather than the client's experience, or the suggestion seems so general as to be impersonal and therefore not requiring a direct response. It is up to the client to adapt in unique ways to the *possibilities* for certain responses raised by the clinician's suggestion. In this way, direct commands for obedience are avoided, and the therapist taps the client's creative ability to form an individualized response.

Content and Process Suggestions

How general or detailed should suggestions be? This next continuum of suggestion structures addresses this issue.

Content Suggestions

Content suggestions contain highly specific details describing feelings, memories, thoughts, or fantasies the client is to experience during hypnosis. Providing details of the suggested experience can assist the client to have a fuller experience.

The generic structure for content suggestions is, "You can focus on these specific details." Examples of content suggestions may include:

- Think of a red rose with soft, velvet petals you can lightly brush against your nose as you inhale its gentle, sweet fragrance.
- Imagine being at the beach on a bright, clear day, feeling the sun warming your skin, smelling the salt in the ocean breeze, and hearing the lapping of the waves upon the shore.
- Can you remember how pleasing it is to bite into a juicy, wet orange, how your mouth waters, how the juice feels as it runs all over your fingers, and how sweet it tastes?

Each of these examples provides specific details about exactly what you are to experience in thinking of a rose, the beach, and an orange. Perhaps those details allowed you to experience the suggestion more fully, in which case they were helpful. However, these examples also illustrate a potential hazard in using content-filled suggestions, namely that the details I directed you to notice may not be the ones you would have chosen to focus on. These may even have negated the experience for you. If, for example, when I said "imagine the beach" you recalled a negative experience you had at the beach, or if you have never been at a beach in your life, then the details will lead you to a negative memory or perplex you (since there is no personal experience to relate to my suggestions) and be disruptive.

The potential problem with content suggestions is simply this: The more details you provide, the greater the probability that something you say will contradict your client's experience. The client will sense that the clinician is not really with him or her, and so will be less likely to benefit from the experience. If I suggest a body scan mindfulness exercise and go through naming specific body parts that can each relax (a technique called a progressive relaxation process in the hypnosis literature), this is a content-oriented approach. If we are focusing on the same parts of the body, things will go smoothly. But if I am ahead of or behind where you are in the scan, it may diminish the experience for you.

Process Suggestions

Unlike content suggestions, process suggestions provide minimal details, encouraging the client to provide them. The generic structure for a process suggestion is, "You can have a specific experience" without saying what the specific experience is meant to be. In response to this deliberate ambiguity, the client projects his or her own personal experiences and frame of reference into the suggestion to make meaning of it. Consequently, process suggestions are considerably less likely to contradict the client's experience. For example, if I would like the client to imagine being in a relaxing place, instead of choosing the beach as a specific place to focus on and then providing lots of details (content suggestions) about what it's like to be at the beach, I can simply suggest that my client imagine being somewhere relaxing. I don't say where that place might be, and so the client can choose the specific place and which particular details he or she would like to focus on. Process suggestions are so general in nature that the client can project personal meaning into them and then relate to them in an individual way.

The following are examples of process suggestions:

- You can have a particular memory from childhood, one that you haven't thought about in a long, long time. (Age regression)
- You may notice a certain pleasant sensation developing in your body as you sit there comfortably. (Kinesthetic sensory association)
- You may become aware of a specific sound in the room. (Auditory sensory awareness)
- Your awareness of the special experience of this moment, what is happening right now, is growing more profound. (General awareness)

None of these suggestions specifies anything—that is, they do not say which memory, sensation, sound, or event the client is supposed to experience. The client chooses a meaningful response to the suggestion. Notice, though, the use of qualifiers such as *particular, certain, specific,* and *special* in process suggestions. They can encourage clients to sift their experiences down to a particular one to focus upon. Process suggestions are especially valuable in doing group GMM and hypnosis processes, where it is virtually impossible to observe each individual's responses to content suggestions.

Authoritarian and Permissive Suggestion Styles

Suggestion style refers to the interpersonal demeanor or attitude of the clinician while offering suggestions. It is a reflection of how the clinician defines his or her relationship with the client. This relationship may be cooperative, one of mutual responsiveness between clinician and client, or the clinician may be the expert and the client's job is simply to comply with the clinician's suggestions. Suggestion styles can be described on a continuum with authoritarian at one pole and permissive at the other.

Authoritarian Suggestions

Authoritarian approaches are the ones people tend to think of when they dismiss hypnosis as too imposing an approach. It is easy to appreciate why people dislike such approaches: The suggestions come in the form of commands. They have all the subtlety of a sledgehammer. The generic structure for an authoritarian style is, "You *will* do X." Authority and power are the key variables the clinician relies on, and the response from the good client is compliance. The following suggestions are structured in an authoritarian mode:

- You will close your eyes when I count to three. (Eye closure)
- You must focus on your breathing and nothing else. (Kinesthetic sensory awareness)
- Be aware only of what is going on in your body right now. (Kinesthetic sensory awareness)
- I want you to let every thought pass through you and hold onto none of them. (Cognitive dissociation)

Directing someone to respond in a specific way that minimizes personal choice does not show much respect for that person's needs or wants. Thus, a strictly authoritarian approach should generally be used sparingly. However, it must also be said that some clients want to be told what to do and will react poorly if you seem uncertain or vague.

Permissive Suggestions

At the other end of this continuum is the permissive style, one that is more respectful of clients' ability to make choices on their own behalf about *whether* and *how* to respond. The generic structure for the permissive suggestion is, "You may do X." The clinician offers suggestions of what clients may experience if they choose. The sensibility of a permissive approach is in knowing that you cannot make someone respond (e.g., relax or focus). You can simply suggest possibilities in such a way that clients, hopefully, choose to avail themselves of those possibilities. Permissive suggestions are intended to raise the probability of a response, and the following examples illustrate the point:

- You can allow your eyes to close, if you would like. (Eye closure)
- You may choose to sit up so you can breathe more deeply and easily. (Postural shift and kinesthetic sensory awareness)
- With each breath you take you may find yourself getting more comfortable. (Deepening)
- It's possible to experience your body differently. (Perceptual shift)

In these examples, the client is offered choices and then makes a decision which the therapist graciously accepts. This tactic makes for a gentle, respectful approach in conducting GMM or hypnosis.

Posthypnotic Suggestions

Whether you call it mindfulness or hypnosis, the experience of being focused and experientially absorbed gives rise to certain phenomena that must be considered in treatment planning. One such primary phenomenon is known as state-dependent learning. When people are absorbed in meditative or hypnotic experiences, the unique and subjective experiences they are capable of generating can be profound. Studies have shown, though, that what people learn in one state of awareness may not transfer to other, more ubiquitous states of awareness. Thus, it is important to include in GMM and hypnotic processes a vehicle for helping the information learned in one state (e.g., deep meditation) transfer to other states (e.g., usual or everyday consciousness). Helping with this extension of learning is the goal of the posthypnotic suggestion.

Posthypnotic suggestions, which are given to clients while they are absorbed, help them take what they are learning or experiencing and extend it to some future context. Posthypnotic suggestions have the generic structure, "Later, when you're in situation A, you'll be able to do B." They are a standard part of nearly every therapy session, given that you will almost always want clients to take something away from the session that they can use elsewhere in the course of daily living.

The following are examples of posthypnotic suggestions:

- When you hear the bell and come out of your deep meditation in a few moments, you can have a deep feeling of self-respect for having discovered new abilities in yourself.
- When you begin to take your examination next week, you can close your eyes for a moment that can seem much longer and take a deep breath, and you can notice the anxiety leaving you as you exhale.
- After you go home tonight, you'll recall a forgotten memory that will make you laugh, and it will feel really good to let off some steam in such an enjoyable way.
- When you find yourself in the next argument with your boss, you can pause, take some deep breaths, and feel more centered and calm than you would have expected.
- If at any time you feel that your mind becomes unfocused, discover how easy it is to come back to focusing on the breath and use this focus to regain a sense of stability.

Each of these examples suggests a behavior or feeling the client is to experience in some future time and place based on the suggestions given during the GMM or hypnosis. Interestingly, some clients may have no conscious memory of the origin of the suggestion (amnesia), yet act on it nonetheless. This experience reflects the automaticity referred to earlier that allows changes to occur smooth-ly, even effortlessly.

Conclusion: Being Mindful of Being Hypnotic

Guiding someone through a mindfulness meditation experience or a session of hypnosis requires encouraging an *experiential* response rather than an intellec-tual one. These processes can be a formality that encourages no real shift in ex-perience on the part of the client; one can *do* hypnosis without necessarily *being* hypnotic. One can encourage greater awareness but the client does not neces-sarily become aware of anything significant.

It takes time to cultivate sophistication with suggestion structures and styles as well as comfort with helping people explore the deeper dimensions of their experience, where data and objectivity just don't mean as much. Learning to use sensory-based language, word play, ways to "invite the person more fully into the experience," an acceptance and skill in acknowledging and utilizing indi-vidual differences in response styles, and an attitude of focusing on what's *right* rather than wrong with someone are all core ingredients of these methods. Valuing stillness and respecting the deeper potentials of clients to become "more" is a foundation for creating an environment between the two of you and within each of you that makes these approaches so potentially powerful.

In the next chapter, I will draw your attention to the suggestive aspects of GMM as conducted by practitioners of these approaches. Based on the con-cepts and terminology presented in this chapter, you are now in a comfortable position to recognize and analyze the suggestions inevitably embedded within these and any other interpersonal processes.

CHAPTER 3

Deconstructing Experiential Processes

It is much easier to ignore the obvious than to renounce the traditional.
Source Unknown

People routinely become absorbed experientially without any formal ritual. One could reasonably argue that the "mindlessness" we are trying to supplant with mindfulness is itself an absorbed state, but in a direction that is not helpful. Focusing on what's wrong, what could go wrong, or what is irrelevant is largely what drives people's problems. Simply put, people's problems are often about focusing on aspects of experience that work against them—perhaps the most compelling reason to learn to conduct experiential processes such as GMM and clinical hypnosis.

As clinicians, we want to redirect focus to what is helpful, positive, and relevant. Interestingly, while mindfulness and hypnosis advocates actively promote the substantial merits of these methods, in reality almost any positive shift in focus and experience of meaningful absorption will provide therapeutic benefits, at least in the short run. Isn't this, at least in part, why people report benefits from praying? Playing with their pets? Walking in nature? Doing crossword puzzles? Surfing the Net? The list of things people can get absorbed in that make them feel better, even if only temporarily, is almost infinite.

So what makes GMM and hypnosis special, each in its own way? They share a purposeful goal-oriented absorption and each provides a structured means for extending key insights and skills across different contexts. The transfer of learning from one context to another, what many in the hypnosis community call the ripple effect, is what we as clinicians strive for. The need to foster transfer of learning is why we don't just solve problems but also teach problem solving, and why we don't just jump in and help someone make a decision but also teach effective decision making. When we encourage mindful living, it applies across many different life experiences, from eating to loving, from walking to sitting, from breathing to smiling.

Setting the Interpersonal Stage

The client is an active force in shaping the interaction, and so the clinician must respond meaningfully to the unique responses of the individual. Guiding the person into internal experience may be the most accurate way of representing the clinician's role. Too many people think of hypnosis as something you do *to* someone rather than *with* them. This myth has intruded into many of my discussions with experts in mindfulness who think of mindfulness as a nondirective process. The experts mistakenly hold the notion that in hypnosis you tell the person what to do and thereby require compliance rather than promote self-discovery.

In the capacity of guide, you cannot know the exact experience the client is having or is going to have, so giving the client room to experience hypnosis and GMM in his or her own way is not only desirable but necessary. How can you demand someone relax, focus, and experience compassion or anything else that cannot just be willed as a response? When Milton Erickson described the therapist as being "the weather," providing a climate for self-discovery, it was an elegant way of defining the clinician as an inevitable and key part of the interaction, paradoxically in supportive and directive roles simultaneously. The process of guiding a person with GMM and hypnosis is a large responsibility to assume: you make yourself a primary focal point, at least initially, because the client is now focusing on the experiences you stimulate through your necessarily suggestive communications. In this respect, GMM and hypnosis overlap completely, with not a crack of light separating them in either form or function.

Stages of Hypnotic (Experiential) Processes

In this chapter, I refer to the structure and intent of GMM and clinical hypnosis sessions as "hypnotic," that is, having the qualities of encouraging focus and absorption in some type of suggested experience, however general (e.g., awareness) or specific (e.g., pain relief in your left shoulder) it might be. Hypnotic interaction can be thought of as taking place in at least seven general stages:

1. Preparing the client (psychoeducation about the experiential process, building expectancy for its likely success, and securing from the client an intent to cooperate with its aims and methods).
2. Orienting to the experience and securing absorbed attention.
3. Hypnotic induction or mindful focusing (building focus, selective attention).
4. Building a response set, that is, an increased tendency to respond positively as the session progresses (building a momentum of responsiveness toward therapeutic objectives resulting in an intensifying or deepening of the experience).
5. Therapeutic utilization (suggestions for change), that is, suggestions given directly or indirectly with the intention to alter the client's experience in some presumably therapeutically beneficial way based on an agreed-upon treatment plan.
6. Contextualization of new behaviors and perceptions, that is, establishing a link or association between new experiences in the session and their relevance to other parts of the person's life (the primary function of the posthypnotic suggestion in hypnosis).
7. Disengagement and reorientation (guiding the person out of the experience).

No matter who is conducting the experiential process, whether a hypnotist or an enlightened spiritual master, these stages and associated intents are an inevitable part of the experience.

The Hypnotic Elements of GMM

We experience life on at least two levels: the empirical and the symbolic. The empirical refers to what we actually see, hear, feel, smell, and taste, that is, our direct sensory experiences. Arguably, the empirical may even include what Jon Kabat-Zinn (2006) called the "mind as a sixth sense," referring to the capacity of the mind to "know" nonconceptually. The symbolic refers to how we represent our empirical experiences in the language we use. Words are symbols of experience, not the experiences themselves. As soon as we begin to describe what we saw, heard, felt, and experienced, we move from the empirical to the symbolic level. Almost everyone has had difficulty making this transition at times, acknowledging with frustration, "I wanted to tell you how I felt, but words got in the way."

The clinical context is a challenging one, to say the least. The client asks for help, trying to explain symbolically (with language) what he or she is experiencing (empirically). The clinician then attempts to use language (symbols) to create meaningful shifts in the client's (empirical) experience. The back-and-forth between levels is difficult enough without buying into the illusion that you, the clinician, can ever really know what someone else is experiencing. So we rely on client reports, whether in response to our queries or our pre- and postsession formal inventories.

An undisguised goal of mine in writing this book is to draw attention to the hypnotic language of GMM and encourage a greater awareness (mindfulness) of the role of suggestion in facilitating the powerful subjective experiences associated with it. It is important to repeat here what I have said elsewhere: the clinical context is different from the spiritual one in important ways, especially the presence of a therapeutic goal orientation and all that it implies; self-directed (independent, *intra*personal) and nonverbal meditations are different from those conducted with someone serving as a guide (*inter*personal); and suggestions are inevitably the vehicle for conducting such interpersonal processes, whether they are verbal or nonverbal, direct or indirect.

We can now turn our attention to the challenge of demonstrating these points directly. In the remainder of this chapter, I provide key sections (the full transcripts would be too long) of the verbatim transcripts of published GMMs conducted by leading experts in mindfulness and Buddhist philosophy. I consider their language from the hypnotic perspective for its suggestive structure and content.

Finally, I provide a hypnosis session transcript of my own that focuses on building a greater acceptance of ambiguity across life experiences. This session's overlap with the concepts and methods of mindfulness will become apparent.

Mindfulness Meditation by Rick Hanson with Richard Mendius

Taken from *Buddha's Brain* by Rick Hanson with Richard Mendius (Oakland, CA: New Harbinger, 2009, pp. 86–87) and reprinted with the kind permission of the author and publisher.

In the excellent book *Buddha's Brain* (Hanson & Mendius, 2009), the authors focus on brain states as they presumably relate to higher consciousness. The authors specifically focus on changing the brain through meditative practice, encouraging readers to develop the "neural pathways to happiness, love and wisdom" (p. 2). The following meditation focuses on the breath as the vehicle for developing a greater attention span, moment-to-moment awareness, and greater compassion toward the self.

Stage 1: Preparing the Client

Hanson and Mendius

"No book can give you the brain of a Buddha, but by better understanding the mind and brain of people who've gone a long way down this path, you can develop more of their joyful, caring, and insightful qualities within your own mind and brain as well" (p. 9).

The authors add, "Since your brain learns mainly from what you attend to, mindfulness is the doorway to

Analysis and Commentary

The direct suggestion is offered that others have changed their brains and improved their lives with these methods and, therefore, you can, too. The indirect suggestion is offered that by studying their stories, following their path, there is legitimate reason to be hopeful for a good outcome.

An indirect suggestion in the form of a metaphor is provided, offering the reader a concrete image of a doorway taking in good experiences and making them a part of yourself" (p. 13).

called mindfulness one can pass through in order to feel better, presumably the motivation of most readers.

Stage 2: Orienting to the Experience

Hanson and Mendius

Prior to introducing this guided meditation to the reader, the authors suggest finding "a comfortable place where you can focus and you won't be disturbed.

It's fine to meditate while standing, walking, or lying down, but most people do so while sitting on a chair or cushion. Find a posture that is both relaxed and alert, with your spine reasonably straight. . . .

Meditate for as long as you like. You can start with shorter periods, even just five minutes. Longer sittings, from thirty to sixty minutes, will usually help you go deeper. . . . Feel free to modify the suggestions that follow" (p. 86).

Analysis and Commentary

A direct, authoritarian suggestion to find a suitable place for the experience, which is defined as "focusing."

A direct, permissive suggestion to find a position in which to meditate is followed by an indirect suggestion to sit "as most people do." A direct, authoritarian content suggestion tells how to sit ("spine reasonably straight").

A direct, authoritarian suggestion says to meditate however long one wishes, but the indirect suggestion is that longer is apparently better since you will likely go deeper. The indirect suggestion is thus given that deeper is better. The direct, permissive suggestion is offered that the suggestions provided can be modified as needed.

Stage 3: Hypnotic Induction or Mindful Focusing

Hanson and Mendius

"Take a big breath and relax, with your eyes open or closed.

Analysis and Commentary

A direct, authoritarian suggestion to breathe and relax is followed by an indirect permissive suggestion for eye closure.

Be aware of sounds coming and going, and let them be whatever they are.

A direct authoritarian suggestion to focus on the auditory portion of experience thereby indirectly suggests a detachment (dissociation) from other elements of sensory experience. A direct suggestion for acceptance of whatever sounds are in awareness indirectly suggests a reduced emotional reactivity.

Know that you are taking this time to meditate. You can drop all other concerns during this period, like setting down a heavy bag before plopping into a comfortable chair. After the meditation, you can pick those concerns up again—if you want to!" (pp. 86–87).

A direct authoritarian suggestion of what the client should know, a direct, permissive suggestion to detach (dissociate) from all usual concerns, and an indirect suggestion through metaphor that one's concerns can concretely be viewed as a "heavy bag" that can be set down. A direct, permissive suggestion says that picking up the bag again is optional, not mandatory.

Stage 4: Building a Response Set

Hanson and Mendius

"Bring your awareness to the sensations of breathing.

Analysis and Commentary

A direct, authoritarian suggestion to focus on breathing is followed by a negative, authoritarian suggestion to avoid controlling the breath willfully.

Don't try to control the breath; let it be whatever it is.

A direct suggestion for acceptance of the breath as it is thereby indirectly suggests detaching from any critical or judgmental self-talk.

Sense the cool air coming in and warm air going out. The chest and belly rising and falling" (p. 87).

A direct, positive suggestion to focus on the kinesthetic portions of breathing (i.e., temperature and physical movements), indirectly suggests a detachment (dissociation) from other aspects of experience related to breathing (e.g., imagery, internal dialogue). The momentum is now building to stay focused on the breath as the vehicle of change.

Stage 5: Therapeutic Utilization (Suggestions for Change)

Hanson and Mendius

Analysis and Commentary

"Try to stay with the sensations of each breath from beginning to end. You may want to softly count your breaths—count to ten and then start over; go back to one if your mind wanders—or note them quietly to yourself as 'in' and 'out.'

A direct permissive suggestion to continue focusing on the breath; a direct, permissive suggestion to associate counting numbers with breathing, pairing the numbers one through ten with each successive breath; and a direct suggestion for the preferred sequence and labeling of the experience the client can adopt.

It's normal for the mind to wander, and when it does, just return to the breath.

A direct suggestion that a wandering mind is normal depathologizes the inevitable and reframes the experience as expected, following the hypnotic formula "accept and utilize" described earlier.

Be gentle and kind with yourself.

A direct, authoritarian suggestion to be kind with oneself.

See if you can stay attentive to ten breaths in a row (usually a challenge at first). After your mind settles down during the first minutes of the meditation, explore becoming increasingly absorbed in the breath and letting go of everything else.

Direct, permissive suggestion to stay attentive to 10 breaths in a row indirectly suggests breaking the experience of being aware of one's breathing as a global and possibly overwhelming goal into a smaller, more manageable task. A presupposition that the first minutes of the meditation will necessarily feature a wandering mind ("After your mind settles down . . .") is followed by a direct, authoritarian, positive suggestion for a deepening of the experience as attention narrows to just the breath, then a direct suggestion to let go of any awareness besides the breath, and an indirect suggestion to thereby detach (dissociate) from all other experiences.

Open to the simple pleasures of breathing, given over to the breath. With some practice, see if you can stay present with the breath for dozens of breaths in a row" (p. 87).

There is a direct, authoritarian, positive suggestion to view breathing as pleasurable, presumably a new emotional association to breathing; this is called an affective reassociation strategy in hypnotic terms. A direct, permissive, positive suggestion that practice will increase one's capacity for focus and attention builds hope for these presumably desirable outcomes.

Stage 6: Contextualization

Hanson and Mendius

Analysis and Commentary

"Using the breath as a kind of anchor, be aware of whatever else is moving through the mind. Aware of thoughts and feelings, wishes and plans, images and memories all coming and going.

A direct, authoritarian, positive suggestion to associate breathing as the foundation of awareness with a greater general awareness for a wide variety of mental activities in the future, is followed by a posthypnotic suggestion for intended aftereffects of the experience.

Let them be what they are; don't get caught up in them; don't struggle with or get fascinated by them.

A direct authoritarian suggestion, as before, for acceptance is followed by a negative authoritarian suggestion (a virtual command) to avoid struggling with or getting fascinated by the various mental activities indicated.

Have a sense of acceptance, even kindness—toward whatever passes through the open space of awareness. Keep settling into the breath, perhaps with a growing sense of peacefulness. Be aware of the changing nature of what passes through the mind. Notice how it feels to get caught up in the passing contents of awareness—and how it feels to let them go by. Be aware of peaceful, spacious awareness itself" (p. 87).

There is a direct authoritarian suggestion to focus on and amplify feelings of acceptance and kindness to associate them with ongoing mental activities and a direct, authoritarian suggestion to amplify the differences in perception between getting caught up and not getting caught up in mental experience. The indirect suggestion, left unstated but implied, is that not getting caught up is better. A direct, authoritarian process suggestion to have an unspecified, abstract "spacious awareness" invites subjective projections on the part of the client as to what that actually means.

Stage 7: Disengagement and Reorientation

Hanson and Mendius

"When you like, bring the meditation to an end. Notice how you feel, and take in the good of your meditation" (p. 87).

Analysis and Commentary

A direct, permissive suggestion to end the experience at will indirectly suggests an internal locus of control is available to regulate the experience. A direct, authoritarian positive suggestion to focus on the kinesthetic or affective dimension of experience in evaluating its merits thereby indirectly suggests detaching (dissociating) from the other elements of experience (e.g., temporal, relational, cognitive, symbolic) that could also be used to evaluate the experience. There is a direct, authoritarian positive suggestion to focus on the presupposition that there was some good to the meditative experience to retain upon its conclusion. This is an indirect suggestion to detach (dissociate) from any negative effects of the experience and an indirect suggestion to become aware of and emphasize only the positive.

Cultivating a Forgiving Heart by Tara Brach

Taken from *Radical Acceptance—Guided Meditations*, an audio CD program by Tara Brach (available from Sounds True and www.tarabrach.com) and reprinted here with kind permission from the author.

The next guided meditation has a more specific intention than awareness: catalyzing the development of a sense of forgiveness toward self and others. Taking the openness and awareness of mindfulness a step further by applying it in a manner meant to elicit a change of heart, a variety of suggestions are offered to facilitate this change.

Stage 1: Preparing the Client

Brach	Analysis and Commentary
"Living with a heart hardened by resentment and blame creates a profound sense of separation and suffering.	The client is provided with a truism about the damage caused by resentment and blame, a suggestion form involving a self-evident truth that cannot legitimately be argued against. A direct, permissive suggestion is offered that any potential we have to be happy and loved will be curtailed by an inability to forgive, thereby establishing a motivation to want to participate in the guided meditation process.
Our capacity for happiness and love is directly related to our ability to forgive.	

While softening and opening our hearts cannot be willed, this guided meditation nourishes a willingness that makes forgiveness possible. It is based on the traditional Buddhist forgiveness practices, in which we first ask forgiveness from others, then offer forgiveness to ourselves and, finally, to those who have caused us injury. "You can practice forgiving informally throughout the day. When you realize you are judging yourself or another person harshly, you might pause and become aware of the thoughts and feelings that trigger blame. Take a few moments to notice them and allow yourself to fully experience the emotions in your body. Then begin offering to yourself whatever message of forgiveness feels most natural. Be patient. With practice, your intention to love fully will blossom into a forgiving heart."

The direct suggestion is offered that a conscious willingness to forgive is not enough, but can be achieved through the guided meditation. This helps establish the positive expectancy that this process is a viable means of achieving the desired goal of success that justifies its being handed down over time and structured (i.e., first this, then this, then this), directly suggesting an established sequence of success in ways other approaches cannot hope to provide. This belief is bolstered by describing this process as "traditional" (thereby indirectly suggesting a long history of success which can instill confidence in the client that "this really works").

Stage 2: Orienting to the Experience

Brach

"Please begin by sitting comfortably. Let your eyes close gently and allow yourself to become present and still."

Analysis and Commentary

These are standard direct suggestions for initiating the experiential process. A direct, permissive suggestion is given to sit comfortably followed by a direct, permissive suggestion to allow eye closure, awareness in the moment, and an experience of stillness.

Stage 3: Hypnotic Induction or Mindful Focusing

Brach

"Rest your attention on the breath for a few moments, relaxing as you breathe in and relaxing as you breathe out."

Analysis and Commentary

A direct, authoritarian suggestion is offered to focus only on the breath, indirectly suggesting a narrowing of attention and a detachment (dissociation) from the surroundings, followed by an associative suggestion to utilize the breath as a means of relaxing.

Stage 4: Building a Response Set

Brach

"Take some moments to sense your intention in this practice . . .

Analysis and Commentary

A direct, authoritarian suggestion is given to focus on the intention of the session, indirectly suggesting it is important to define the goal and keep the goal in mind as the session progresses.

the sincere wish to not leave anyone, including your own being . . . out of your heart."

A negative content suggestion is given—that is, don't leave anyone, including yourself, out of the process. Forgiveness is indirectly given a specific location in the next associative suggestion—it is in the heart, further indirectly suggesting this will be an emotion-based experience rather than an intellectual one.

Stage 5: Therapeutic Utilization (Suggestions for Change)

Brach

"Beginning by bringing to mind a situation in which you've caused harm to another person.

Analysis and Commentary

A direct, positive process suggestion to retrieve a specific memory (age regression, hypermnesia) to focus on as the context for attaining forgiveness,

You might have intentionally hurt someone with insulting words . . . by hanging [up] the phone in a fit of anger. . . . Perhaps you caused pain unintentionally, in the way you ended a relationship . . . or by being preoccupied not realizing your child needed some special attention. Take some moments to remember the circumstances, whatever they were . . . in a way that you've caused injury to another. . . . And it may be circumstances that have continued over and over through the years.

indirectly suggests a detachment (dissociation) from the current time. Content suggestions of common examples of interpersonal harm, intentional or not, a past episode or ongoing, are offered to further encourage a specific memory.

As you reflect on these circumstances, let them be close up . . . so that you can really sense . . . how you've caused harm to another, sense the feelings of that person's hurt, or disappointment, or feelings of betrayal.
. . . Now holding this person in your awareness, begin asking for forgiveness. You might mentally whisper his or her name and then say . . . *I understand the hurt you have felt and I ask your forgiveness now, please forgive me.* . . .

A direct, positive, permissive suggestion to bring the memory "close up" indirectly suggests the client has and can use an internal locus of control to manipulate both location and intensity of the memory.

A presuppositional direct suggestion to "hold the person" in awareness suggests the memory's parameters should involve a single individual, rather than a group of people (e.g., a team, perhaps work or sports, of which one is a member) or a pet. A direct, authoritarian suggestion to ask for forgiveness followed by a direct, permissive suggestion to whisper the person's name is followed by a direct, authoritarian content suggestion stating what the language should be in asking for forgiveness.

With a sincere heart, repeat several times this request for forgiveness . . . *I understand the hurt you have felt and I ask your forgiveness now, please forgive me* . . . Taking some moments of silence . . . letting yourself open to the possibility of being forgiven . . . of feeling forgiven."

There is an indirect, permissive process suggestion to access a "sincere heart," that is, a suggested specific emotional frame, for conducting the memory work, then a direct, authoritarian suggestion to utilize the following period of silence to absorb the direct, positive, permissive suggestion to develop the feeling of being forgiven. The indirect suggestion, implied but not stated, is that in order to feel forgiven by someone following asking for forgiveness, the injured person must be able to offer forgiveness. How this is done is implied but not specified through process suggestion. This follows the traditional sequence suggested at the outset ("We first ask forgiveness from others, then offer forgiveness to ourselves and, finally, to those who have caused us injury"), presumably moving from a less difficult to a more difficult challenge over the course of the process. Hypnosis sessions follow this same general structure, generally moving from less direct to more direct as the session progresses, and from less to more emotionally charged as the session unfolds.

Brach, Continuing Stage 5, Therapeutic Utilization
". . . Now bringing to mind some aspect of yourself . . . that feels unforgiveable.

Analysis and Commentary
A direct, permissive process suggestion is given to now shift the focus to a new domain of concern: an aspect of the self that feels unforgiveable;

then an indirect, permissive suggestion to split off (dissociate) one part of experience from the whole of the person and to define it by its associated affect ("*feels* unforgiveable," which is malleable compared to "*is* unforgiveable").

Content suggestions are offered to provide examples of common pathways into feeling unforgivable.

Perhaps you can't forgive yourself for how you've hurt another person . . . for being judgmental . . . for being a controlling person . . . or you might hate yourself for being cowardly . . . for not taking the risks that might make your life more fulfilling . . . or maybe it's difficult to forgive yourself for how you feel like you're ruining your life with an addictive behavior. Whatever it is . . . allow yourself to sense how you've turned on yourself . . . sense what feels so bad about your unforgivable behavior or emotion or way of thinking. What's so wrong about it? How does this part of yourself make you feel about who you are? How does it prevent you from being happy? Now explore more deeply what is driving this unacceptable part of your being.

A direct, positive, permissive suggestion is provided to reframe a lack of self-forgiveness as having "turned on yourself," a more negatively charged perspective inviting greater resistance to lacking forgiveness and increased motivation to be more self-accepting.

If you've wounded another person, did you act out of hurt and insecurity? If you've been addicted to food, alcohol, drugs, what need are you trying to satisfy? What fear are you trying to soothe? As you become aware of underlying wants and fears . . . allow yourself to feel this human vulnerabil-

A reframing is offered through indirect suggestion by the use of what are termed accessing questions and conversational postulates in hypnotic terminology; these are questions one asks the person to consider experientially, with no expectation for a verbal response. In this case, Brach reframes

ity . . . directly in your body, your heart, your mind.

Begin to offer a sincere message of forgiveness to whatever feelings, thoughts or behaviors you're rejecting. You might mentally whisper the words, '*I see how I've caused myself or others suffering . . . and I forgive myself now*,' or you might simply offer the words '*forgiven, forgiven*.'

If it helps to put your hand on your heart, let the gentle touch of your hand help to communicate this message of mercy of forgiveness, then do that.

"unforgiveable" as "unacceptable," a step toward eventual acceptance. She further reframes this unacceptable part through the indirect suggestion as having been motivated by understandable, hence acceptable, drives such as hurt, insecurity, an unspecified need, or fear. These are process suggestions, because every human being is troubled by these feelings, inviting the listener to project these feelings into the damaged interaction and offering an emotional rationale for bad behavior. The reframe is complete when the listener is able to say, in essence, "I behaved badly, but now I understand why."

A direct, positive, authoritarian suggestion is given to offer a "sincere message of forgiveness," followed by a direct, permissive content suggestion to mentally whisper the suggested words to elicit the internal state of forgiveness.

A direct, permissive content suggestion for putting the hand on the heart is given to associate this action with the feeling of the "mercy of forgiveness." This is a suggestion for a behavioral cue, what some in the hypnosis literature call a kinesthetic anchor, essentially a specific conditioned response meant to associate the emotion of forgiveness with the direct physical contact of touching the heart.

"In these moments, meeting whatever arises . . . fear or judgment, shame or grief . . . with the message of forgiveness . . . forgiven, forgiven. Allowing the hurt, the vulnerability . . . to untangle in the openness of a forgiving heart.

"As you practice you may feel as if you're going through the motions and are not actually capable . . . of forgiving yourself. You might believe you don't deserve to be forgiven. You might be afraid that if you forgive yourself you'll just do the same things again. Maybe you're afraid that if you really open and forgive yourself you'll come face to face with an intolerable truth about yourself. . . ."

An indirect, permissive suggestion is offered through metaphor of the "untangling" of the hurt and vulnerability. This metaphor utilizes the imagery of something knotted coming untangled, providing the listener a concrete means for knotted-up feelings of being unforgiveable getting smoothed out. Direct, permissive suggestions are given to address any lingering feelings of resistance to the process by accepting and utilizing feelings of unworthiness as a further catalyst for forgiveness by again reframing them as rooted in understandable doubts and fears rather than malice. This same theme continues through the remainder of Brach's guided meditation, which turns to the final step of the forgiveness sequence by focusing on an experience of having been "wounded . . . deeply disappointed or rejected, abused or betrayed . . . in a relationship." In this phase, suggestions are given for developing feelings of compassion toward the person who committed the act of harm. The injury is reframed as an act of an "imperfect human." Brach offers the suggestion that "no one causes suffering unless they're suffering." If the listener accepts that suggestion, then feelings of compassion can more easily follow, giving rise to forgiveness.

Stage 6: Contextualization

Brach	Analysis and Commentary
"If these doubts and fears arise . . . acknowledge and accept them with compassion. Then say to yourself '*It's my intention to forgive myself when I'm able.*'	A direct, authoritarian process suggestion is given to respond to doubts and fears with compassion, an undisguised posthypnotic suggestion for future possibilities based on this meditative experience. A direct, positive content suggestion is given regarding what the self-talk wording should be.
Your intention to forgive is the seed of forgiveness. This willingness will gradually relax and open your heart. . . .	A truism is provided to suggest that an intention to forgive is almost as good as forgiveness, directly suggesting it is an inevitable precursor ("seed") in the gradual established forgiveness sequence.
As you practice, let whatever arises . . . whatever reactions or thoughts, feelings . . . sensations in the body be included with a forgiving heart,	An indirect, positive suggestion to practice this process is given and to make it as multidimensional as possible by now including thoughts, feelings, and body sensations associated with a "forgiving heart."
You might gently whisper, '*forgiven-forgiven*' to whatever place feels conflicted or vulnerable."	A direct, permissive content suggestion is offered regarding what to say to oneself, another undisguised posthypnotic suggestion, when feeling conflicted or vulnerable in the future.

Stage 7: Disengagement and Reorientation

Brach	Analysis and Commentary
". . . Now let go of all ideas of self, of other and simply rest in the experience of tender awareness. If a thought or feeling arises, sense the capacity to	A direct, authoritarian process suggestion to "let go" of (dissociate from) preconceived notions of self and others is given, and instead to focus on

include this entire living . . . dying world . . . in the vast space of heart.

"We'll close with the words of the poet Rumi: 'Out beyond ideas of wrongdoing and right doing, there is a field. I'll meet you there. When the soul lies down in that grass, the world is too full to talk about. Ideas, language, even the phrase "each other" doesn't make any sense.'"

(associate to) a "tender awareness" of an unspecified nature, followed by a process suggestion to filter everything through the "vast space of heart." The direct suggestion "we'll close" signals the imminent ending of the session on the cue of the final word of the poem.

Recognizing and Tolerating Ambiguity: A Clinical Hypnosis Session by Michael D. Yapko

Adapted from *Treating Depression With Hypnosis* (New York: Brunner/Routledge, 2001, pp. 53–57).

Each of us makes decisions in the face of uncertainty (ambiguity) on a daily basis, but not everyone deals with uncertainty equally well. Uncertainty invites projections—hypotheses—about what's going on and how to best respond. But anxious and depressed people, in particular, are known to project negative, self-damaging interpretations into ambiguous circumstances (for detailed discussions of this phenomenon see Yapko, 1997, 1999, 2001a, 2010).

For as long as an individual is unable to tolerate uncertainty, he or she will be motivated to continue forming meanings about life experience with little or no insight into the interpretive process and thus suffer the mood consequences when those meanings are negatively distorted yet accepted as true. Thus, one of the most basic goals in treating therapy clients in general, and anxious and depressed clients in particular, is to teach them how to recognize and tolerate ambiguity. The client needs to become more comfortable with having no conclusions, that is, reduce the drive to have an answer, rather than reflexively forming conclusions without evidence or merit. Jon Kabat-Zinn used different language but the identical construct when he suggested, "meditating is about not knowing who you are and being comfortable with not knowing" (2006). He suggested, therefore, the development of a "beginner's mind," one that is open and curious rather than bogged down with preconceptions, particularly self-limiting ones.

The following is a clinical hypnosis session, making abundant use of deliberate and carefully worded suggestions designed to elicit the beginner's mind in the client, that is, a frame of mind that makes recognition and acceptance of the ambiguities of life easier. Just like the guided meditations presented earlier, this hypnosis session progresses in clearly identifiable stages. Through discussions with the client, the clinician can identify relevant patterns of self-organization, such as cognitive or relational styles, in order to determine how that particular client may best respond. The more feedback from the client about his or her personal phenomenology a clinician uses in formulating an approach, the more likely the intervention can be tailored appropriately (Yapko, 2003).

Stage 1: Preparing the Client

Yapko

"Life offers all of us countless opportunities. Which opportunities we choose to pursue is clearly a reflection of our value systems and the things we've been taught to view as important. Thus, from the choices we make, both large and small, we are the ones who give our lives meaning. . . . The need to explain things in order to understand them is a basic human requirement. People want things to make sense, and they want and need to understand what's going on. . . . Through all the things that you do each day, you're continually engaged in a process of explaining to yourself about yourself, about others, and about events in the world around you. . . .

Analysis and Commentary

A truism is provided to establish agreement at the outset. An indirect suggestion is offered through the truism that we make choices among opportunities, directly but permissively suggesting an internal locus of control, that is, a participation in the process and capacity to influence it. Further truisms support the same point, but the suggestions move from general and impersonal to general and personal when the direct, positive process suggestion is given that each day the client is continually engaged in a process of meaning making. The indirect suggestion is that this process may be flawed and require renewed consideration, building motivation to want to pay attention to the issue.

The feelings you have are closely related to how you explain the things going on *around you* and *within you* . . . situations that are ambiguous represent risk factors . . ."

The frame is established with a direct, positive process suggestion that making meaning can affect feelings. A direct, positive process suggestion links ambiguity directly to risk factors. The indirect suggestion is offered through implication that the meanings we make are malleable and can be changed, establishing the hope and expectancy of some therapeutic value for participating in the session.

Stage 2: Orienting to the Experience

Yapko

". . . Have you experienced hypnosis, guided meditations or other similarly focused states before? Whether you have or haven't had such wonderfully absorbing experiences before, you're capable of allowing yourself to find a comfortable position in which to sit . . ."

Analysis and Commentary

The question about previous experience orients the client to this type of intervention and the implied directive, a form of indirect suggestion that gently tells the client, "I hope and expect to do this with you now." The client's experience, whatever it may be, is accepted and utilized with a direct, permissive process suggestion to sit comfortably.

Stage 3: Hypnotic Induction or Mindful Focusing

Yapko

Analysis and Commentary

The induction process is whatever means a clinician uses to absorb and direct the client's attention. Inductions can be structured (e.g., body scans or countdowns) or conversational ("Can you recall how good it feels to close your eyes and get absorbed in relaxing images?"). The chief function of an induction is to facilitate some degree of dissociation in the client, an increased capacity for multilevel responding, so the actual induction method employed is a secondary consideration. The primary consideration is the client's ability to relate well to it and get absorbed in it, whatever it is.

In this case, I used an induction process called "accessing previous hypnotic experiences." As I direct the person to think of a past experience, and he or she gets absorbed in it, the same or similar feelings and responses can begin to build in the present, which I can notice and amplify with further suggestions.

"... Sometime in your life, you've had the experience of getting absorbed in some experience you found relaxing ... comforting. ...

A direct, positive process suggestion is offered to find some previous experience (an indirect suggestion for age regression) on which to focus.

Perhaps it was the many sensory pleasures of being someplace you found beautiful and rich with things to appreciate ... or perhaps it was a deep absorption in some activity that seemed to delight every part of you ... and soothe you ... and comfort you ... all at the same time ...

Direct, permissive process suggestions are offered as to what types of experiences might have given rise to the experience of comfort.

and as you begin to focus on that experience ... it's quite possible that you'll find yourself re-experiencing some of those same sensations of comfort ... and you can become fully aware of them in this moment ..."

A direct, permissive process suggestion is offered that the responses of the past could extend into the present.

Stage 4: Building a Response Set

Yapko

Analysis and Commentary

The building of a response set is the means for establishing a momentum in client responsiveness. To expect the client, following an induction, to instantly be able to relate to and absorb new ideas isn't usually realistic. Most clients need time to progressively develop their hypnotic responsiveness over the course of a session, and the goal of this step is to deliberately assist in that process. Here, I provide an example of the most commonly used response set, the so-called yes set, a means for building agreement and receptivity in the client to further suggestions. The client may be offered a series of truisms (i.e., suggestions so obviously true there is no legitimate basis for rejecting them) that he or she naturally will agree with, establishing a momentum in the direction of more easily agreeing with whatever else the clinician might say later.

"... There are many different things I could say intending to help you relax ... and I don't know which of them would be the most valuable in helping you get deeply comfortable ... and you don't know exactly what I'm going to talk about that will be helpful to you ... and you don't know quite yet how you'll come to think differently about yourself ... and you don't really know at just what moment

The truism is offered that "there are many different things I could say," a statement the client must accept as true. The next statement directly establishes the "I don't know" frame for what is to come, an indirect suggestion that not knowing is inevitable and that even a so-called expert can openly acknowledge and even embrace not knowing. Within that same statement is the indirect, permissive you'll find yourself so wonderfully comfortable with the possibilities you'll discover here . . ."

suggestion that despite not knowing it will be possible for the client to get deeply comfortable. The next truism again asserts the client doesn't know what I will say, but offers the indirect suggestion through a presupposition that it will be helpful. Next is the indirect suggestion through presupposition that the client will learn to think differently about himself or herself. What follows then is another suggestion in the same format, an indirect suggestion through presupposition that the client will be comfortable with possibilities. Notice how these preliminary suggestions are offered in a manner consistent with the larger goal of the session to increase awareness and acceptance of uncertainty. In each suggestion, uncertainty is amplified but also associated to positive possibilities.

Stage 5: Therapeutic Utilization (Suggestions for Change)

Yapko

". . . And as you start to become aware . . . much more fully aware . . . in moment-to-moment experience . . . you can start to see where the uncertainty is in everyday situations . . . and where the different possibilities are in life. . . .

You can comfortably consider an everyday example, for almost everyone has had the experience of calling

Analysis and Commentary

The direct, permissive process suggestion is offered to start to become more aware of the presence of uncertainty in life and its relationship to triggering an awareness for possibilities.

A simple, nonthreatening example is introduced through the metaphor of an unreturned phone call. Wondering someone ... getting his or her voice mail because the person is unavailable ... and leaving a message ... and when the person doesn't call back in a time frame you think of as reasonable ... you might naturally wonder what it means ...

what it means is framed through a direct suggestion as natural, depathologizing the process and indirectly suggesting the problem is not in wondering.

and it can be so comforting to recognize instantly that you can wonder ... but not know what it means. ... You can consider whether the person is busy ... or whether voice mail worked properly ... or whether the person is alright ... or even whether the person is avoiding you for some reason ... or any of *many* possible reasons for not returning your call as quickly as you'd like

The next direct, positive suggestion underscores that point by directly suggesting one can wonder but also instantly recognize one doesn't know. A direct suggestion linking comfort to not knowing is offered, called an affective reassociation strategy in hypnotic terms. Content suggestions are offered as examples of possible reasons why someone might not return a call, indirectly suggesting that in the face of ambiguity, multiple possible explanations or viewpoints may all be plausible but are not necessarily objectively true.

... and how do you know what the real reason is? ...

Asking the rhetorical question regarding how you know which explanation is true indirectly suggests plausible is simply not good enough.

But it's human nature to speculate about what things that happen mean ...

A truism is offered regarding human nature and the tendency to speculate, again an indirect suggestion for depathologizing projection and reducing any potential for self-criticism.

and the real skill is knowing when you're speculating ... and when you have evidence to affirm your interpretation. ... After all ... you want to

A direct, positive suggestion frames the salient skill as knowing one is speculating, a new and therapeutic awareness that can lead to seeking out react to something on an informed basis . . .

and whether you want to understand something like why someone doesn't call back, or something much more complex such as why people do what they do . . . or how the mind works . . . it's one of human beings' greatest strengths . . . that they strive to understand . . . and make sense of the things that go on around us . . . and the fact that you can generate so many different explanations for why someone doesn't call back . . . gives you an opportunity to realize you don't know why he or she didn't call back. . . . You can make lots of guesses . . . but you really don't know for sure . . .

and when you really don't know how to explain something precisely . . . with evidence . . . it's perfectly alright to say you don't know. . . . After all, no one really expects you to know why someone else doesn't return a phone call. . . . It's a gift of honesty and clear thinking when someone says, "I don't know" instead of quickly making up an answer that might well be wrong . . . and even hurtful . . . and if you think about it . . . there are so many times in life you'd rather be given no answer than a wrong one . . . and it makes it so much easier to evolve a calm acceptance for the way things are . . .

more objective information, a helpful strategy in terms of both treatment and prevention.

This key learning is then broadened with a direct, positive content suggestion to other areas of life, such as examining human motives or mental functions. Direct, positive suggestions reinforce the message.

These lead into a direct, permissive, positive suggestion to accept not knowing as all right, and with an indirect, positive content suggestion lift the stigma of ignorance. In fact, the direct, positive, permissive content suggestion is offered as a reframing that it is virtuous at times to not know, a gift of honesty and clear thinking. A direct, permissive, positive process suggestion is given that no answer is often better than a wrong one, a realization that can give rise to feelings of calm acceptance.

when you realize you really don't know how things are . . . in some areas of your life . . . and that some questions we can ask . . . will never be answerable . . . allowing a calm acceptance . . . and a mindful awareness . . ."

A truism is offered that directly suggests some questions can't be answered, again reinforcing the direct, permissive, positive suggestion for a calm and mindful acceptance of things as they are rather than fighting against them.

Stage 6: Contextualization

Yapko

Analysis and Commentary
The function of the posthypnotic suggestion is to link a new thought, feeling, or awareness with some context in which it will serve to enhance the person's experience.

". . . So, in the future, when you face some important situation or event . . . and you reflexively generate multiple ways of looking at it . . . and can mindfully hold the moment of not knowing in your awareness

A direct, permissive, positive process suggestion is given to face future situations skillfully by instantly recognizing uncertainty in the form of multiple possible meanings then taking a moment, an indirect suggestion for utilizing some impulse control, before reacting.

. . . before you reach a conclusion, *any* conclusion . . . you can gently ask yourself, 'How do I know?' and if your answer is simply, 'I just feel it's so' or 'I just believe it'. . . then know you are forming a subjective conclusion . . . and you can comfortably wonder whether there is a more objective reality waiting to be discovered . . .

A direct, positive content suggestion is given as to what the self-talk can be to guide the process of better distinguishing the subjective from the objective, followed by a direct, permissive, positive suggestion to wonder about whether an objective perspective is somewhere to be found. The indirect suggestion is an implied directive to use objectivity when possible while acknowledging that sometimes there is no objectivity to be found.

that you can use your curiosity to explore . . . and maybe there will be or maybe there won't be, but you can notice the quality of your explorations and conclusions getting better and better over time . . . just as your appreciation for your life experience grows ever greater."

A direct, positive, permissive suggestion to associate curiosity to the process and a frame of going exploring is an indirect suggestion to be open to discovery without reacting out of either preconception or reflex. Finally, the direct, permissive process suggestion is given that, with practice, decision making will improve as will life satisfaction.

Stage 7: Disengagement and Reorientation

Yapko

". . . Now, I've talked about many different possibilities for recognizing and tolerating the uncertainties in life . . . and being comfortable . . . and, in just a few moments . . . we can bring this experience to a comfortable close. . . .

You can take whatever time you'd like to process and integrate what would be helpful to you . . . and then, when you're ready to do so, you can start the process of re-orienting yourself . . .

fully aware . . . and present . . . and whenever you feel ready to do so . . . you can allow your eyes to open . . ."

Analysis and Commentary

These are standard suggestions for closure. An anticipation signal is offered by saying "in just a few moments" the session will end, gently orienting the client to the disengagement to come.

A direct, positive process suggestion is given to integrate the learnings, an indirect suggestion for the possibility of evolving an automaticity. An internal locus of control is reinforced and directly suggested in permissive form by saying the process of reorienting is initiated at the client's readiness. Direct, positive suggestions are given for heightened awareness and a reiteration that the client is in control and can choose when to respond to the direct, permissive suggestion for opening the eyes.

Conclusion

This chapter's transcripts provide compelling evidence that any GMM or clinical hypnosis session must be viewed as a highly suggestive process. Furthermore, it is an interpersonal process with clearly delineated roles of guide/therapist and student/client. It does not and should not diminish the merits of mindfulness to acknowledge the role of suggestion in GMM. On the contrary, the awareness and sense of empowerment that arise during GMM speak for themselves in terms of GMM's therapeutic value. An awareness of hypnotic language and phenomena inevitably embedded within these processes can only add to that value.

CHAPTER 4

The Forces Behind the Power of Focus

Even though hypnosis has always been an enigma, it is still one of the seven wonders of psychology.

William S. Kroger, M.D. (2008, p. 26)

Is mindfulness a special state distinct from other states of mind, or is the experience of mindfulness on the continuum of everyday experiences? What about hypnosis and the manifestation of hypnotic phenomena such as dissociation, analgesia, and time distortion? For many years people have wondered whether to attribute hypnotic experiences to some special state or to the same cognitive processes and situational demands that influence actions and experiences in the course of everyday living. The state-or-trait debate in hypnosis has quieted recently after decades of consideration: The evidence suggests both are important in influencing hypnotic responses.

Mindfulness is caught on the horns of the same dilemma, though mindfulness practitioners may not really be aware of it yet. Mindfulness is at once considered a "special state" that "holds the promise of both alleviating our suffering and making our lives rich and meaningful" (R. Siegel, 2009, p. 5) and an ordinary everyday experience as well:

I could use the [mindfulness] practice to notice the trees as I walked to class, taste my food in the dining hall, and connect more intimately with my friends.... . While making time for formal meditation is important, mindfulness can also be practiced as part of our ordinary routine, while brushing our teeth, driving to work, walking the dog, or waiting in the check-out line ... (R. Siegel, 2009, pp. vii–ix)

Context matters, of course. If the merits of GMM were contingent on becoming a Buddhist and applying it as part of a spiritual evolution, it would not have as much appeal to clinicians. Many patients showing up at mindfulness centers and integrative medicine centers are not particularly interested in Buddhism or spiritual learning. They simply want help for their problems and have accepted the suggestion, from wherever it might have come, that here they will learn something that may be helpful. It is therapists, though, who have long been searching for a credible way to integrate spirituality into psychotherapy and who now have found a legitimate means for doing so. Mindfulness is both spiritual in nature and clinically effective. Will either suffer if the underlying suggestive mechanisms are better understood? I don't believe so.

Swapping Trances

As scientific inquiry into hypnosis and the nature of hypnotic phenomena has progressed over the last three-quarters of a century, differing viewpoints have naturally evolved to describe the phenomenon. The so-called trance state, the nature of consciousness, the nature of the unconscious, the capacity for hypnotizability within and across individuals, the clinical merits of facilitating hypnotic phenomena (ranging from simple relaxation processes to complex anesthesias) in treating a wide variety of diseases and disorders, the durability of such interventions over time, and many, many other aspects of hypnosis have been well addressed in the literature. As the analyses of hypnosis and hypnotic phenomena have grown progressively more sophisticated over time, supplemented by newer neuroscientific discoveries, the view of hypnosis as a special state has been seriously undermined. Even the use of the word *trance* is declining in the literature as the evidence grows that it simply does not represent people's reported experiences very well and reinforces the unfortunate myth that somehow the person will be unaware of what he or she is doing (Lynn & Kirsch, 2006; Yapko, 2003).

With this evolution in understanding, the view of hypnosis as an aberration of some kind, a mental trap to hold us prisoner and prevent us from being fully awake, has all but disappeared as new scientific findings illuminate the discovery of how, essentially, we do not "awaken" from a trance; rather, we just develop another one that is potentially more helpful.

Hypnosis is less about whether we believe than about what we believe, and how these beliefs serve us for better or worse. "Awakening to the truth" is really about becoming absorbed in yet another belief system; hopefully one that helps us despite the fact that it may not be any more objectively true than the last belief system we embraced. Whether we "awaken" to experience the "smile of the Buddha" in our soul, or feel the Holy Spirit move through us, or discover who we were in hypnotic past life regressions that ostensibly "prove" reincarnation, or sleep with crystals under our pillows that provide us with "healing energy," or absorb ourselves in countless other belief systems ranging from plausible to implausible that have the power to transform us, they *all require us to* believe. What we believe to be holy, sacred, or true isn't a statement about that thing. It's a statement about us.

No one person has cornered the market on truth; we each have our individual versions of the truth simply because so many of the key issues in life are inherently ambiguous. How do you prove in an objective sense what the purpose of life is, or what happens to us after we die, or even simpler things like whether it is better to go out to a movie tonight or stay home and watch TV?

The Sociocognitive Model of Hypnosis

The sociocognitive model of hypnosis goes a very long way in describing the kinds of subjective experiences people report in their guided meditations and clinical hypnosis sessions. The sociocognitive perspective holds that the subjective experiences generated during hypnosis are goal directed, as are those of everyday life experiences, and involve the same social and cognitive processes as routine life experiences (Lynn & Green, in press). These special experiences come about in response to the various intrapersonal, interpersonal, and contextual factors to which I have been alluding all along, which are detailed further in Chapter 5. Such experiences can be subjectively experienced as therapeutically beneficial at least, transformative at most. Indeed, in this respect they *are* special. But they are not outside the realm of everyday experiences. The relationship between the person and context, ultimately, is what gives experiences the ascribed significance.

Theodore ("Ted") X. Barber was a prolific and profound hypnosis researcher in the 1950s and 1960s who can be credited with setting the stage for the development of the sociocognitive viewpoint. His research made it clear to him that the notion of some vaguely defined and esoteric phenomenon called trance was unnecessary to explain hypnotic behavior. Instead, Barber proposed that the phenomena of hypnosis were best understood in social terms. His research demonstrated that when the setting was appropriate, and subjects were motivated to carry out the suggested task, their responses were not significantly different from those who had gone through the rituals of hypnosis. He wrote, "We can view hypnosis in its broader context, as a social phenomenon par excellence, when we see how much of it is explained by basic principles of the social sciences which have been thoroughly documented by several generations of cultural anthropologists, sociologists, and social psychologists" (Barber, 2000, p. 232). Other sociocognitive researchers have also emphasized the importance of social as well as cognitive processes regarding hypnosis and have shown convincingly how hypnotic responsiveness is markedly influenced—and can even be enhanced—by these processes (Gorassini & Spanos, 1999; Spanos & Chaves, 1989; Spanos, Robertson, Menary, & Brett,1986; Wagstaff, 2004).

States and Traits in GMM

The hypnotic phenomena on display in GMMs described below are the building blocks of human experience—*all* experiences, whether arising in the context of clinical hypnosis sessions or GMM. These experiences arise in the course of everyday living as traits and they manifest as special state experiences during deep meditation. These experiences are structurally the same across contexts but are given quite different interpretations and characterizations across differing expert viewpoints. They are assembled and weighted differently in different religions, philosophies, and psychotherapies, but all utilize to one degree or another the following hypnotic phenomena:

- Age regression (defined as the experiential utilization of memory)
- Age progression (defined as the experiential utilization of expectancy)
- Analgesia (defined as a diminished awareness for kinesthetic experience)
- Catalepsy (defined as the inhibition of movement, the stillness of the absorbed person)
- Sensory alterations (defined as increased or decreased sensory awareness)
- Positive hallucinations (defined as sensory experiences arising despite no external cause)
- Negative hallucinations (defined as the absence of a sensory experience despite the objectively presence of a stimulus)
- Time distortion (defined as perceptual changes regarding the passage of time such as a sense of timelessness)

Automaticity in Responding: Unconscious Goal Setting?

Two of the foremost hypnosis experts and sociocognitive theorists today, Steven Jay Lynn and Irving Kirsch, have been instrumental in expanding our understanding of the social and cognitive processes influencing responsiveness to hypnotic procedures. People in hypnosis respond in a manner that is consistent with their aims and what they believe about such experiences, and "ultimately exhibit exquisite control of their thoughts, feelings, and behaviors, despite the fact that their experiences during hypnosis often have an automatic or involuntary quality" (Lynn & Green, in press). When sophisticated responses spontaneously arise during the course of GMM or hypnosis sessions, where do they come from? For example, if you focus on the client's breath by suggesting "becoming aware of the breath, the rise and fall of the chest, the warm or cool temperature of the air," and the person's breathing slows down although that was not part of the suggestion, the individual may report that it "just happened."

One of the most intriguing aspects of training people to develop focus in their lives, whether through techniques of mindfulness or hypnosis, is how the phenomenon of automaticity surfaces during the process. Tobis and Kihlstrom described automaticity as comprised of "effortless execution and parallel processing. . . . In principle, automatic processes do not interfere with other ongoing processes precisely because they do not consume attentional resources that are required by those other processes" (2010, p. 369). One simply cannot be aware of everything all at once; thus, having the ability to carry out goal-directed activities without conscious effort is essential. *Someone does not need to be consciously focused on a goal to still be operating in a goal-directed manner.*

Many people use the general term "habit formation" to explain how something that is repeatedly performed consciously may eventually become automatic, that is, an unconscious, dominant response. Yet one of the most common observations documented in the hypnosis literature is how, even on the basis of a *single* hypnotic experience, a new perceptual or behavioral response is readily absorbed and repeatedly acted upon for a time span that may range from only a short while to an entire life span. Even more intriguingly, the person does not necessarily have any conscious awareness of having responded to a suggestion to do so. It is both curious and puzzling to observe such responses, much less try to explain them. What is it about the unconscious that allows automaticity of responses to arise? This is an exceptionally important question to consider if one is to practice approaches such as mindfulness and hypnosis skillfully.

To even begin to address the phenomenon of automaticity, we must briefly transition into the domain of cognitive psychology. Psychology professor and cognitive scientist James Uleman provided an overview of how cognitive psychology is changing our understandings of the unconscious mind and, in so doing, our understandings of ourselves:

> The development of cognitive science across disciplines . . . discovered a great deal about complex unconscious mental phenomena and provided rigorous methods for studying them. . . . The new unconscious is much more concerned with affect, motivation, and even control and metacognition than was the old unconscious. Goals, motives, and self-regulation are prominent. . . . And the new unconscious includes the causes of the phenomenal experience of having intentions and free will, of attributing these to oneself and others. (2005, p. 6)

As Uleman alluded, the evidence is growing that, as much as we like to think we can be in control of our judgments and behavior, in actuality we are largely influenced by automatic cognitive processes that shape our responses to life experience. These automatic processes influence what we like and dislike, how we perceive other people (especially when unconsciously responding to biases based on race or gender, for example), how we react emotionally, and how we orient to the goals we establish (Bargh, 2006). Consider the power of self-fulfilling prophecies, placebo, and nocebo effects.

Cognitive scientists consider it an attribution error to see self-control and free choice when often we are acting out of unconscious, and even unknowable, forces. In fact, University of Virginia professor Timothy Wilson, in his book, *Strangers to Ourselves: Discovering the Adaptive Unconscious* wrote:

> People possess a powerful, sophisticated, adaptive unconscious that is crucial for survival in the world. Because this unconscious operates so efficiently out of view, however, and is largely inaccessible, there is a price to pay in self-knowledge. There is a great deal about ourselves that we cannot know directly, even with the most painstaking introspection. (2002, p. vii)

When the oft-stated goal of meditation is to discover the truth by being open and fully aware, in light of advances in cognitive science and neuroscience, is such a goal plausible? Silvia and Gendolla (2001) provided a substantive review of the evidence that suggests introspection does *not* lead to more accurate reports about the self. It is a practical question: How much of our own unconscious can we become aware of and regulate? Cognitive scientists make a distinction between automatic and controlled mental processes. With some exceptions, nonconscious thinking is regarded as automatic, and most conscious thinking is considered controlled, requiring attention and awareness. Is more attention and awareness an illusion? Perhaps so. Daniel Wegner (2003), author of *The Illusion of Conscious Will*, wrote (in Hassin, Uleman, & Bargh, 2005) that we are most likely to believe we are doing something—including being mindful—when three principles are in play: (1) a priority principle which states that intentions precede actions; (2) a consistency principle which states that intentions and actions are consistent with each other; and (3) an exclusivity principle which states that there are no other obvious causes of action besides the intentions.

Ruud Custers and Henk Aarts of Utrecht University in the Netherlands published an article challenging the conventional view that the decision to act produces the actions themselves (Custers & Aarts, 2010). They showed that, under some conditions, actions are initiated even when we are unconscious of the goals for which we are striving or how these goals motivate our behavior. Practitioners of solution-oriented therapy have described how much improvement people would note just between scheduling a first appointment and showing up for it (de Shazer, 1985, 1988). As Steven Jay Lynn and Joseph Green pointed out, "Because most people are unaware of the automatic nature of their responses . . . they tend to attribute the automatic or involuntary nature of their responses during hypnosis to an altered state of consciousness, trance, or the power of the hypnotist" (in press). Similarly, they can attribute it to the meditative state or the guru.

Why is this important? For many reasons both philosophical and procedural, none of which is more important than appreciating how the interaction between therapist and client triggers a wide variety of responses on many different levels, most of which are likely to be—and remain—unconscious. Here is another example of how what practitioners *think* they are doing and how they explain it may be quite different than what they *actually* do. I'm hoping to encourage a greater congruity between thought and practice by acknowledging salient sociocognitive principles that are evident yet largely unacknowledged in the methods of mindfulness.

Automaticity in Treatment

Different forms of treatment deal with the phenomenon of automaticity differently. Some approaches, such as cognitive-behavioral therapy, place a great deal of emphasis on taking unconscious elements of experience, especially our so-called automatic thoughts, and bringing them into conscious awareness for identification and, if necessary, refutation. Cognitive distortions are automatic thoughts that involuntarily surface in our awareness and misrepresent some aspect of life experience, thereby exacerbating symptoms. In cognitive-behavioral therapy, a primary goal of treatment is to correct distorted thoughts and replace them with a more insightful and rational understanding of how to perceive and consciously interpret sensitive situations with a greater level of accuracy. Automaticity follows effortful and repeated practice.

Is it possible to instill positive automatic thoughts as a means of replacing negative ones? Rather than striving to identify and correct distorted unconscious thoughts, is it possible to influence the unconscious processes that can give rise to beneficial automatic positive thoughts? How might it change the practice of psychotherapy to absorb people in the kinds of experiences that allow them to develop automatic responses more quickly and easily? The potential for fostering positive automatic thoughts is an area of considerable overlap between mindfulness and hypnosis. Through structurally identical processes, as you discovered in the previous chapter, both approaches attempt to instill positive perceptual and behavioral reflexes that give rise to healthier and more meaningful responses.

I use the term *automaticity* to describe reflexive responses that are developed on nonconscious levels. These reflexive responses can develop in a variety of ways. They can be deliberately or accidentally conditioned as we have learned from behavioral research, they can be suggested, or they can be acquired through both conditioning experiences and suggestion working in tandem.

First, a Tiny Bit of History Regarding Hypnosis and Automaticity

Questions about how people are able to evolve purposeful, meaningful, and goal-directed unconscious responses have been at the heart of the art and science of clinical hypnosis from its earliest days as a serious domain of clinical practice and research. More than a century ago, Sigmund Freud found his way to the two primary schools of hypnosis at the time, the Salpêtrière school of Jean-Martin Charcot in Paris and the Nancy school of Hippolyte Bernheim, named for its location in the French city of Nancy. These two schools were the leading centers of neurological inquiry in the late 19th century. Hypnosis was de rigeur for studying neurology then, because it was an obvious means of producing unusual physical responses that triggered valuable insights into dissociation and the nature of what was called hysteria at the time. Thus, these meccas of the study of hypnosis were instrumental in shaping the understanding that people could respond to suggested behaviors and perceptions without necessarily having conscious awareness of doing so. Interestingly, Freud was so taken with the works of Charcot and Bernheim that he translated their books into German upon returning from their respective schools to his home in Vienna.

In the 125 years since the early demonstrations of the capacity of hypnosis to generate what was then presumed to be some form of hysteria-based responses, hypnosis has been extensively studied in the laboratory in an effort to understand how meaningful and deliberate responses can be generated outside awareness through suggestive procedures. Nonvolitional responses have also been studied in the context of clinical practice by generations of practitioners of clinical hypnosis who have directly influenced their patients to develop responses on cue that defy reasonable expectations, such as "You can now stop the bleeding at the wound site."

The late psychiatrist Milton H. Erickson diverted from the classical views of hypnosis and began to develop his unique understandings of the nature of hypnosis and hypnotic phenomena in the 1920s. As an innovator, he chose a different path for delivering treatment compared to his contemporaries. Rather than analyzing the presumed meanings of people's symptoms, or the defects in their psyches, Erickson developed a unique style for encouraging change rather than insight. Of course, change and insight are not mutually exclusive, but it was unique to Erickson's approach to emphasize the value of experiential and unconscious yet goal-directed learning.

When one performs hypnotic inductions or GMM, the principles and methods that Erickson pioneered are immediately relevant. He catalyzed a deeper and broader view of the unconscious in the psychotherapy context than anyone either before or since his pioneering innovations. He described the unconscious this way:

> Now, the unconscious mind is a vast storehouse of memories, your learnings. It has to be a storehouse because you cannot keep consciously in mind all the things you know. Your unconscious mind acts as a storehouse. Considering all the learning you have acquired in a lifetime, you use the vast majority of them automatically to function. (Zeig, 1980, p. 173)

Erickson's characterization of the unconscious is neither positive or negative—it simply acknowledges that our experiences can serve as resources. The use of hypnotic methods to gain access to and mobilize these dormant resources, as well as develop new ones, is of even greater interest now that we have growing evidence such experiences change not just minds, but brains as well. Current research on such topics as neural plasticity, unconscious processing, priming, social influence, expectancy and treatment response, and many others relevant to clinical practice can directly and indirectly trace their origins to hypnosis in general and often to the work of Erickson in particular.

Dissociation as a Context for
Facilitating Hypnosis and Mindfulness

Whether one is a practitioner of mindfulness or hypnosis, a principal goal of treatment is to encourage the development of behavioral and perceptual responses that give rise to more adaptive, expansive, self-enhancing responses to ongoing life experiences. Dissociation in both mindfulness and hypnosis helps make this possible.

Hypnosis pioneers Charcot, Bernheim, William Kroger, Ernest Hilgard, André Weitzenhoffer, Herbert Spiegel, Helen and Jack Watkins, Erickson, and too many others to name here made seminal contributions immediately relevant to practitioners of mindfulness, including their enlightened consideration of the phenomenon of dissociation and its relationship to automatic responding. In the remainder of this chapter, I explore how structured experiences in combination with well-designed suggestions can influence specific automatic responses.

What Is Dissociation?

Most psychotherapists only learn about dissociation in the context of studying psychopathology. They learn about dissociative identity disorder, fugue states, psychogenic amnesia, and other such dissociative phenomena. In such instances, dissociation is viewed as a defensive reaction, an attempt to cope with some overwhelming trauma. Some have termed this pathological dissociation and suggest that it "involves the ability to segregate and idiosyncratically encode experience into separate psychological or psychobiological processes, with associated alterations in identity" (Vermetten, Bremner, & Spiegel, 1998, p. 136). The potential to dissociate by shifting attention and engaging with one element of experience while simultaneously disengaging from others is a consequence of our having multiple levels of awareness, an ability to both absorb and respond to information on multiple levels, including levels outside of awareness. The fact that a variety of life experiences can be intense enough to catalyze a splitting of the different levels of awareness is no surprise.

However, it is vital to appreciate that dissociation is not always a defensive mechanism for coping with stressors. It is a human capacity that can be utilized for therapeutic benefit. Deliberately shifting attention away from a painful body part to experience the suggestion that the part can seem detached, thereby encouraging pain relief, is a fantastic and valuable use of physical dissociation. Detaching from negative thoughts in order to see them harmlessly float by, thereby reducing emotional reactivity, is a great use of cognitive and emotional dissociation. Thus, dissociation may be regarded as a neutral phenomenon, capable of helping to generate both positive and negative experiences.

The salient question regarding dissociation is how attentional absorption allows the formation of goal-directed, unconscious responses to suggested experiences. The person in hypnosis who is focused, whose attention is fully engaged, can respond appropriately, on cue, on time, in context, to a meaningful suggestion for which he or she may have little or no awareness (e.g., "in one minute you can experience your left arm as pleasantly numb"). Surely, automaticity is a basic function of mental processing, given how many of our responses are formed unconsciously. Beyond everyday automatic responses, however, it is a special case to describe how a nonvolitional response can arise in response to suggestions given during meditative and hypnotic experiences.

Dissociation involves cognitive and perceptual detachments arising from shifting one's attention. When you suggest to someone that he or she focus on some specific stimulus, you are directly and indirectly suggesting some degree of dissociation. If I draw your attention to *this*, then I am separating your attention from *that*. When you suggest that someone experience a sense of detachment from some thought or feeling, you are directly and indirectly suggesting dissociation.

Realistically, each and every experience we have as human beings comprises many different components. What can you experience that cannot be broken down into ever smaller units of analysis? Even the effects of mindfulness itself are now being broken down into tissue and molecular components by those who favor biological explanations and neurological evidence for its merits (Hanson & Mendius, 2009; D. Siegel, 2010b). Similarly, much of my professional life has focused on the problem of major depression. Some experts take a *macro* sociocultural view of the disorder, and others focus on the *micro* level of analysis by researching depression's neurochemistry. Even a mood can be broken down to a molecular level—and, by doing so, if one focuses on only the biology, then one effectively detaches depression from the larger social context in which it appears, is defined, and can be successfully treated. The focus on the biology of depression to the exclusion of other factors contributing to the disorder ad-

vanced by some clinicians and researchers is an unappealing example of bioreductionism (for a fuller discussion of this complex issue, see my book, *Depression
Is Contagious*; Yapko, 2009).

Out of All There Is to Focus On . . .

Of all the different things there are to pay attention to at a given moment, the
critical factors of what we choose and how we choose to pay attention play an
enormous role in how we feel and react. Accordingly, one of the principal reasons why a mindful awareness of being in the moment is so therapeutic is that it
fosters the best type of dissociation, a natural dissociation that allows the noise
of life to recede into the background, replaced with a soothing engagement with
the breath, the body, the soul. The implicit self-suggestion is, "I'm more than
what is going on out there right now . . . and *I* get to choose where I focus."

Consider your experience at this very moment as you read this. You may be
reading, but reading is a global term that encompasses many different associated
aspects of experience: Are you sitting comfortably? Are you aware of different
parts of your body as you read? Do you notice the quality of your breathing as
you read? Do you know whether you turn the pages with your left or right
hand? Do you turn them from the top, middle, or bottom of the page? Does
your mind wander as you read? Does it drift to personal experiences you've had
that surface as memories as you read, or do you find yourself focused on new
thoughts and ideas that surface in response to things you read? I could ask
10,000 questions about different aspects of your physiology, emotions, cognitions, and behavior that collectively—associatively—form your integrated, global experience of reading.

Each experience that we as human beings have is similarly composed of many
different elements. The implications are profound for whether we focus on one
element versus another: what a difference to focus on self-acceptance rather
than self-criticism! Or peace rather than violence, or what is right rather than
what is wrong. Perhaps one of the simplest ways of describing what goes on in
both GMM and clinical hypnosis sessions is that we shift the quality and direction of focus from one element of experience to another. Most typically, of
course, we attempt to shift the client's attention deliberately from some elements of experience that cause discomfort to other elements of experience (e.g.,

a philosophy of acceptance, a kinesthetic awareness of breathing) that might provide relief.

Here's a simple example: consider the experience of flying. I fly a lot and I'm comfortable flying. I read, watch movies, listen to music, even take a nap. I can relax. But, on so many flights, there's someone across the aisle from me who is anything but relaxed, barely containing intense anxiety. We are both exposed to the same conditions, namely an experience of flying in an airplane. Why am I all right when the other person is on the verge of a breakdown? In the early days of my career I used to actually get up and go ask such people, "What are you doing in there?" The answer was always the same: they were visualizing the plane taking off, the wings falling off, slamming into a mountain, and then seeing in gory detail the mountainside strewn with body parts, including their own. They became hypervigilant, a little *too* mindful of every noise and bump, judgmentally viewing these as added evidence that a plane crash was imminent.

The person who focuses on the imagery of an impending plane crash inevitably has the experience of suffering higher levels of anxiety that make flying a miserable experience. In contrast, the person who focuses on the freedom to read or snooze, or on the destination and the experiences awaiting there, will enjoy or simply tolerate the flight as a means to an end and not have much reaction to flying, either positive or negative. What a huge difference to focus on imagined dangers versus imagined benefits. Dissociation is what makes it possible to separate different elements of experience from one another to amplify awareness of one element (e.g., benefits) and thereby deamplify awareness of another (e.g., dangers).

Many of the exercises that people are taught in the name of mindfulness have the explicitly stated intention not only to increase awareness, but to do so while absorbed in a frame of mind that is accepting and nonjudgmental. Out of the literally hundreds or thousands of pieces of information available to our sensory systems and minds at a given moment, which ones hold the potential to raise consciousness helpfully? The standard advice is to "come back to the breath." When things get overwhelming, when starting to spin off into worry or anger, "come back to the breath." This is a reasonable, calming, stabilizing suggestion. But how worried or angry should one be before diverting to breath awareness? What is the process of selective attention in the practice of mindfulness meditation and how does one learn to select? Consider the following parable told by the Buddha:

A man traveling across a field encountered a tiger. He fled, the tiger after him. Coming to a precipice, he caught hold of the root of a wild vine and swung himself down over the edge. The tiger sniffed at him from above. Trembling, the man looked down to where, far below, another tiger was waiting to eat him. Only the vine sustained him.

Two mice, one white and one black, little by little started to gnaw away the vine. The man saw a luscious strawberry near him. Grasping the vine with one hand, he plucked the strawberry with the other. How sweet it tasted! (Reps & Senzaki, 1998, p. 38–39)

Panic is not going to help his situation, but neither is a strawberry. By tasting the strawberry and enjoying the moment, did he delay effective problem solving? Did he give the mice extra time to gnaw away the vine and thereby, by his passivity, help decide his fate? The salient clinical issues are quite different than the philosophical issues. There is a balance to be struck between them.

People Differ in Their Dissociative Capacities

If you consider the aims of GMM and structured hypnosis sessions, you can appreciate that the psychotherapist is attempting to redirect the client's attention in presumably positive directions. To suggest to troubled clients that they can begin to focus more on breathing right now than on trying to solve all of their problems today requires that they be able to *separate a focus on the breath from everything else*. For highly self-critical perfectionists to focus on a message of loving kindness toward themselves requires the ability to *set aside the usual self-criticism and instead focus on the message of compassion* toward the self. Can anyone do this? Under what conditions and to what degree? Is it a learnable skill that all people can acquire with a good teacher and lots of practice? Or is the capacity for dissociation a stable trait that changes little over time no matter how much you practice?

It is well established in the hypnosis literature that people differ substantially in their capacities to experience the dissociation of hypnosis meaningfully. Hypnosis experts agree that people differ in hypnotic responsiveness. Where the experts differ, however, is in their interpretation of what these differences mean. Is hypnotic responsiveness a genetically or biologically determined phenomenon, as some suggest? Is it determined by the context in which hypnosis is applied? Or is it a combination of these two and perhaps other variables as well? The same questions are immediately relevant in striving to understand people's responses to GMM.

Learning to be mindful depends heavily on dissociation. Likewise, hypnosis necessarily involves dissociation as a core element of any suggestive procedure. People often think of hypnosis as always involving relaxation, probably because relaxation is so commonly used as a vehicle for encouraging hypnotic responsiveness. However, relaxation is *not* necessary for hypnosis to occur. Hypnotic procedures can be carried out while the client's eyes are open and he or she is physically engaged in activities that are anything but relaxing, such as riding a stationary bike. The person is pedaling away—and simultaneously generating complex hypnotic phenomena such as sensory hallucinations. These are typically called waking hypnosis processes. One can do hypnosis without suggesting relaxation, but one cannot do hypnosis without suggesting dissociation.

Utilization of Unconscious Resources

As we are discovering, when GMM and clinical hypnosis focus people's attention and bring into their awareness things that had previously gone unnoticed, they may benefit profoundly from the experience. Just focusing on the breath can remind people that there is a reliable life-sustaining process they can enjoy and count on. Just performing a body scan, in which people are encouraged to focus on different parts of their body in turn, can remind people they are capable of greater physiological control than they sometimes realize and that the body can be a source of comfort and even pleasure. But what makes greater conscious awareness an important goal to strive for? Considering the earlier discussion of our conscious limitations and what may be an illusion of free choice, it makes good sense both philosophically and therapeutically to employ methods that encourage greater utilization of unconscious resources.

The work of Milton Erickson challenges the conventional wisdom that higher consciousness is *better* consciousness. Erickson evolved his own unique style of conducting psychotherapy utilizing hypnosis in creative and highly effective ways, an approach that has come to be called Ericksonian psychotherapy, also known as the utilization approach. It is extremely popular with experts in hypnosis and strategic forms of therapy.

Erickson was a maverick back when being a maverick was more than just a political gimmick. He rejected the negative views of the unconscious prevailing at the time, as well as the view of people as pathological simply because they experienced symptoms. He could see their strengths, too. His own history is a classic tale of the "wounded physician." Born color blind, tone deaf, and dyslexic, Erickson came very close to dying from the ravages of polio in his late adolescence. He undertook a long course of physical rehabilitation, which he credited for teaching him to be an extraordinary observer and skilled interpersonal tactician. After walking into a graduate course on hypnosis while still an undergraduate, taught by renowned learning theorist Clark Hull, Erickson was immediately hooked on the expansive possibilities of hypnosis. Erickson evolved a gentle, often indirect, even conversational way of eliciting hypnotic responsiveness, in sharp contrast to the direct and authoritarian styles of suggestion commonly employed at the time, which he found distasteful. He wasn't always "doing" hypnosis, but he was always "being" hypnotic, that is, recognizing and respectfully employing suggestions even in routine conversations. In the time since his death in 1980, his work has been refined and expanded in ways he could little have imagined. There are now well over 120 Milton H. Erickson Institutes around the world dedicated to advancing Erickson's teachings, the hub of the wheel being the Milton H. Erickson Foundation in Phoenix, Arizona.

Erickson commonly made use of structured amnesias in hypnosis. He would typically address his patients' issues by creating experiences—in or out of hypnosis—that would expand their views of themselves, their life options, or their capacities to respond differently and meaningfully to challenging situations. He would often provide experiences through hypnosis that would help his patients resolve their problems, and often facilitate amnesia for some or all of their hypnotic experiences. Patients would then go out into the world and carry out new responses, which served them well, that were learned through Erickson's interventions, but would experience these new responses as arising spontaneously (unconsciously) and independently. Patients would feel that they had solved the problem themselves, not Erickson. Erickson's view was that unconscious resources could be mobilized and directed in a client's behalf through the hypnotic experience, and that greater consciousness was less important than the ability to better utilize the unconscious. He said, "Consciousness does not have available all the knowledge that is in the unconscious, which actually governs our perceptions and behavior" (Erickson & Rossi, 1979, p. 367).

Erickson considered the conscious mind to be the most limited part of a person. To Erickson, the goal of expanding conscious awareness was of less interest than the goal of developing varied and innovative ways of utilizing unconscious resources. He wanted people to be able to move through life experiences more easily, more automatically in beneficial ways. (See Haley, 1973/1986; Zeig, 1980, for compelling introductions to Erickson and his strategic approaches.) His was a substantially different viewpoint about the best way to help someone, and it made far more deliberate use of dissociation than other approaches typically do. Interestingly, though, GMM seems to work in a parallel way: the client has a moving, expansive experience while in a focused state, may or may not remember some or all of the experience, yet feels empowered somehow and then reports the spontaneous discovery of new subjective responses indicating some improvements that seem to just happen.

Encouraging Nonvolitional Responses in Hypnosis and Guided Mindfulness Meditation

In hypnosis, dissociation is especially evident when people respond nonvolitionally, that is, without conscious effort, to a suggestion. A clinician might suggest an experience of arm levitation, offering suggestions for the client to focus on allowing the experience of his or her arm becoming lighter and lighter until it actually begins to lift. The client is not aware of expending any effort; the arm seems to just lift by itself. Typically, the first time a client has a dissociative experience—an unconscious, goal-directed response that is detached from conscious intention or effort, such as an arm levitation in hypnosis—he or she is truly amazed. It is a potentially profound discovery to find that there are elements beyond your conscious experience that can generate meaningful responses in a directed fashion. Put simply, people discover there is more to themselves—more resources, more potential—than they previously realized. Clients experience this realization as empowering, motivating, intriguing, and enjoyable. It is a concrete example of the power of suggested dissociation to create a context for developing unconscious responses. Part of the person is responding, but not all. How is it possible to access an individual's unconscious through hypnosis to suggest a specific response that the person provides without any sense of effort in forming that response? This has been the million-dollar question in hypnosis since its earliest days in both clinical and research contexts.

In GMM, dissociation similarly becomes evident when people are able to separate themselves from their usual frames of reference. When people are able to lose the sense of self when focused narrowly on just the physical experience of breathing, that sense of depersonalization is a dissociative response. When people are able to externalize their thoughts by seeing them "like clouds in the sky," the separation of self from their thoughts is a powerful experience of dissociation with the potential for great therapeutic benefit. It is a critical step in reducing emotional reactivity, building impulse control, increasing frustration tolerance, and expanding skills in reality testing.

There are many different forms of mindful meditation, of course, but they share the common denominator of fostering some degree of dissociation to make them experientially meaningful. The most basic starting point to introduce dissociation into someone's experience is a suggestion to "focus on this." Both hypnosis and GMM employ the mechanism of selective attention as the catalyst for dissociative experiences. Thus, it becomes immediately important to consider the role of attention in GMM and hypnotic experiences, which I explore in Chapter 5.

Global Cognitive Style and Dissociative Abilities

The ability to dissociate in useful ways during experiential processes of hypnosis and mindfulness is affected by many different variables, such as attentional style, expectations, willingness to engage, personal history, competing environmental stimuli, level of stress, and coping style. Arguably however, the single greatest factor influencing one's capacity for dissociation is cognitive style. Cognitive style, the patterned ways one tends to think, plays a powerful role in shaping many of the variables just mentioned. A number of different qualities of cognition are relevant, but none more so than one's tendency toward what is referred to in the literature as overgeneral thinking, or what I prefer to call a global cognitive style.

It is obvious that different people think differently. Cognitive neuroscientists have been attempting to distinguish between different styles of cognition for decades. Their efforts inform our educational system and our business environments, and hold the potential to inform our clinical interventions involving mindfulness and hypnosis. One of the best articulated and developed aspects of the modern practice of clinical hypnosis revolves around the question of how best to formulate suggestions in a manner that will more easily be taken in and responded to by the client? This represents the artistry of clinical hypnosis. The ability to adapt one's delivery to the client requires many different skills, including observational skills to determine the client's information processing style and the verbal skills to take a message and tailor it to the client's style. No matter how many times you have conducted a body scan during a GMM, it will always require modification because people respond idiosyncratically. It is important to adapt your methods to individual differences.

People's thinking styles differ in terms of how general or specific their thoughts are. Certainly thinking styles can vary with the context: One can have a general, global view of relationships and a very specific view of money management, for example. But it is often possible to describe people in terms of their general or typical cognitive styles. Some people have a strong desire to know the details, whereas others are quite happy to simply skim the surface of different life experiences. Let's consider the implications of these stylistic differences for techniques of GMM and clinical hypnosis.

The person with a global cognitive style is more likely to have difficulty breaking global experiences into their component parts, a skill necessary to achieve meaningful dissociation. Global thinkers may not know how to recognize what they are specifically feeling or thinking, and simply react globally and emotionally to circumstances without insight. People responding globally to multiple stressors may become overwhelmed by all the difficulties they are facing, and experience emotional paralysis and the inability to break overwhelming global issues into specific problems to solve. The person who responds globally emotionally, who says, in essence, "All of me feels this way," is more likely to overreact. People who defines themselves globally, who think, "All I am is this job or relationship," are far more likely to suffer terribly when that job or relationship is jeopardized or lost. The research literature has been unequivocal about the relationship between overgeneral thinking and the associated increased risks for anxiety, depression, and post-traumatic stress disorder (PTSD). It is a common task in therapy to address global responses that define common disorders by breaking them into manageable smaller components and teaching the skills of then addressing and resolving specific issues.

In performing GMM and hypnosis sessions, the quality and direction of the client's global cognitive style will influence how well he or she will be able to respond. In mindfulness sessions, clients frequently report that they could not maintain focus because mundane and irrelevant thoughts sidetracked them. The mindful therapist gently assures the client that this is normal, to be expected, and that regular practice will increase focus and decrease distractibility. In hypnosis sessions, clients report exactly the same thing and are similarly assured that not only is it normal to get sidetracked, but it should be allowed because whatever the conscious mind may miss can still be absorbed and responded to meaningfully by the unconscious.

If the goal, though, is to facilitate deeper hypnotic experiences and meditative states, then it becomes desirable to foster deeper dissociations to counter ineffective global responses. In fact, practitioners of hypnosis have paid a great deal of attention to the depth of the hypnotic experience. Until relatively recently, many assumed a deeper experience was a better experience. As alluded to earlier, the depth of an experience is not about the degree of relaxation, nor about how nonverbal it was or how enlightened the person felt. Rather, it is about the degree of attentional absorption and attentional redirection achieved. We are interested in how able a client was to flexibly detach from his or her usual frame of reference to become absorbed in another, presumably more therapeutic, quality of experience. The capacity to separate oneself in this way to engage with one element of experience to the exclusion of most or all others is the essence of attentional and experiential absorption. Whether one does this as a meditation on a raisin or a Zen koan, or a self-hypnosis session for pain management, the capacity to detach from one perceptual frame to become immersed in another is key.

Another way to name this capacity for dissociation through attentional absorption is with the synonymous term *compartmentalization*, which is the ability to focus on one element of experience and keep it functionally separate from other immediate experiences. Compartmentalization is a necessary skill for living life well. We need to be able to focus on one thing right now and let other things recede into the background. In fact, one way of thinking about the nature of PTSD is as a lack of skill in compartmentalization. Anyone who suffers PTSD symptoms has material (e.g., visual images, emotions, body sensations) from the past intruding into the present in an uncontrolled, distressing fashion. The traumatic experience is not compartmentalized as a past event. To the contrary, the past event continues to spread into and contaminate current experience as if it was still occurring. It is routine in the treatment of PTSD, regardless of therapeutic modality employed, that a primary goal of treatment is to teach and help the client acquire compartmentalization skills to better separate past from present.

GMM emphasizes compartmentalization skills, though not with this terminology. To derive benefit from GMM, a person must learn to compartmentalize. To focus on just the breath requires compartmentalization, as does a focus on acceptance rather than self-criticism or a focus on feelings of compassion rather than anger or hurt. The benefits of teaching our clients the methods of mindfulness and hypnosis as vehicles of selective attention and enhanced control are great and hold the potential to be even greater as dissociation's role in nonvolitional attentional processes becomes better understood.

Is Compartmentalization a Good Thing?

It is important to appreciate the role of context in determining the value of dissociative experiences. Dissociation may allow us to distill experiences to their essence, but is that a good thing? The answer, it seems, depends on whether the dissociation serves to enhance experience or diminish it.

Both mindfulness and hypnosis have paid substantial attention to ways of assisting with pain management. Hypnosis in particular has a very broad and deep literature on pain management (Barber, 1996; Patterson, 2010) that lends substantial empirical support to the merits of hypnosis in reducing or even eliminating the subjective experience of pain across many types of conditions. The way that hypnosis uses dissociation to manage pain overlaps the way mindfulness uses dissociation to reduce suffering, but differs in its methods for actively transforming subjective perceptions of the body and the pain sensation itself. Yet both employ dissociation as a principal means of promoting comfort.

When deliberately applied, dissociation in the service of pain management is a wonderful means of helping. But the same mechanism of dissociation for pain reduction can be misapplied. Consider an individual who self-mutilates. This person can literally take a knife and slice into his or her own flesh with no apparent pain or suffering. If you ask directly, "Doesn't that hurt?," the person typically replies, "No. It feels good. It's how I get my feelings out. It's the only thing that makes me feel alive." This is a clear example of how compartmentalization, the sense of detachment from part of one's body, can play a central role in disordered thoughts and self-mutilating behavior.

The fact that various hypnotic phenomena can be used to generate symptoms as well as solutions requires a better than global consideration of their role in effective applications of mindfulness and hypnosis. Without specificity, meaning a clear goal and specific guidelines for delineating and following the steps to achieve that goal, an intervention runs the risk of simply becoming another global perspective that may or may not be helpful across different contexts. To offer a concrete example, it may be valuable to teach someone self-hypnosis or a meditation promoting a "radical acceptance" that can provide detachment from pain, but no therapist would want a client so educated to use this strategy for self-mutilation.

Specific guidelines regarding when to employ such strategies constructively must be considered a necessary ingredient in treatment. But not all clinicians care to—or can—provide such guidelines. Many promote certain pop psychology clichés, which grab hold of the public, who do not think critically about their merits or limitations. Instead, the public accepts them noncritically and adopts them as a philosophy of life. Promoting global beliefs such as, "You are responsible for everything that happens in your life" actually discourages making meaningful discriminations between what you are and are not responsible for. Without the ability to go beyond the global statement, people too easily unfairly blame themselves for situations or events for which they are not to blame, such as being laid off when a factory closes or their car being stolen.

Clearly we must go beyond attractive philosophies and think more critically about the process of focusing people lest we generate unintended outcomes. Any therapeutic process that breaks people's global experiences into their component parts runs the same level of risk. As soon as we start using the language of dissociation, intentionally or otherwise, we will amplify and deamplify parts of a person based on our beliefs and therapeutic framework. The "parts" metaphor of human experience has potential clinical utility, and every therapy model promotes a selective attention to some parts rather than others. The therapist's assumptions about the nature of human experience in general and the client's experience in particular will lead him or her to suggestively direct the client's experience, even while denying doing so.

Suggesting Dissociation

In hypnosis, the generic suggestion for dissociation is, "part of you is experiencing this while the rest of you is experiencing that." Using the arm levitation example offered earlier, as soon as the therapist suggests that the arm is getting lighter, dissociation is being indirectly suggested. The therapist is saying, in essence, "Part of you [i.e., your arm] is experiencing lightness while the rest of you is experiencing your usual weight." As soon as the therapist suggests that you have parts (optimistic or pessimistic, compassionate or self-critical, accepting or rejecting, masculine or feminine, child, adult, or parent, serious or playful, etc.), he or she is encouraging a dissociation, possibly even multiple dissociations.

One of the ways of describing psychotherapy, any psychotherapy, is in terms of what it dissociates the client *from* and, simultaneously, what it associates the client *to*. In GMM, for example, the client may be told to identify a part of the self that is self-critical. The client may further be told to identify a part that is capable of great compassion. GMMs that focus on compassion will structurally strive to help the client dissociate from self-criticism and associate to compassion. But if these two parts of the self are not adequately developed and compartmentalized to be reorganized in this way, the process is unlikely to succeed to the degree it might otherwise.

Another Look at Priming the Unconscious

Now that we have taken a look at selective attention, dissociation, and unconscious processing from several different angles, let's return to the issue of deliberate attempts to influence the unconscious. This potential has been studied for decades, primarily by memory experts, language experts, social psychologists, and neuroscientists. A principal means of studying the relationship between the unconscious exposure to specific stimuli and the influence of those stimuli on later behavior and perception has been through the study of priming. Priming involves exposing experimental subjects (or clients) to words, images, or even objects in the environment, at levels outside of conscious awareness (subliminally), then exposing them to some task during which or after the unconscious influence might be observed in their responses. For example, in one study (Epley, Savitsky, & Kachelski, 1999), graduate students in psychology were asked to generate topics for possible research. The researchers then exposed the students to subliminal images (i.e., brief flashes on a screen delivered too quickly to notice consciously) of either the smiling face of a friendly colleague or the obviously dissatisfied face of their faculty supervisor. Next, they were asked to evaluate the merits of the research topics they generated. With no conscious understanding of why, students who had been exposed to the dissatisfied face rated their own ideas more harshly than those who had been exposed to the smiling face. What does this suggest? It suggests, at least in part, that a stimulus with an affective valence (i.e., an emotional component) can affect one's emotions and perceptions at an entirely unconscious level. The emerging field of affective neuroscience is providing interesting insights regarding emotional states, neurological functioning, and the decision-making strategies people employ.

One study (Williams, Bargh, Nocera, & Gray, 2009) may have profound implications for the practice of mindfulness in particular. It addressed the question of how likely someone is to reach a goal when the goal is nonconscious compared to when the goal is consciously pursued. When individuals were nonconsciously primed to be goal oriented for the purpose of encouraging emotional regulation, their behavior was every bit as goal oriented as those who had consciously oriented themselves to attaining a specific goal. The researchers wrote, "Across a variety of goal contingents, non-consciously operating goals have been found to produce the same outcomes, and in the same manner, as when those goals are consciously pursued" (p. 847).

Malcolm Gladwell's (2005) popular book, *Blink*, caused many to question the merits of conscious decision making versus relying on intuitive, unconscious decision making. Some researchers have come to the conclusion that, in some domains of decision making, nonconscious processes may produce even better outcomes than a conscious analysis of the same information. Their rationale is that conscious thinking is limited by the lesser capacities of working memory and the typically linear nature of conscious process. Unconscious thought processes do not share these limitations. It is to Milton Erickson's credit that he formed the same conclusion more than half a century ago, well before the development of modern research protocols and sophisticated studies examining the merits of unconscious processing.

In another study of priming, researchers manipulated objects in a room to assess their potential influence on people's behavior. Research subjects were given the task of working together as a group to achieve a shared goal. When the room contained a briefcase on a table, group members behaved much more competitively with each other than they did when a backpack was on the table (Kay, Wheeler, Bargh, & Ross, 2004). Similarly, in a classic study, people behaved much more aggressively when there were guns on a nearby table than when there were badminton racquets (Berkowitz & LePage, 1967).

Verbally Shooting in the Dark

What complicates matters substantially is the inability to predict what might serve as an agent of priming. It is often the case conducting guided meditations or formal hypnosis sessions that one simply does not know which words, phrases, images, or realizations will be the ones to have a lasting therapeutic impact. I can offer suggestions directed at specific goals and, just as often as not, the client generates responses I did not necessarily intend. Perhaps more remarkable is how often the responses clients generate are more sophisticated than what I had in mind. Thus, I have come to appreciate how important it is to use mindfulness and hypnosis strategies as a vehicle for creating possibilities, allowing for the possibility that the person's response may well be the most useful one for him or her.

Conclusion

From this chapter's focus on the roles of attention and dissociation in providing a context for the therapeutic benefits of GMM and hypnosis, a different frame is established for helping to understand these experiences. Clearly, practitioners of mindfulness have different explanations for what they do and how it works than practitioners of hypnosis do. But these differences are of little consequence when we focus on what practitioners of either approach *actually say and do* rather than what they say that they say and do. This has been routinely observed across psychotherapies: therapists do far more that is alike than different in clinical practice, despite their very different theoretical and philosophical descriptions of what they do.

In this chapter's focus on the foundational role of dissociation in catalyzing the therapeutic benefits of GMM and clinical hypnosis, practitioners can learn to recognize and better utilize their emphasis on amplifying and deamplifying parts of a person in their treatments. Building a "compassionate part," for example, necessarily precedes learning how to relate to it beneficially. By immersing the person in a focused, dissociated state in which conscious and unconscious processes function more independently of each other, and where an automaticity of responses is thereby increased, the ability to further develop compartmentalized parts becomes more pronounced. Which parts one assists in creating and how one organizes them for therapeutic benefit will necessarily differ from client to client based on need and personal style. And they will necessarily differ according to the clinician's belief system about which aspects of a person's experience are the most valuable ones to develop.

CHAPTER 5

Guided Mindfulness Meditation and Clinical Hypnosis: Shared Structures and Functions

Hypnosis is a state of hyperacuity. Most people think about it being a detached, unaware kind of state. It's not. It is a highly focused state, wherein sensory and motor capacities are altered in order to initiate appropriate behavior.
Kay F. Thompson, DDS (2004, p. 12)

As a longtime practitioner of hypnotically based methods, I have been deeply impressed by the significant therapeutic gains that such methods offer my clients. Many people benefit, and benefit quickly. However, it is inevitable that any practitioner of such methods will run into the differences in quality and magnitude of response across individuals. As experienced practitioners of mindfulness will also acknowledge, whereas almost everyone can benefit from all that mindfulness has to offer, not everyone will benefit to the same degree or at the same rate. There are inevitable individual differences in responsiveness to *any* approach.

In this chapter, I explore some of the intra- and interpersonal factors inherent in conducting GMM or clinical hypnosis sessions that influence individual responses to them. Beyond the clinician's intention or underlying philosophy of approach, the subjective phenomenology of the client's experience is what determines whether the experience is regarded as helpful.

There is no doubt that the Buddhist underpinnings of mindfulness provide a sophisticated and elegant framework for integrating mindfulness into one's life. Likewise, there is no doubt that the malleability of human experience highlighted through hypnotic methods is enormously powerful in facilitating meaningful personal growth. Developing a deeper insight into some of the structures of subjective experience that are amplified through experiential learning processes can help clinicians better adapt their methods and thereby increase their effectiveness.

You're Unique . . . Just Like Everyone Else

Many mindfulness practitioners regularly provide GMMs in their workshops and writings, and also in the form of DVDs, recorded audio CDs, and downloadable MP3 programs. These scripted or prerecorded formats are known as standardized approaches. A standardized approach is, in essence, a one-size-fits-all method. All individuals are exposed to the exact same procedures without variation, as if all of them can or will respond in the same way.

In fact, the limitations of standardized approaches contributed in no small way to the popularity of Ericksonian hypnosis. One of Milton Erickson's most often quoted caveats about psychotherapy referred to this issue: "Each person is a unique individual. Hence, psychotherapy should be formulated to meet the uniqueness of the individual's needs, rather than tailoring the person to fit the Procrustean bed of a hypothetical theory of human behavior" (Zeig, 1982, p. vii). The field of hypnosis has paid significant attention to the standardization of methods, especially because so much hypnosis research has taken place in the laboratory where standardization and tight control of methods are imperative. In the laboratory, many individuals exposed to an experimental condition are compared with many that are not (the controls). Accordingly, any significant differences that are found between the experimental and control groups on the variables under consideration are attributable to the treatment received. But the assumptions and methods in studying larger populations are quite different than those in treating individuals in therapy. Differences of opinion exist regarding the extent to which laboratory research findings are applicable to clinical practices serving individuals seeking help in a clinical context.

If a standardized approach is applied, whether it has been tested in a lab or not, what should we conclude about individuals who do not respond in any meaningful way? Should they be deemed resistant? Is it evidence of secondary gain, that is, a motivated lack of response? Does the failure to respond highlight the irrelevance of the technique for this particular individual who might well respond to a more personalized one?

Whether one addresses and how one answers these questions speaks volumes about how one applies these experiential approaches. If we view a minimal response to an approach as evidence of something lacking in the client, then there's no need to modify our approach. The method is assumed to be sound and the difficulty is with the client. But if we consider that the approach might be sound in general, but not for this particular client, then striving to adapt our methods to the individual will become an integral part of practice. When striving to tailor our experiential processes to the individual client, the factors described in this chapter become important to consider.

Individual Neurobiology and Paying Attention

Clinical hypnosis and GMM are highly similar in the way they focus attention, each giving rise to similar qualities of experience that people describe as different from usual consciousness. These qualities include a sense of detachment, a sense of timelessness, and absorption in the experience. Not surprisingly, the neurophysiology of hypnosis and meditation is also similar. How we pay attention, and how well we pay attention, have become hot topics in the field of neuroscience. Some neuroscientists strive to identify morphological differences between the brains of people who manifest an obvious ability to focus well and the brains of those who have difficulty paying attention. Other neuroscientists are interested in how changing the immediate environment influences brains and minds that are tasked with focusing exercises.

Jean Holroyd of UCLA, in an excellent review of the mindfulness and hypnosis literature, described similarities in studies of both hypnosis and meditation:

The neurophysiology of deep hypnosis and deep meditation is similar.... Often there is cortical inhibition, as evidenced by very slow EEG theta waves.... High band theta is related to hypnotizability, and theta power often increases as people (both high and low hypnotizables) go into hypnosis.... EEG theta waves are also prominent in deep states of meditation.... The far frontal cortex and the anterior cingulate gyrus on the midline surface of the frontal lobe are areas where theta figures prominently in meditation studies.... In both the meditation and hypnosis investigations, areas where theta is prominent (frontal cortex and especially anterior cingulate cortex) are also perfused with blood, which means that they are working hard. (2003, pp. 115–116)

Most important, though, are these statements:

When meditation involves activities other than just concentration, EEG patterns change over the relevant cortical sites, *depending on the meditation activity*. In a direct parallel, when hypnosis involves suggestions, the appropriate sensory and motor areas of the brain may be activated even more than in the non-hypnotic condition. (2003, p. 117; emphasis added)

The reason these last two sentences are so important is that much of the uniqueness of GMM disappears as soon as suggestions are given to develop some perception or perspective, whether it be compassion or something else. The biological lines separating hypnosis and mindfulness at the level of clinical practice, where suggestions are routinely given for developing self-enhancing experiences, are not readily distinguishable.

In their book *Neuro-Hypnosis*, C. Alexander Simpkins and Annellen Simpkins (2010) also pointed to a shared neurobiology between meditation and hypnosis, emphasizing the brain structures associated with focus and attention. Their book does an excellent job of bridging the gap between brain and mind, and uses the growing body of evidence regarding brain plasticity to suggest ways to maximize brain function with hypnosis.

It is currently difficult to assess how many of the conclusions regarding the neurophysiology of meditation and hypnosis can be considered objectively true. As Williams et al. pointed out, "researchers' understanding of the specific meaning of neurophysiological activity is still rudimentary" (2010, p. 334). Despite the presumption of a substantial overlap between the brain signatures of mindfulness and hypnosis, different forms of meditation (e.g., concentrative, expansive) and different forms and aims of hypnotic suggestion make it difficult to accurately compare the neurophysiology of mindfulness and hypnosis. It is simply premature to form a conclusion that they are neurophysiologically either the same or different. It is reasonable to predict, though, that these experiential processes that share a common language and a common phenomenology will also likely share a common neurophysiology (Spiegel, White, & Waelde, 2010).

Holroyd (2003), in her comparative article, described the phenomenological similarities found in studies of meditators and self-hypnosis practitioners alluded to above. Though the meditation was of a different type than mindfulness, specifically a Kundalini form that involves concentration and imagery of energy moving through the body, the results are germane:

> Both meditation and deep self-hypnosis were associated with … alterations in state of awareness, self-awareness, time sense, perception, and meaning; with changes in imagery vividness and rationality; and both processes were accompanied by feelings of joy and love. (2003, p. 113)

Perhaps it goes without saying, but I think it important to say anyway: The goal is not to encourage an alignment with either hypnosis or mindfulness, in a forced either/or choice. In pointing out the overlapping language, neurophysiology, and phenomenology of clinical hypnosis and GMM, the goal is to maximize the benefits to the client by integrating insights and methods from both fields. The merits of such an integration have been well described by Lynn et al. (2006), Otani (2003), and Williams et al. (2010).

Individual Differences in Paying Attention

Developing and utilizing attentional focus is a primary emphasis of both mindfulness and hypnosis:

> All of us have the capacity to be mindful. All it involves is cultivating our ability to pay attention in the present moment. . . . Think of mindfulness as a lens, taking the scattered and reactive energies of your mind and focusing them into a coherent source of energy for living, for problem solving, and for healing. (Kabat-Zinn, 1990, p. 11)

The capacity to pay attention is obviously a critical component, indeed, the defining component of mindfulness. Does everyone pay attention in the same way and to the same extent? Intuitively, one knows the answer is no. Research on attention confirms the intuition in this case (Dietrich, 2003; Heap, Brown, & Oakley, 2004; Raz, 2005).

Without the ability to pay attention, we would be overwhelmed by the vast amount of information available in sensory experience at any given moment. When people suffer disorders that affect their ability to focus, such as attention-deficit disorder, physical pain, or severe anxiety, the resulting distress and impairments tend to be obvious. Clearly, the capacity to focus in a meaningful way varies across individuals. How do variations in attentional capacities influence a client's response to GMM and hypnotic interventions? To what extent will innate attentional capacities vary when exposed to differing procedures? Furthermore, will your expectations for and subsequent treatment of clients differ based on how you view their capacity to pay attention?

Beyond the individual differences evident as a result of physical and mental states, the hypnosis literature suggests attention and responsiveness will vary, even at a neurophysiological level, based on the type of suggestions offered (Barabasz, 2000; Barabasz et al., 1999; Oakley, 2008). The role of standardization again becomes significant here. If one adopts a structured approach, one that is delivered in much the same way across different individuals, variations in responsiveness will inevitably surface. When an individual's response is minimal, does that reflect the limitations of a standardized approach to meet individual needs, or does it indicate some personal limitation? Or is it a combination of the two?

Responding to Individual Differences

Practitioners typically respond in two distinct ways to differences in client responsiveness. One response is to debrief the individual about the experience after the session to learn something about how to structure such experiences to increase their personal meaning. The other response is to maintain one's belief in the merits of the particular process and suggest to the client that the technique is well established and he or she is somehow blocked and will require help and lots of additional practice to develop the desired response.

There is a third possible response, however: talk to the client *during* the experiential session, get feedback about his or her experience, and use it to adjust the process while it is still ongoing. It is a routine part of modern clinical hypnosis training to engage the client in this way based on the recognition that if you wait until the session is over to debrief the client's experience, it is too late. The session is already finished and there is no opportunity to adjust one's approach and continue the session. Beginners in hypnosis are fearful they will disrupt the session by engaging the client this way, but what they discover in practice is that when they give the client suggestions to make it easy to speak about their experience and even deepen their experience further as they do so, the interaction does, in fact, deepen the experience for the client. It requires flexibility as a practitioner to be willing to engage in this way and use the information to change one's methods midstream when the client's feedback suggests this would be helpful.

In many of the GMMs reviewed in preparing this book, and in many of the books introducing mindfulness to the reader, whether professional or layperson, the typical advice provided is to practice, practice, practice. The assumption is that the mindfulness technique is sound and one's skill in performing it will improve if practiced regularly. This same viewpoint pervades the hypnosis literature, in which it is routinely suggested that regular practice will increase responsiveness, presumably by making selective attention a more well developed, reliable skill. Thus, individual differences are acknowledged and seen as bridgeable, narrowing toward greater similarity across people with repetition, called the practice effect.

Paying Attention Involves Choice

If you know the phrase, "He only sees what he wants to see," then you are already aware that people can notice what they choose to notice. By implication, we can also not notice what we choose not to notice. This perceptual phenomenon is referred to as selective attention, that is, the ability to voluntarily focus on one portion of an experience while tuning out the rest. Focusing on a specific stimulus (e.g., words, gestures, silence, images, sounds, textures, memories) to the exclusion or near-exclusion of other ongoing stimuli is the foundation of meditative and hypnotic experiences upon which the other phenomena rest.

Even when the focus is on having no focus, that is, just a general heightened awareness for whatever one happens to notice, there is, paradoxically and inevitably, still a focus on *something*.

A number of complex factors determine what works its way into awareness, including the degree of sensory stimulation (how weak or strong the stimulus is), the novelty of the stimulus, the person's response tendencies (arising from a complex interplay of socialization and genetics), the person's motivation to attend in the context under consideration, the person's mood, and the kinds and amounts of other sensory stimulation coexisting in the environment. This is why practice is so important in regulating attention; there will virtually always be multiple things available to attend to at a given moment. In training oneself to be skilled in meditation or self-hypnosis, one learns how to regulate attentional abilities.

As neuroscientists focus on the nature of attention, they commonly describe different attentional subsystems in the brain. These different subsystems lend substantial support to the influence of dissociation in multiple-level responding. In fact, one of the premier pioneering hypnosis researchers, Ernest Hilgard, PhD, first described in modern terms the role of dissociation in hypnotic responding. Hilgard was known for many key contributions to the field, including codeveloping with André Weitzenhoffer the hypnotizability test that remains the gold standard in the field today, called the Stanford Hypnotic Susceptibility Scale. His formulation of the neodissociation theory of hypnosis has special relevance here (Hilgard, 1977). Hilgard postulated that an "executive system" serves as the decider among conflicting inputs on different, lower levels of attentional processing. Current neuroscience research supports the existence of different levels by identifying three attentional subsystems in the brain, the first of which is an executive attentional subsystem. Its function is defined as conflict monitoring (Raz, Fan, & Posner, 2005). An implication for real life: What suggestions might you offer to someone caught in the conflict of emotionally wanting to avoid the unpleasant when intellectually he knows that avoidance only makes things worse?

A second attentional subsystem is the orienting subsystem, whose function is to orient the individual spatially. If I say, "Look here," I am directing your attention to a specific location (Posner & Peterson, 1990). An implication for real life: What suggestions can you offer someone who gets sidetracked by the irrelevant, such as ambient noise in the environment in which you are conducting your session?

A third attentional subsystem is the alerting subsystem, which orients the individual temporally. If I say, "Look at this *now*," I am orienting you in terms of both space and time (Simpkins & Simpkins, 2010). An implication for real life: What might you suggest to someone who is wrapped up in rehashing the past or overplanning the future while you're conducting your session?

It is curious that focused attention can readily give rise to unconscious responses to suggestions. It is also interesting, but hardly surprising, to discover from the neuroscience that different areas of the brain regulate the different types of attention. Thus, it is predictable that there are differences in brain activity across different types of meditation as well as different types of hypnotic experiences. In the same way that one's quality of attention regulates emotion, cognition, and motor activity, *one's quality of attention will necessarily activate different regions of the brain depending on the content of one's focus.*

The Capacity for Absorption

In the practice of mindful meditation, and often in self-hypnosis as well, it is a frequently stated goal to develop what some call "flow" and what others call a "sense of selflessness." Whatever terminology one prefers, the experience of the person in deep meditation or hypnosis may be a profound sense of experiential absorption. In other words, the person is so absorbed in the experience that he or she can temporarily lose a sense of self as an active agent in the process. As you now know, dissociation is a defining element of this quality of experience.

Other elements of experience are also vitally important in facilitating absorption. In the hypnosis literature, imaginative involvement is often a foundation for generating therapeutically meaningful associations (Bowers, 1992). In mindfulness, an *open presence* allows experiences to arise that can have great spiritual meaning, an obvious parallel (Brach, 2004). In hypnosis, the client is encouraged to create an internal atmosphere that is supportive, gentle, and empowering. In many GMMs, the emphasis is on compassion, as the client is taught to do no harm. Again, the parallels are obvious.

Wanting to encourage meaningful absorption as a vehicle to enlightenment or well-being is an obvious goal of employing mindfulness and hypnosis. But, just as people differ in their capacities to focus and engage meaningful attention, they differ in their capacity for absorption. When one considers all the obvious barriers to developing and maintaining absorption, especially such factors as physical pain, high levels of anxiety, and feelings of deep despair, it is easy to appreciate how absorption can be negatively affected by the very symptoms the person hopes to alleviate through the experience of absorption. The person may try to generate a meaningful experience of absorption, yet be unable to do so in the first attempts. If the client experiences low frustration tolerance or makes negative attributions about the experience (e.g., "I'm incompetent. I'll never get the hang of this and it means I'm always going to suffer"), whatever suggestions were offered with the best of intentions have the potential to be a painful episode in the client's experience, particularly if he or she subsequently gives up trying to experience and benefit from hypnosis or meditating.

Can one learn to create flow states at will? Those who have practiced meditation over long periods of time maintain that the answer is yes. Studies of long-term meditators lend impressive support to their claims. Likewise, people who have practiced self-hypnosis over long periods of time report similar capacities for self-regulation and higher awareness (Holroyd, 2003; Williams et al., 2010). It is easy to believe them when they demonstrate dramatic hypnotic capabilities, such as the ability to undergo surgery without any chemical anesthetic. The important corollary question is, can anyone learn to create flow states at will?

The salient issue concerns the modifiability of responsiveness to these methods. While this question has not yet been substantively explored in the mindfulness literature, it has been in the hypnosis literature. The capacity for hypnosis has been shown to be modifiable. Nicholas Spanos, a primary researcher in this area and a strong proponent of a social psychological view of hypnosis, showed how research subjects who previously tested low or even as unhypnotizable could become suitably responsive if they were provided with new information that changed their unrealistic or negative expectations (Spanos et al., 1986). These findings suggest that how one introduces and describes the goals and methods of hypnosis and GMM plays a powerful role in shaping client expectations and responses to these experiential processes.

Predictably, however, we also encounter profound individual differences in responding to experiential methods that strongly suggest that even with substantial practice some individuals will simply not develop focusing and absorption abilities to a meaningful degree (Gibbons & Lynn, 2010). Thus, we have to further consider how to explain these inevitable differences both to ourselves and our clients. Leading clients to believe that they will eventually "get it" if they practice enough can make each failing, or simply unsatisfying, experience increasingly painful. No matter how many times the clinician charitably assures clients that "no experience is a failing experience," some clients simply will not believe it to be true. Worse, leading people to believe that they are somehow defective because of the inability to generate dramatic and impressive responses can create emotional distress and demoralization.

The Capacity for Emotional, Cognitive, and Spiritual Depth

Another of the important ways people differ is in their capacities for deep, or profound, experiences on different levels. Is everyone equally capable of deep thought, deep emotional awareness, or spiritual enlightenment? It does not seem unfairly judgmental to acknowledge that people differ markedly in their capacities for having deep experiences, just as they differ in other characteristics (e.g., intelligence, empathy). There are differing viewpoints about human potential, of course, and there are those who are philosophically opposed to the idea that some people are simply not capable of deeper experiences. If we are to deal with the issue of individual differences in capacities for deeper experiences realistically, then putting aside idealistic philosophies will be necessary.

It is tempting to believe that each person is capable of deep and rich experience. It is tempting to want to believe that under the right conditions everyone is equally capable of profound experiences such as spiritual enlightenment, a connection to God, and an awareness of universal truth. Even if such idealistic beliefs had merit, in practical terms there are people who have no interest in spiritual matters, intellectual pursuits, or emotional awareness. Personal philosophies and psychological explanations for such individuals aside, it is important in the way one conducts one's clinical practice to consider the goodness of fit between one's therapeutic intentions and a client's capabilities.

The clinical literature is replete with demoralizing examples of clinicians having sold individuals in certain diagnostic categories short. As an example, consider so-called borderline clients, whom many argued were too severely pathological to help, given their volatile emotions, self-destructive behaviors, unpredictability, and difficulty in maintaining relationships. However, given the advances in the treatment of borderline personality disordered and other diagnostically severe individuals, especially evident in the dialectical behavior therapy model (Linehan,1993; Dimeff & Koerner, 2007), it may be imprudent to suggest that a client has predetermined limits on his or her potential. However, it is also wise to be realistic in appreciating that not everyone is capable of everything. Too often, we look at people who excel in some way and then suggest that this individual represents the human potential of all people. The danger is in erroneously believing that because *one* person can excel, *all* people can excel similarly.

There are some people whose style of thinking, information processing, and relating not only lack depth but may even preclude the potential to develop depth. People may argue whether this deficit is genetically, psychologically, culturally, or multifactorally determined, but attempting to explain the lack of ability to achieve depth does not change this fact: Some people will be exposed to deep procedures, whether clinical hypnosis or GMMs designed to foster higher awareness, and their response will, nevertheless, be superficial. Across many different experiences, in fact, ranging from tragic to inspirational, their response is equally superficial. Shouldn't this be taken into account when attempting to promote deep experiences?

I am not suggesting that it is futile to strive to promote meaningful experiences. I am suggesting, however, that clinicians should not be surprised when some people's reaction to experiences that many find powerful and life transforming is, essentially, "So what?" Many clinicians, it seems, operate on what I call the "hidden gem" hypothesis. They have the idealistic belief that if you dig deeply enough, you can find the hidden gem of a deeper self inside anyone. It may sound cynical, but I think it is actually realistic to say that some people are very superficial and will remain that way even in the face of what others might call powerful and transformational experiences.

Internal and External Orientations and Differing Versions of Reality

An *internal orientation* is the term used to describe the heavily subjective focus of a client. Utilized skillfully, an internal orientation can help one be more self-aware and make good decisions accordingly. However, one can be *too* internally oriented when habitually focused on one's feelings, perceptions, and beliefs at the expense of noticing and responding skillfully to more objective information that may be available from the outside (e.g., the physical and social environment).

As an example, depression is a disorder that is largely rooted in subjectivity. The depressed person typically processes information idiosyncratically and regularly reaches conclusions that are both self-harming (e.g., "Everyone hates me") and often at odds with the facts (e.g., "I can tell because a person in the back row yawned during my lecture"). It is no coincidence that cognitive therapy, which teaches clients how to think more clearly and use available information more skillfully (i.e., reality testing), has such a strong track record in treating depression successfully. Cognitive therapy encourages a greater *external* orientation, an ability to go outside oneself and use available information to form more helpful responses. There is a great deal of truth to the point that much of what drives human experience is too heavily subjective, whether for better or worse.

Spiritual awareness is a subjective experience. Truth is in the eye of the beholder. Higher consciousness is subjective. As impressive as subjective experiences may be, it is a constant struggle in the context of psychotherapy to try to answer the question, "Do you want to feel better, or do you want to know the truth?" For example, someone can be unrealistically optimistic, which feels good and may even benefit the person in specific ways, but is unrealistic nonetheless. Some people resolve this dilemma by suggesting that in order to feel better they must know the truth, further suggesting that the truth is knowable. But is it? The world is at war because of differing views of the truth that seem entirely incompatible. People are at war with themselves when they face inevitable multiple truths about themselves, some of which are entirely contradictory. The ubiquitous tendency to experience internal conflict is what makes acceptance, even radical acceptance, potentially so powerful an intervention (Brach, 2004; Hayes, 2004).

Often, what changes someone's subjective experience in meaningful ways is new information, new experiences, and new insights catalyzed by connecting with the world in a novel way. Teaching clients to be more observant about the world around them, and to develop more of an external orientation in some key situations, is a common therapeutic theme. Teaching clients how to gather information rather than simply make inferences is another common therapeutic theme. As soon as clinicians orient clients externally in order to go beyond subjective experience, and to use facts instead of feelings or subjective perceptions, which may or may not be accurate, they empower clients.

One of the most compelling reasons, though, to use methods of mindfulness and hypnosis is their ability to respond to and incorporate the malleability of subjective experience. Many different theories explain how uniquely subjective experiences can arise during hypnotic procedures, and one of the more compelling theories is the reality testing perspective (Shor, 1959; Yapko, 2003). People continually process a great deal of information both consciously and unconsciously that orients them in space and time. If I ask whether you are sitting down or standing up at this moment, you instantaneously know the correct answer. You have absorbed information on multiple levels that orients you to your body and spatial experience. But when someone gets deeply internally absorbed and thereby dissociated from external cues, as is typical in mindful and hypnotic experiences, reality testing is diminished or suspended. Time loses its meaning, the person feels selfless, and the environmental cues become unimportant and typically drop out of awareness. Thus, the individual suspends the ongoing process of reality testing, which allows exploring and developing subjective experiences that may have little or nothing to do with other things objectively going on in the immediate context or environment. So, for example, someone may be in an office undergoing hypnosis during the course of a therapy session, and to relax the client the therapist suggests imagining being at the beach (a content suggestion). The client may imagine the scene readily, and may even manifest a measurable warming of the skin in response to the suggestion to feel the sun's warmth. The person's imagination translates the suggestions into specific and measurable physiological responses (called ideodynamic responses), a remarkable phenomenon shared by GMM and clinical hypnosis.

The therapeutic value of intensifying growth-oriented and highly subjective experiences is readily apparent. Therapists are not limited to immediate objective realities to catalyze meaningful experiences. Thus, therapists can suggest healing white lights that travel through the body, heartfelt conversations with Buddha or a deceased parent, a freeing of the soul to cross time and space, and countless other experiences that can have deep personal meaning but still undeniably be a product of suggestion. The opportunity to act as if something were real can be a gateway to deeper feelings and issues appropriate for therapeutic intervention as well as to developing a sense of enlightenment.

The capacity for intense subjective experiences that have no relation to objective reality can also pose a danger to the client. It is possible for clients to have subjective experiences that may seem enlightening but are also damaging. There is no better example of this than the repressed memory controversy mentioned previously. Too often due to the therapist's (mis)guidance, but sometimes alone while striving to understand their anger or feelings of victimization, many individuals searching for "the truth" about themselves came to an entirely erroneous and horribly traumatizing conclusion that they had been sexually abused as children and repressed the memories. They believed they discovered the "truth," yet it was nowhere near the actual truth of what objectively did and did not happen to them. Any therapist unclear about the potential of human beings to make up vividly detailed and highly emotional experiences that seem to be true needs to study this chapter in the history of psychotherapy especially closely.

Does truth matter? The answer, it seems, is that the relative value of truth depends on the context. When I have posed the question whether someone would rather feel better or know the truth, many have answered that they would prefer to feel better. It is basic to human nature to want to avoid what is unpleasant. However, avoidance as a coping strategy, unfortunately, is inherently disempowering. It says, in essence, "This problem is more powerful than I am, and I can't deal with it, so I will retreat from it." A major strength of mindful approaches is that they deliberately teach people to face reality and, more than that, strive for a higher level of acceptance of that reality. This striving for acceptance of undisguised reality is how empowerment evolves in one's life.

The larger point I am making here concerns the potential to overemphasize the merits of subjective experience, particularly when placed in a potentially hazardous frame of truth seeking. Psychiatrist Martin Orne, MD, one of the most prolific researchers and theorists in the field of hypnosis, made a seminal contribution to the literature in this regard. He advanced the notion that one of the most important attributes of hypnotic experience is the ability to comfortably tolerate incongruities or inconsistencies in suggestions that in the usual, so-called waking state would be disruptive or disturbing. He termed this phenomenon *trance logic* and described it this way: "an important attribute of hypnosis is a potentiality for the [subject] to experience as subjectively real suggested alterations in his environment that do not conform with reality" (Orne, 1959, p. 297). For example, in one demonstration of trance logic, Orne suggested to the research subject that he could see through another research subject sitting in a chair across the room. The subject reported, "This is very peculiar: I can see

Joe sitting in the chair and I can see the chair through him." Despite thinking it was peculiar, the subject was untroubled by the experience. He simply accepted the unusual perception without feeling any need to explain, justify, or rationalize it.

In fact, many people will vigorously defend their lack of need to analyze such highly subjective experiences, adamant that the experience is entirely justifiable simply because they had it. In the case of recovered memories of abuse, some people "recovered" entirely implausible memories, such as being forced to breed babies for a satanic cult despite clear medical evidence that they were still virgins. On the basis of this sort of twisted trance logic, alleged victims took their bewildered parents to court, splintered their families, and did so with confidence that this was their experience, their truth, providing them reason enough to proceed. It was shocking to me, as an expert witness in many of these gut-wrenching cases, how often therapists on the witness stand attempting to justify their unjustifiable methods would say, "What really happened doesn't matter to me. What matters to me is that this is my client's truth." A client's truth matters, but if you're going to take someone to court on charges of heinous crimes, then real truth matters more.

The Need for Clarity and Certainty

People differ markedly in their responses to uncertainty; some people tolerate it well and other people become so anxious and uncomfortable that they develop lots of strategies to prevent having to deal with it. Many hypnosis and mindfulness experts have addressed the issue of coping with uncertainty, particularly when people are looking for guidance and feedback about their understandings of core elements of their spiritual path, such as openness, acceptance, inner freedom, and insight (Kabat-Zinn, 2006; D. Siegel, 2010 a). Whether looking to a lama or a psychotherapist for guidance, how one manages ambiguity is a key variable in the process. (It is why I included a hypnotic process in Chapter 3 that encourages having an easier time managing ambiguity.)

Both social psychology and common sense have taught us that when people experience uncertainty, other people become very important sources of information. The old saying, "When in Rome, do as the Romans do," reflects our reliance on other people's judgments and behaviors as models of what to do when faced with uncertainty about what is correct or best. Uncertainty is a catalyst for conformity, whether it is a gawky adolescent smoking to be cool or a reasonably competent adult being swayed to vote for an unknown candidate just because a seemingly knowledgeable friend recommends doing so.

The principle of increased conformity in the face of uncertainty is immediately relevant to the clinical context. This is particularly true in highly abstract domains such as spirituality. Many people rely on organized religions to define religious truth and the rituals necessary to perform to honor those truths. Unclear about God or how to pray or meditate, the "experts" are looked to for guidance and structure. The experts define the goals and procedures of meditation or hypnosis and what is supposed to happen when you participate in these experiences. It is no coincidence that so many mindfulness meditation authors directly address the issue of how to respond to concerns that someone "isn't doing it right" (Hanson & Mendius, 2009; D. Siegel, 2010). The expert may say, "You're experiencing what you're supposed to experience," which is reassuring, kind, and compassionate. It also fulfills the role of expert in that relationship.

The role of clinician carries a big responsibility with it. That is true even when the therapist defers this responsibility by denying he or she has any influence on the client.

Expectancy as a Predictor of Response

The power of expectation has been demonstrated in numerous places and called by many names, as described in Chapter 2 (Kirsch, 1990, 1999; Weinberger & Eig, 1999). Virtually all models of psychotherapy emphasize the value of positive expectations in enhancing treatment results. The same is true for all religious and spiritual practices that have this same core suggestion at their base: *Believe and you will* (be saved, bask in God's love, be redeemed, reach nirvana, experience fulfillment, discover the God within, touch the sacred, know peace, find love, live the truth, cultivate equanimity, transcend the merely physical, attract wealth, and on and on). The power of establishing hope and expectancy in clients is why the framing (i.e., the explanation given) for one's procedures is so important. Telling someone "this is the way of the Buddha" only matters if someone cares. Would the way of the Buddha be attractive to a conservative Christian any more than a Jewish person is likely to have a vision of the prophet Mohammed?

Responses to GMM and hypnosis are greatly influenced by the clients' beliefs and expectations. Thus, as the hypnosis research shows, a good hypnotic induction is one that the client believes is a good one, and a good hypnotic experience is one that fits with what the client believes one to be (Lazarus, 2010; Lynn & Kirsch, 2006). Skillfully finding out what a person needs in order to build positive expectations can be a major catalyst to achieving good outcomes with these experiential processes.

Conclusion

As we have seen, many of the changes associated with mindfulness and hypnosis surface in the domains of memory, awareness, absorption, rationality, imaginative ability, imagery, and attention. As we have come to appreciate, many different factors influence the magnitude and direction of an individual's response. There is a great deal of social psychology at work in the utilization of GMM and clinical hypnosis, which can only be ignored if one is overly attached to the idea that all such experiences occur entirely within the person. If more than one person is involved in the process, whether performed live or on a recording, it becomes necessary to consider interpersonal factors. But, as we will see in Chapter 6, this point highlights one of the paradoxes found in the domain of experiential processes: "I'm doing this with you, but it's all about you."

Paradoxes (or Are They?) Evident in Practice

Yapko: What would you do with a depressed woman with a dependent personal-
*   ity disorder and dysfunctional relationships?*
Haley: I wouldn't let her have those problems.

What is a paradox? The *Random House College Dictionary* provides a basic definition: "A statement or proposition seemingly self-contradictory or absurd, and
yet explicable as expressing the truth" (1973, p. 964). The seemingly irreconcilable
nature of two conflicting inputs can pave the way for a higher-order realization.
In his book *Paradoxical Strategies in Psychotherapy*, Leon Seltzer skillfully described the essence of paradox:

> Perhaps more than anything else, paradox leads to defeat of one's "commonsensi-
> cal" expectations.... And thus are the reactions of confusion and surprise often
> intimately associated with paradox; in fact, they are virtually a *prerequisite* for per-
> ceiving a thing as paradoxical.... Paradox is essentially a subjective phenomenon.
> It derives not from the accumulation of facts but from human perception.... That

which is alien to one's common sense (i.e., one's assumptions about reality) is correctly identified as "paradoxical." (1986, pp. 6–7)

Alan Watts was the director of the American Academy of Asian studies in the early 1950s when he presented a series of lectures called Eastern Philosophy and Western Psychology. He was an authority on Zen Buddhism, one of the few in the West at the time, and in 1961 wrote a book many considered a classic, *Psychotherapy East and West* (Watts, 1961). Also in the early 1950s, Jay Haley, a pioneer in strategic therapy and a founder of family therapy, joined anthropologist Gregory Bateson's research project on communication. Haley was particularly interested in the topic of paradox and how people's classification systems for defining their experience gave rise to their sense of paradox. Haley began to study with Watts, and they reciprocally developed an interest in the relationship between therapy and Zen. Watts became an informal consultant to the Bateson project, and paradox became a shared focus.

Watts (1961) described how paradox was evident in the way the master relates to the student by not resisting the position (i.e., beliefs, assumptions) of the naive or unenlightened student. Rather, the master first *accepts* the student's position and even encourages it to the point that it becomes an untenable position to maintain and so must be abandoned.

> Ironically, the teacher of liberation instructs not by rational explanation but by indicating new behaviors grounded on the student's false assumptions until the student finally comes to recognize their falsity.... Liberation is not facilitated by efforts, however strenuous, to escape one's pain or sense of confinement but by facing it squarely, making friends with it, and then working through it. (Seltzer, 1986, p. 12)

In 1953, the same year Haley discovered Zen, he also attended his first seminar with Milton H. Erickson on hypnosis. It seems inevitable that Haley would come to see the methods the Zen masters used to encourage enlightenment in their students as being virtually the same as those utilized by Erickson in his hypnotic interventions with his patients. Haley wrote a classic article on this subject, "Zen and the Art of Therapy," first published in 1992 (in Zeig) and recently reprinted in *Jay Haley Revisited* (Richeport-Haley & Carlson, 2010). Haley wrote, "I found the premises of Zen to be just about the only way of explaining Erickson's directive therapy, which at that time was quite deviant in the [psychotherapy] field" (Richeport-Haley & Carlson, 2010, p. 316).

Paradoxical interventions may be relatively new to the therapy field, with its primary emphasis on rational thinking, but paradox has played a central role in Buddhist teachings for over 2,500 years. Stories, tasks, and paradoxical statements are considered essential vehicles for taking steps along the path toward enlightenment. The well-known koan is an example, a paradoxical saying frequently used in Buddhist practice as a focus for meditation and training in reaching enlightenment. The familiar Zen koan, "We know the sound of two hands clapping. But what is the sound of one hand clapping?" is an example of a confusing statement that seems to have no rational reply, only an *experiential* one. It stretches the mind and encourages a different quality of subjective experience. On the path toward enlightenment, paradox has a decidedly spiritual foundation. Applied in the context of psychotherapy, spirituality is less the focus than is facilitating a specific therapeutic outcome.

Expanding Views of Hypnosis

In older views of hypnosis, the induction was something a hypnotist did *to* a subject by employing specific incantations or prepared scripts. The assumption was that the "induction ritual" was necessary for hypnosis to occur. In modern clinical practice, the ritualistic aspects of hypnosis have all but disappeared. Milton Erickson is widely credited with transforming the clinical practice of hypnosis from such ritualistic approaches to a more refined, natural, *conversational* hypnosis defined in broader interactional terms. Hypnosis, in this view, is a result of a focused and meaningful interaction—the relationship—between clinician and client. The clinician, to be successful, must recognize and respond to the unique attributes of the client and tailor the approach accordingly.

Virtually every form of psychotherapy acknowledges the therapeutic relationship (i.e., alliance) as a primary vehicle for facilitating results: This relationship is especially intense in the use of hypnosis and GMM. Practitioners of these methods commonly tout the importance of the therapeutic relationship, but we can only guess at the reasons why. Does it promote a greater intimacy for the therapist to tiptoe through someone's unconscious? Is it the vulnerability of sitting with eyes closed while allowing someone else to guide your experience that accounts for the potency of the relationship? Is it a transference reaction of some sort? The hypnotic relationship is one of interdependence, both clinician and client following each other's leads while, paradoxically, at the same time leading. By focusing research on the relationship dynamics of successful hypnosis, the emphasis in hypnosis quickly broadened to include communication structures and styles, including the use of paradoxical communications and their effects on subjective experience.

The field of clinical hypnosis expanded decades ago from an obsolete methodology ("do hypnosis to someone") to a modern approach ("do hypnosis *with* someone"). To make that transition successfully, hypnosis had to give up some of its early ideas about itself. Perhaps the most important change was when the notion of hypnosis as a special state gave way to the recognition that hypnotic experiences arise routinely in the course of living. Erickson termed these spontaneous periods of absorption everyday trance experiences, complete with manifestations of so-called classical hypnotic phenomena such as regression or anesthesia. Hypnosis researchers, especially Theodore X. Barber (1969) and Ernest Hilgard (1965), lent support to this notion when they demonstrated convincingly decades ago that whatever people can experience with the formal induction of hypnosis, they can also experience without it. By eliminating the hypnotic rituals and substituting suggestions for imaginative involvement instead, researchers were able to regularly elicit hypnotic phenomena in subjects. Paul Watzlawick (1985), one of the pioneers of systemic approaches and a communications expert, expanded on this theme in his classic article, "Hypnotherapy Without Trance." Here's a paradox that joins hypnosis and mindfulness together in both form and function: You don't need to do hypnosis in order to do hypnosis. Suggestions can transform experience, whether the processes they are embedded in are called hypnosis or GMM.

The "everyday trance" seems to overlap with "everyday enlightenment." Consider the old Zen proverb, "Before enlightenment, chop wood, carry water. After enlightenment, chop wood, carry water." "Zen doesn't confuse spirituality with thinking about God while one is peeling the potatoes. Zen spirituality is just to peel the potatoes" (Watts, 1957/1999). So just how special is the special state of either hypnosis or enlightenment?

When people are first exposed to both hypnosis and meditation, they typically ask, "Am I doing it right?" and "Is this what I'm supposed to experience?"

The assumption is there *has* to be more, something profound and deeply moving. An awareness of breathing, used routinely in hypnotic inductions as well as in GMM, just doesn't strike people as profound or mysterious enough to justify all they have heard about the "amazing" experiences of mindfulness and hypnosis. They may even express disappointment: "Is that all there is?" A leading Buddhist teacher, Shunryu Suzuki, said as much: "To have some deep feeling about Buddhism is not the point; we just do what we should do, like eating supper and going to bed. This is Buddhism!" (1988, p. 76). When the focus shifts from sophisticated philosophy to actual experience, a shift from "special" to "meaningful" can take place. Is that shift enlightenment? I honestly don't know. However, it presents another paradox: What makes it special is that it isn't special.

Jay Haley, Gregory Bateson, John Weakland, and later Don Jackson, Paul Watzlawick, Richard Fisch, and the other brilliant members of the famed Palo Alto group studied paradox in depth. They were especially interested in double binds and their impact on perception and behavior. The double-bind theory, first published in 1956 by Bateson, Jackson, Haley, and Weakland in a seminal article called "Toward a Theory of Schizophrenia," described communication as occurring on multiple simultaneous levels. The possibility thus existed that two or more of these levels could conflict and generate a double bind, a seemingly unresolvable paradox: "Damned if you do, damned if you don't." The following is an example of a double bind Haley offered: "[There] was the family whose supposedly 'psychotic' son sent his mother a Mother's Day card which said, 'You've always been like a mother to me.' The mother brought it with her to a session, saying, 'There's something wrong with this.' It was *that* paradoxical level of communication that interested us" (Yapko, 2001b, p. 186).

But Haley had already found his first double bind years earlier. He found it in hypnosis. "In fact, in hypnosis was the first double-bind we ever found. Bateson had this idea of the double-bind, but we couldn't find one. I remember when I realized that a hypnotist wås directing a person to behave spontaneously that that was a double-bind. That was a classical paradoxical conflict" (Yapko, 2001b, p. 188).

What Haley began to document through his study of hypnosis in general and his study of Erickson in particular was a seemingly unique attribute of hypnosis: people could be exposed to multiple and seemingly conflicting messages in hypnosis and somehow manage them comfortably—and even be enlightened by them. (Recall the earlier discussion of the phenomenon called trance logic.)

They could focus on several competing messages and in a nonverbal, transcendent display of what might reasonably be termed higher consciousness, reach understandings that ordinary linear conversations could not have hoped to stimulate. In this way, the patterns of hypnosis and the patterns of mindfulness share more common elements than most realize.

It is important to keep the focus on the interpersonal dimensions of both hypnosis and GMM. Quiet individual meditation or self-hypnosis as intrapersonal processes are necessarily different and are not my focus here. A koan is delivered by a teacher to a student in a relationship in which the koan is defined as meaningful, however puzzling it might be. Likewise, a therapist using hypnosis might deliver a metaphor or task assignment that seems irrelevant or even crazy yet is defined as meaningful.

When a teacher behaves in a seemingly paradoxical way or delivers a paradoxical communication to a student, there is an implicit suggestion that there is a deeper meaning to be uncovered, a new awareness to be discovered and *experienced*. Student and teacher do not have a relationship of equals, any more than client and therapist do. The social psychology of unequal relationships, encompassing factors such as power, influence, conformity, prestige, self-fulfilling prophecies, and obedience to authority become vital factors shaping the relationship and what occurs between the members of that relationship. When someone is in a position of influence but denies that influence, power can too easily be misapplied. Jon Kabat-Zinn (2006) addressed this issue nicely when he spoke to the ethics of mindfulness: "A core motivation of mindfulness is non-harming ... [instead] an attitude of generosity, compassion, openness." Similarly, the ethics of psychotherapy are found in the oath "First, do no harm."

In the remainder of this chapter, then, let's consider just a few of the paradoxes, double binds, and incongruities shared by GMM and clinical hypnosis.

Paradox: Don't Change; Accept . . . So Things Can Change

Acceptance is one of the core foundational elements of mindfulness-based approaches. Instead of trying to change, improve, modify, or fix things, which is viewed as a certain path to unhappiness, cultivating an attitude of acceptance can provide a means of detaching from focusing on problems. Acceptance is a means of getting off the seemingly never-ending treadmill of striving for self-improvement and getting on a path of greater compassion, tolerance, and patience toward the self and others. Buddhist teacher Tara Brach uses the term "radical acceptance" to emphasize the fuller benefits to be obtained when global compassion is the vehicle of relationships with self and others.

Acceptance has been explored over the centuries in many different contexts, ranging from religion and philosophy to psychotherapy. Acceptance as a means of cultivating compassion became especially important to psychotherapists in the 1960s when Carl Rogers (1986) spearheaded the humanistic psychology movement with the development of his client-centered therapy. Rogers placed a premium on what he termed "unconditional positive regard" as the primary ingredient in forming effective therapeutic attachments. He also had the notion that the therapist was, in essence, a mirror that could reflect back to clients in ways that would allow clients to see themselves more realistically. In this sense, acceptance and compassion were vehicles to help one discover the "truth."

As mindfulness-based treatment is integrated into structured clinical programs for stress reduction or depression treatment, it will inevitably lose at least some of its spirit and self-identity as special and simply become just another therapy modality. Mindfulness-based cognitive therapy (MBCT; Segal et al., 2002), as just one example, is already structured as an eight-session program involving classes that are 2.5 hours long plus one all-day practice session held between the sixth and seventh classes. Participants are expected to practice between classes for about an hour daily. An ever-present challenge is how to acknowledge the uniqueness of each person when running a standardized program. "You're a unique individual—just like everyone else" captures the essence of the multi-level lesson to be learned.

The primary paradox under consideration in this section, though, is how promoting acceptance—essentially a message not to change—becomes the catalyst for change. On one level, the therapist says, "Don't try to change anything; instead accept the inevitable." On another level, the therapist says, "By not trying to change things, you will change." Australian psychologist George Burns quoted the Dalai Lama addressing the power of acceptance in this way: "If you have a problem that you can change, you don't have a problem. And if you have a problem that you can't change, you don't have a problem" (Burns, 2010, p. 310).

Acceptance is an important element of treatment. In fact, in the field of clinical hypnosis, it has long been recognized that the most important ingredient in establishing the therapeutic alliance is acceptance. More than half a century ago, Milton Erickson wrote, "The purpose and procedures of psychotherapy should involve the acceptance of what the patient represents and presents. These should be utilized to give the patient impetus and momentum so as to make his present and future be absorbing, constructive and satisfying" (Erickson, 1954, pp. 127–128). Erickson's concept of utilization was relatively straightforward: "Whatever the patient presents to you in the office, you really ought to use" (Erickson & Rossi, 1981, p. 16). Utilization means acknowledging and building into the process whatever defines the client as unique. So, one can utilize the client's language, behavior, history, imagination, desires, or whatever aspect will serve the individual in the process. Accordingly, utilization is a highly respectful approach that is carefully tailored to the individual client, in marked contrast to standardized one-size-fits-all approaches.

The fascination with Erickson's methods has given rise to a broad and deep literature attesting to the merits of acceptance as the framework for conducting meaningful psychotherapy. The influence of Erickson's methods on the fields of brief therapy, strategic therapy, family therapy, and clinical hypnosis is extraordinary. His approach uses many of the same methods as Buddhist teachers and great teachers across many disciplines and with many of the same goals, including the goal of fully experiencing what is available in the present moment.

> Erickson's goal was to have people respond to their impulses in the present without being concerned about whether or how they were doing so. In the same way, the primary goal in Zen is simply to live rather than to be preoccupied with how one's living. The goal is to recover from self monitoring. In fact, it is said, "when you are really doing something, you are not there." (Haley, 1992/2010, p. 325)

Since Erickson's passing away in 1980, the utilization of hypnosis and strategic forms of therapy have continued to expand in complexity yet, paradoxically, in simplicity. Their relevance to any endeavor, whether enlightenment or symptom relief, is only now beginning to be more widely understood and appreciated.

If one accepts the notion that acceptance is a precursor to change, then the question naturally arises, how does acceptance also create change? It seems apparent that acceptance can diminish and perhaps even gradually eliminate depressing or anxiety-provoking thoughts. In fact, acceptance has already been integrated into a variety of treatment approaches, including solution-oriented therapy (de Shazer, 1988), acceptance and commitment therapy (Hayes, 1987, 2004; Hayes, Strosahl, & Wilson, 1999), and MBCT (Segal et al., 2002). In these approaches, distressed patients are taught to disengage from whatever thoughts, images, or feelings trigger distress. Frequently, they are taught through the familiar hypnotic methods of dissociation and metaphor. Dissociation provides the structure for detachment, and metaphor provides the content that drives the process. For example, Stephen Hayes (1987) offered this metaphor as a means for detaching from negative thoughts and viewing them as both temporary and malleable: He advises clients to imagine that their thoughts are written on signs carried by parading soldiers. The thoughts are accepted as being present, but the capacity to distance from them is utilized as a means of managing them skillfully.

From this vantage point, acceptance is a precursor, a stepping stone to effective utilization. By paving the way for detachment, or greater emotional distance (lowered reactivity, better impulse control), acceptance becomes part of a larger intervention, not an end in itself.

Paradox: The Goal . . . Is to Have No Goal

In a presentation for the employees of Google, Jon Kabat-Zinn (2007) made the point at the outset that he faced challenges in bringing meditation into mainstream medicine. As Americans, he said, we are go-getters who need to learn how to be "human *beings*" rather than what we mostly are, "human *doings*." He said we live with "stone age minds in a digital world," out of touch with dimensions of the universe, out of tune with ourselves, and needing to "tune the self" through mindful meditation, as if tuning an instrument before we can hope to play it well. But, he said, it is challenging because mindful meditation is outside of cultural norms; too many people feel there is "something weird about stillness, quiet, self-reflection." I think he is right.

As I suggested in my book *Depression Is Contagious* (Yapko, 2009), and as Kabat-Zinn alluded to when he discussed a culture of "human doings," the forces of socialization inevitably, inescapably, operate on each of us, for better or worse. How we manage these forces, embodied in our marriages, families, friendships, workplaces, and social and political institutions, can serve to either increase or decrease our vulnerability to disorders like depression and stress-related diseases. We are each challenged by the increasing complexity of life. We each have to find a way of managing ourselves, in fact, our *many* selves. The merits of taking time to "just be" are always evident, but now take on a growing urgency as the pace of life continues to escalate.

As clinicians, we acknowledge that we hope to influence people to learn to manage themselves differently in some way. Why try to attract new students to a study of Buddhism, if not because of the belief that people will benefit from such study? Why give a presentation at Google, if not to attempt to influence at least some members of the audience to recognize the merits of meditation and motivate them to want to learn and practice how to be more mindful? Likewise, in the world of psychotherapy, what are the various methods we use to attract clients? What are the promises we make that encourage our clients' integration into our programs and their cooperation with the treatment plans we generate?

The question of the promises we make has been especially interesting and personal for me as I have researched this book and spoken to many experts in mindfulness. In regard to my book's focus on the relationship between mindfulness and hypnosis, one such expert said the goals of the processes are different because people seeking hypnosis are concerned with specific outcomes such as symptom relief while meditators are interested in cultivating equanimity, insight, love, and the capacity for inner freedom. I find this a curious distinction and not at all a persuasive one. Rather, I believe a quest for spiritual growth and enlightenment is every bit a goal as is hoping to benefit from therapy in some way that leads to a symptom resolution. The path may differ, but not the longing that leads one to walk it.

Similarly, Kabat-Zinn said in his 2007 Google lecture that people often come to study meditation to get better at something, or to find a solution to a problem, and he dismissed this as an idealization, an apparently incorrect application of the method. So when he advised people to "stop doing, even for a moment, to drop into just being," he added that they need to "give up wanting anything else to happen." He said, "Don't try to get there . . . you're already here." This is a repeated theme in his approach, for in his audio CD program, *Mindfulness for Beginners*, Kabat-Zinn (2006) said, "When you practice mindfulness, you immediately become aware of how much we do is mindless. . . . The challenge of mindfulness is to be yourself and the irony is, you already are. . . . There's no great place to get to; you're in the greatest place there is—this moment."

A core element of mindfulness approaches is to dissuade meditators from having a goal. The underlying philosophy of nonstriving drives this teaching. So people are told, "There's no place to go, nothing to attain.... It's realizing you are already here so there's no place else to go.... What happens now is what matters.... The future we want is here now—we're already in it" (Kabat-Zinn, 2006).

Curiously, though, in the opening minutes of his program, Kabat-Zinn said, "There has to be some underlying impulse that longs for a certain knowing or way of being. Otherwise, you wouldn't bother to pick up a program like this." This is the incongruity, the paradox: Denying both the presence or need for a goal, when a goal is inarguably implicit in the way the context and relationship between student and teacher are defined. The double bind is stating on one level, "I want you to have a goal," while saying on another level, "You shouldn't have a goal"; You should have the goal of not having a goal.

As stated many times already, there is a huge difference between people who seek spiritual growth and higher consciousness and those who come to therapy just trying to get through the day without breaking down. Mindfulness will serve both populations, but in different ways. It is important in the clinical context to appreciate that the client has a reason for being there; the therapist has decided to teach mindfulness as a means of helping the person change in some meaningful way, whether through greater acceptance, awareness, or compassion, and the therapeutic goal is (or should be) well defined.

Frankly, one of my major concerns has been that therapists may use mindfulness methods while denying their influence on the process. To conduct a guided meditation, an interpersonal process involving at least two people, and then deny one's influence on what the client experiences may be highly self-deceptive. If you are in the room with someone, you are part of the experiential process. The language you use, why and when you introduce these methods, the demeanor you have in applying them, and many other factors all influence what happens.

When someone diagnosed with cancer and hoping to overcome it goes to an integrative medicine center that teaches mindfulness, he or she has a goal. When someone who is depressed and can barely function goes to therapy to find a mindful way through depression, he or she has a goal. When someone is suffering pain from some disease or accident and wants to learn to manage pain and reduce suffering with mindfulness, he or she has a goal. Would it diminish the value of mindfulness methods to state the goal explicitly? Obviously not, because many mindfulness practitioners do. Does it tarnish mindfulness to suggest that clients want symptom relief but "true" meditators want inner freedom? Is there really a significant difference? Again, I make the disclaimer that I am addressing the clinical context, the use of these methods in the course of treatment, whether in psychotherapy or behavioral medicine. I would be willing to bet, though, that even when attending Buddhist retreats for spiritual purposes, each person will have a goal that guides his or her focus and direction.

I raise this paradox about "the goal of no goals" as an issue for a specific reason: Here is the greatest overlap between GMM applied in a goal-oriented way and clinical hypnosis. Hypnosis is an overtly goal-oriented process. In fact, that is one of its strengths, because when hypnosis is well applied, it establishes an expectation and then gently guides the client (with direct or indirect suggestions) on a path toward fulfilling that expectation. As you saw in Chapter 3, when GMM is explicit in its goals, its methods are every bit as suggestive as hypnosis.

Isn't the goal-oriented nature of both methods a compelling reason to formulate suggestions as skillfully as possible? This is what the study of clinical hypnosis emphasizes. Hypnosis (1) defines the goals of treatment in terms that make success more likely; (2) adapts to the uniqueness of the individual's way of being and doing; and (3) encourages the recognition and development of inner resources that can empower people. These are just a few of the compelling reasons to integrate patterns of mindfulness with hypnosis in doing clinical work. Lynn et al. further summarized the merits of integrating mindfulness and hypnosis:

> We suggest that a mindfulness approach can serve as a template or springboard for generating an array of suggestions that provide cognitive strategies to contend with a variety of problems in living and to ameliorate stress and negative affect more generally. . . . Mindful attention can play a pivotal role in modifying response sets, a goal that is of paramount importance to virtually all psychotherapeutic endeavors. . . . Hypnosis and mindfulness approaches are complementary in key respects. Our discussion implies that mindfulness can deautomatize response sets and create the mental workspace for the formation of new ones. Hypnosis is also a viable method for creating positive response sets as well as deautomatizing dysfunctional response sets. (2006, pp. 146, 153)

Paradox: Do as I Suggest . . . but Behave Spontaneously

In both mindfulness and hypnosis, an explicit expectation is established by the teacher that active engagement in the process will spontaneously give rise to new understandings and actions. Whether offered by a spiritual guide or a therapist, GMM, hypnosis, koans, and homework assignments provide a deliberate climate for spontaneous discovery.

> The therapist, or Zen master, must influence the person to change "spontaneously" and so escape the helping relationship. This is the essential paradox of Zen and of therapy. One solution is the example of a student who attempted again and again to answer a Zen master's koan, only to be informed each time that he was wrong. Finally, he simply sat down beside. That was the answer, since he was behaving as an equal. (Haley, 1992/2010, p. 322)

Erickson had a memorable way of describing the role of the therapist: "It is the patient who does the therapy. The therapist only furnishes the climate, the weather. That's all. The patient has to do all the work" (Zeig, 1980, p. 148). The therapist may be tasked with offering potentially useful suggestions, but the client is tasked with finding a way to integrate them. Good therapists and teachers are careful to provide an environment that increases the likelihood that the student will get it, but they also know they are not in control of what the person gets. Thus, it is important to have a variety of ways of creating a helpful climate (e.g., by being patient, accepting, motivating, supportive, generous, compassionate, open) as well as a variety of tools to guide and teach.

Note these structurally similar paradoxes of the therapeutic relationship: (1) "I cannot help you, but I can help you help yourself"; (2) "I want you to follow my advice not to take anyone's advice"; (3) "I'm not going to tell you what to do, but this is what I think you should do." The parallels to what happens in the teaching relationship supporting someone on the road to enlightenment are likely self-evident.

For more than half a century, practitioners of hypnosis have been stating the paradox, "All hypnosis is self-hypnosis." Practitioners conduct a hypnosis session, offer a variety of suggestions to clients about what they could experience and learn, then deny having any influence by defining the interaction as entirely regulated by the client. The double bind is clear: "I will influence you to believe I do not influence you." The intention, of course, is benevolent: It is an attempt to empower clients to believe they are in full control, primarily as a reaction to the old myth that someone in hypnosis gives up personal control. Benevolent intention aside, though, the statement just doesn't ring true: The hypnotist's suggestions do have an impact. If I say, in or out of hypnosis, "Don't think of an elephant," you naturally do. I have to take some responsibility for bringing up that image in your mind.

This leads us to the paradox "Do as I suggest, but behave spontaneously." The relationship between two unequals—teacher/therapist and student/client—is imbalanced for at least one very specific reason: the student/client wants what the teacher/therapist appears to be able to provide (e.g., insight, support, "the secret"). This refers to expert power, the capacity for influence arising from one's perceived expertise (Aronson et al., 2009). If you want to learn hypnosis, and you perceive me as a credible expert from whom to learn, then you will likely give me the power to direct your learning experience. If you want the wisdom and spiritual enlightenment you think I have to offer, then you will likely give me the power to direct your spiritual journey. I will give you tasks to fulfill, things to read, things to practice doing and experiencing, and, in the end, the sense of getting it will (hopefully) arise from within you in some seemingly spontaneous fashion.

The paradox of following directions to have a spontaneous experience is evident in both the mindfulness and hypnosis literature. The parallels are sometimes extraordinary, as in the following two examples, the first one from an article by Milton Erickson, reprinted with the kind permission of the *American Journal of Clinical Hypnosis*, and the second an ancient Zen story.

> Another Utilization Technique was employed during the lecture and demonstration before a medical student body. One of the students proceeded, at the beginning of the lecture, to heckle the writer by denouncing hypnosis as a fraud and the writer as a charlatan, and he declared that any demonstration using his fellow students would be a prearranged hoax perpetrated upon the audience. . . .
>
> Since he persisted in his noisy, adverse comments as the lecture proceeded, it became necessary to take corrective action. Accordingly, the lecture was interrupted and the writer engaged in an acrimonious interchange with the heckler, in which the writer's utterances were carefully worded to elicit an emphatic contradiction from the heckler, either verbally or by action.

Thus he was told that he had to remain silent; that he could not speak again; that he did not dare to stand up; that he could not again charge fraud; that he dared not walk over to the aisle or up to the front of the auditorium; that he had to do whatever the writer demanded; that he had to sit down; that he had to return to his original seat; that he was afraid of the writer; that he dared not risk being hypnotized; that he was a noisy coward; that he was afraid to look at the volunteer subjects sitting on the platform; that he had to take a seat in the back of the auditorium; that he had to leave the auditorium; that he did not dare to come up on the platform; that he was afraid to shake hands in a friendly fashion with the writer; that he did not dare to remain silent; that he was afraid to walk over to one of the chairs on the platform for volunteer subjects; that he was afraid to face the audience and smile at them; that he dared not look at or listen to the writer; that he could not sit in one of the chairs; that he would have to put his hands behind him instead of resting them on his thighs; that he dared not experience hand levitation; that he was afraid to close his eyes; that he had to remain awake; that he was afraid to go into a trance; that he had to hurry off the platform; that he could not remain and go into a trance; that he could not even develop a light trance; that he dared not go into a deep trance, etc.

The student disputed either by word or action every step of the procedure, with considerable ease until he was forced into silence. With his dissents then limited to action alone and caught in his own pattern of contradiction of the writer, it became relatively easy to induce a somnambulistic trance state. He was then employed as the demonstration subject for the lecture most effectively. (1959/2009, pp. 352–353)

The parallel to this Zen story from the book *Zen Flesh, Zen Bones,* by Paul Reps and Nyogen Senzaki, is obvious:

The master Bankei's talks were attended not only by Zen students, but by persons of all ranks and sects. . . . His large audiences angered a priest of the Nichiren sect because the adherents have left to hear about Zen. The self-centered Nichiren priest came to the temple determined to debate with Bankei.

"Hey, Zen teacher," he called out. "Wait a minute. Whoever respects you will obey what you say, but a man like myself does not respect you. Can you make me obey you?"

"Come up beside me and I will show you," said Bankei.

Proudly, the priest pushed his way through the crowd to the teacher.

Bankei smiled. "Come over to my left side."

The priest obeyed.

"No," said Bankei, "we may talk better if you are on the right side. Step over here."

The priest proudly stepped over to the right.

"You see," observed Bankei, "you are obeying me and I think you are a very gentle person. Now sit down and listen." (1998, p. 23)

These two stories share the common denominators of being respectful of the needs for autonomy and acknowledgment, yet use paradox as the vehicle for the teaching. The paradox is evident in the statement, "I want you to obey me by disobeying me." As Haley stated, "If a person says, 'disobey me,' the responder cannot classify that in a way that allows either obedience or disobedience. The person who disobeys is obeying as instructed. To obey requires disobeying" (1992/2010, p. 320).

The simultaneous directives "Do as I say" and "Discover something meaningful spontaneously" are especially interesting in light of the earlier discussion about conscious and unconscious responding. The fact that someone in a state of absorption can generate context-appropriate responses (e.g., analgesia in a specific suggested location) without any awareness for how he or she did so is one reason why we use experiential approaches such as mindfulness and hypnosis. When people discover resources they didn't know they had, or rediscover resources they had forgotten how to use for their own benefit, the resulting sense of empowerment can indeed be transformative.

Paradox: This Metaphor Is Not About You . . . but This Metaphor Is About You

A woman in her early 60s was struggling to make a decision about her marriage of nearly 40 years. She was unhappy and wanted to leave, and at the same time she was afraid to be out on her own when considering all the challenges she would face ranging from financial to social. She had been agonizing over this decision for many years. She had the idea that, somehow, one day it would all be clear to her and she would be able to make the "right" decision without discomfort. Of course, this was an entirely unrealistic expectation. Even when two people are both crystal clear that a divorce is necessary, it is still a hurtful process.

What justifies the pain, if not believing you will somehow eventually be better off as a result? In hypnosis, I told this woman the following metaphor:

> I remember years ago being deeply affected by reading the book . . . and then see-ing the movie . . . *Inherit the Wind* . . . the story of the "Scopes monkey trial" in Tennessee early in the last century. . . . Spencer Tracy's character, Henry Drum-mond, is an attorney defending the biology teacher who dared to teach the theory of evolution in a school in a deeply religious town whose citizens were quite literal in and deeply devoted to their interpretation of the Bible. At one critical moment in the trial, Drummond turned to the jury . . . and he said, "Ladies and gentlemen of the jury . . . knowledge, progress, has a price." . . . And then he went into a sort of reverie . . . talking at the jury . . . but not to them . . . so self-absorbed . . . as he was saying out loud . . . "It's as if there's a little man who sits behind a table and dishes out the price of progress . . . who says, 'Yes ma'am, you can have the vote . . . and you can participate as an equal in politics . . . *but* . . . then you won't be able to hide behind your apron anymore. . . .' And, 'Yes sir, you can have an airplane . . . and travel great distances quickly. . . . *But* . . . the clouds will smell of gasoline . . . and the birds will lose their wonder. . . .' And 'Yes ma'am, you can have a telephone . . . and you can share information instantly with others. . . . *But* . . . you'll give up some of your privacy . . . and distance will lose its charm. . . ." (Yapko, in Burns, 2007, pp. 75-76; the DVD of "The Case of Carol" is available from Zeig/Tucker Publishers, www.zeigtucker.com.)

The implicit message was clear to her: no matter what decision you make, whether to stay or go, there will be a price to pay. The right decision will *not* be painless. But it will be justified by whether it leads to a better quality of life one way or the other. By the time she came out of hypnosis, her decision was made: She would set the fear aside and leave her unhappy marriage. Frequent follow-ups over the next 18 months indicated she was happy with herself for taking prompt action and happy with how her decision had affected her quality of life. Notice, though, that I did not tell her what to do; I merely offered a story about how any step forward will mean inevitably leaving something behind. There is indeed a price to pay for moving forward and avoidance will not change that fact. *The story wasn't about her, though.*

Metaphor is clearly an indirect form of communication. Instead of speaking directly to someone about his or her concerns, or instead of directly suggesting that someone respond in a particular way, metaphor uses indirection as a means of stimulating the subjective associations of the listener. The listener is told a story about someone (or something) else in some other circumstance, or is provided an elaborate analogy that only indirectly relates to his or her concerns. I say only indirectly because even stories that are perfect parallels (a client comes in for help with anxiety and the therapist tells a story about another client coming in for help with anxiety) are still one step removed; I'm not talking about you—I'm talking about someone else like you. The field of clinical hypnosis has been particularly interested in the potential of therapeutic metaphors as a communication device. In fact, most people who utilize hypnosis regularly employ them as a vehicle for facilitating therapeutic goals, from encouraging identification with story characters to encouraging alternative viewpoints of some situation, even to suggesting solutions to a problem (Lynn, Neufeld, & Mare, 1993; Yapko, 1983, 2003; Zeig, 1980).

Consider the biological metaphors regarding brain functions offered by psychiatrist Dan Siegel in his superb book, *Mindsight: The New Science of Personal Transformation*. As Siegel explains the way the brain is structured and how various brain structures function independently and synergistically, he tells a story with a message:

> The mind uses the firing patterns in these various parts [of the brain] to create itself. It bears repeating that while the physical property of neurons firing is correlated with subjective experience we call mental activity, no one knows exactly how this actually occurs. But keep this in the front of your mind: Mental activity stimulates brain firing as much as brain firing creates mental activity. (2010b, p. 39)

Siegel's message is clear: You are not a victim of your brain. You can create experiences, particularly through the mindful meditations he advocates. The metaphor he employs, the structures of the brain activating as they give rise to the mind, is sprinkled liberally throughout the book. He even uses the neuroscience model (i.e., metaphor) when explaining his own "hijacked" feelings in an angry episode with his kids in a story he called the "Crepes of Wrath":

> Let's look at my meltdown again in terms of how my mind was riding the waves of my (mis)firing brain. A likely explanation is that I experienced a temporary brain dysfunction.... In that kind of dysfunction ... the "limbic lava" from the fiery emotional centers below the cortex, just beneath the middle prefrontal area, can explode in out of control activity. (2010b, pp. 26–27)

The brain story is a metaphor; it is told with charismatic flair and the compelling imagery of a volcano erupting with explosive lava. This powerful imagery helps establish an association in the reader's mind: There is a brain dysfunction that accounts for overreactions, and it has to be acknowledged and steps taken to correct it if and when it erupts.

Is the brain story Siegel tells really a true story? Is a brain dysfunction really the reason for the overreaction? Maybe ... but maybe not. The unidirectional relationship in the observation that "brain firing creates mental activity" seems to challenge the other piece of the bidirectional metaphor—namely, how mental activity stimulated his brain firing. One could just as easily—and plausibly—argue that his apparently unrealistic expectations for how his child should behave caused his "limbic lava" to flow.

If the brain story is true, is that the best metaphor to employ, that is, the one that will be most helpful to people who are trying to get a handle on their anger? Predictably, for some people the answer will be yes but for others, no. Some will only hear the first part of the story (it is a brain dysfunction) and never hear the second part of the story (you can change your brain). Some people do not wonder about their brains or reactions. Instead, they wonder why other people are such jerks. The power, as you can see, is not in the metaphor. It is in people's reactions *to* the metaphor. Furthermore, with a client in a focused (relaxed, dissociated, attentive) state, would the imagery of a volcano erupting followed by centuries of dormancy and a regrowth of the devastated areas be as effective in calming someone as using the brain's ability to rewire itself as the subject of the metaphor? Again, for some people, yes. For others, no.

When we offer people explanations for why they are the way they are, these seemingly sophisticated ideas are merely models or theories. They are metaphors. There is no id, ego, or superego in the real world. They are representations, symbols of experience. Likewise, there is no inner child. It's a metaphor. If you're not pregnant, then you don't have an inner child! There is no limbic lava. It's a metaphor. And, as with all metaphors, we have to consider whether the metaphor serves to enhance or diminish the client's perceived options. If the belief in an inner child makes you treat yourself better, as if you were caring for yourself as a delicate being, then the metaphor helps. If, on the other hand, it leads you to be childish, then it would be a good idea to wonder when the inner child will *grow up and move out*.

Psychotherapy is filled with what many, including me, call psychobabble, that is, abstract, metaphor-based verbiage that does not translate into real experience very easily. "Ego strength," "healing the wounded soul," "personal boundaries," and lots of other jargon of the trade sound so deep. What about the abstract metaphors, such as "full awareness," "enlightenment," or "the compassion of the Buddha" that people strive to grasp? Is metaphor truth? There is an inevitable gap between the theoretical construct and actual experience.

The metaphor presented earlier, taken from *Inherit the Wind* (Lawrence & Lee, 2003), is one I paraphrased during a hypnosis session (Yapko, 2007). It makes the point that as we advance our scientific and social knowledge, there is a price to be paid for doing so. Recall that in the movie, Spencer Tracy's character, Henry Drummond, is the attorney defending a teacher who broke a law forbidding the teaching of the theory of evolution. Drummond offered the observation that as our knowledge grows, it may mean that we have to revise or even give up previously cherished ideas. Although that may be uncomfortable at times, he advised, our discomfort should not lead us to choose a more comfortable ignorance. I think this metaphor applies to many of the points I am making in this book. I am encouraging some revisions of how we think about both mindfulness and hypnosis.

The key factor in using metaphors, whether in the context of seeking spiritual growth under the guidance of a lama or in the course of therapeutic intervention, is the inherent, though never directly stated, paradox: I'm telling you a story that is clearly not about you. It's about somebody else. But the story really *is* about you, which is why I'm taking the time to tell it to you. There is a message in the story that can help you when you "spontaneously" discover its meaning.

Paradox: Confusion Gives Rise to Clarity

Jon Kabat-Zinn (2006) pointed out that Buddha wasn't a Buddhist. Kay Thompson (1985), a longtime colleague of Milton Erickson's and a superb teacher of his methods, pointed out that Erickson wasn't an Ericksonian. Each had a system of thought that engendered certain possibilities—and precluded others. One of the elements shared by Buddhist teachings and Erickson's utilization approach involves the paradoxical role of confusion: When clarity is desired, confusion is necessary.

Koans are a wonderful vehicle for stimulating confusion and eventual clarity. For example, in a clinical demonstration of hypnosis I conducted, a woman was feeling terribly mistreated by her employer. She reported becoming increasingly anxious and depressed, finding it more and more difficult to go to work, and feeling trapped in her job. In hypnosis I told her the koan of the Zen master holding a stick over the trainee's head who said, "If you say this stick is real, I will hit you. If you say it is not real, I will hit you. If you don't say anything, I will hit you." Fear of getting hit amplifies the confusion about what to do when, at first consideration, all available options lead to getting hit. After a long pause, my partner in the demonstration had the idea that she should find another job. Not coincidentally, in my story, the trainee reached up, grabbed the master's stick, and took it away from him.

Confusion is the basis for the help-seeking behavior of clients ("What do I do now? I don't know what to do. . . . Help!"). Likewise, confusion is the basis for undertaking the spiritual quest for enlightenment ("What is the meaning of life? How am I supposed to live my life? How do I make sense out of this bewildering existence?"). As with all other aspects of human experience, people differ widely in how they deal with confusion. Some people welcome it as an invitation to learn; some manage to ignore it; others retreat into artificial levels of certainty, feeling deeply certain about things that probably should preclude such certainty.

Erickson said that confusion "is the basis of all good techniques" (Erickson et al., 1976, p. 107). As a master of communication, a brilliant observer of human nature, and an exceptionally skilled practitioner of hypnosis, Erickson was very aware that there was an inverse relationship between an individual's level of certainty and level of responsiveness to therapeutic suggestions. In plain language, the more certain someone is, the more deeply entrenched in a particular viewpoint, the more difficult it is to introduce other perspectives. Certainty works against suggestibility. And, as any clinician knows, too often the problem with clients is how absolutely sure they are about something—and how absolutely *wrong*.

The field of social psychology has generated many wonderful insights from some very ingenious research about the conditions under which people are most likely to conform to the perceptions of others. Experiments designed to generate role confusion, sensory confusion, social protocol confusion, personal identity confusion, and cognitive confusion have all made the same point: When most people (not all) are confused, they tend to look for guidance from others. It is human nature to seek clarity. Confusion generates the anxiety of uncertainty, and how well or poorly people tolerate this anxiety is a powerful factor in predicting how responsive they are likely to be to the guidance of others, whether a therapist or spiritual guide.

When Kabat-Zinn (2006) defined meditation as being about "awareness," "discernment," "clear seeing and wisdom," and "knowing the actuality of things," he directly suggested there is an actuality that is knowable. Others also speak to the issue of meditation as a means to "know the truth." The implicit promise is that from confusion will come enlightenment.

On the other hand, in the same program Kabat-Zinn provided the reassurance that "there are no experts in mindfulness." Best of all, in my opinion, is his direct statement that "meditating is about not knowing who you are and being comfortable with not knowing. . . . Not knowing isn't a bad thing [because] you have to admit what you don't know in order to discover or create." This is a valuable observation about the inevitability of ambiguity in life and how it can serve as a catalyst for growth and discovery. When he discussed the beginner's mind, he said there are infinite possibilities in the beginner's mind, but few in the mind of the expert, a well-known saying from the Zen master Suzuki (1988): Kabat-Zinn unambiguously suggested that "expertise gets in the way of knowing what we don't know." In his 2007 lecture at Google, Kabat-Zinn stated the premise directly: "It's not what you know but what you're willing to know you don't know."

Buddhist teachers may or may not describe it this way, but hypnosis practitioners certainly do: Confusion can be deliberately induced as a means for promoting insight, understanding, or change even in the absence of insight. Consider this example of a clever therapeutic intervention by Erickson involving confusion and change in the absence of insight: A 14-year-old girl developed the idea that her feet were much too large. Over the preceding 3 months, she became so self-conscious that she refused to go to school or anywhere else outside the house. Her mother came to see Erickson to ask what to do to help her, since the girl was unwilling to discuss the problem with anyone, much less a doctor. Erickson arranged with the mother to visit the home under the pretext that he was coming to examine her because of flulike symptoms she was having. Erickson made a big show of examining the mother with the daughter present. The daughter was very concerned about her mother and watched the examination intently. Erickson then asked the daughter to fetch a towel and stand by him in case he needed her help, which she promptly did. Erickson finished his exam, maneuvered the girl behind him, and accidentally (on purpose) backed into her, clumsily stepping on her foot. Erickson said she "squawked with pain." In apparent fury, Erickson wheeled on her and yelled, "If you would grow those things *large* enough for a *man* to see, I wouldn't be in this sort of situation!" (Haley, 1973/1986, p. 198). Haley reported, "That afternoon, the girl told her mother that she was going out and she went to visit friends and returned to school. Apparently she was enlightened" (1992/2010, p. 332).

Confusion, when deliberately invoked, causes uncertainty, and thus paves the way for a change in attitude and behavior. When people are confused, they typically stop what they are doing and then develop an internal focus, essentially a spontaneous experience of hypnosis, as they quickly sort through everything they can to try to resolve the confusion. While the person's conscious mind is so preoccupied with trying to make sense of something, the unconscious is more readily available for any suggestion that will reduce the dissonance. There is much more to the power of confusion to transform experience than dissonance reduction, of course, but in a nutshell, that is the mechanism of confusion techniques.

The paradox of confusion: Knowing is not knowing.

Conclusion

The role of paradox in religion, philosophy, literature, and psychotherapy has received far more in-depth treatment than I have provided here. However, this chapter has made the point in a variety of ways that both mindfulness and hypnosis share an emphasis on paradox as a vehicle of growth. It is striking how, as Kabat-Zinn (2006) described in *Mindfulness for Beginners*, monks will begin their lessons by modestly declaring, "I know nothing," despite their many years of experience, study, and wisdom. Equally striking is how experienced practitioners of clinical hypnosis will often begin a hypnosis session by saying, "I don't know . . . I don't know what the best position is for you to sit in to get comfortable. . . . I don't know just when you might want to close your eyes . . . and I don't know what you'll experience that will be meaningful for you . . ."

It takes a long time and lots of focused study to "not know" *really well.*

CHAPTER 7

The Art of Discrimination: Strive to Accept, Strive to Change—or Do *Both*?

Muddy Road

Tanzan and Ekido were once traveling together down a muddy road. A heavy rain was still falling. Coming around a bend, they met a lovely girl in a silk komono and sash, unable to cross the intersection.

"Come on, girl," said Tanzan at once. Lifting her in his arms, he carried her over the mud.

Ekido did not speak again until that night when they reached a lodging temple. Then he could no longer restrain himself. "We monks don't go near females," he told Tanzan, "especially not young lovely ones. It is dangerous. Why did you do that?"

"I left the girl there," said Tanzan. "Are you still carrying her?" (Reps & Senzaki, 1998, p. 33)

This classic story has been handed down in Buddhist teachings over the centuries because of its simplicity in addressing an issue that is anything but simple. The important teaching embedded in the story is about letting go rather than holding on to that which is worrisome or troubling. It teaches the importance of action over contemplation; it models the ability to bend the rules flexibly when circumstances may warrant doing so; and it illustrates the merits of decisiveness over second guessing.

Consider the story of Tanzan and Ekido from a psychotherapeutic perspective. As monks, both Tanzan and Ekido have taken a vow of celibacy. They are taught to avoid contexts where they may be tempted to violate their vows. Tanzan seemingly harmlessly engages with a young woman in a way that might well have crossed the line of what was deemed appropriate behavior for a monk, and Ekido questions him about it. Tanzan's response is, in essence, "Let it go." Instead of offering some insight into his reasoning process regarding his decision to cross the line in this exceptional instance, he simply says, "Let it go." Instead of using it as a teaching opportunity to educate Ekido about when to follow rules strictly and when to bend them based on varying circumstances, he simply says, "Let it go." Instead of compassionately acknowledging that Ekido has a legitimate basis for wondering about the protocol violation, or perhaps even praising Ekido for his thoughtfulness in contemplating the episode rather than just impulsively attacking him for what he did, Tanzan's reply suggests he is above questioning and it is therefore Ekido's problem for still thinking about the episode.

Imagine that Tanzan and Ekido come for psychotherapy to resolve their differences about this episode with the woman. How many therapists would listen to the story of what happened and then join Tanzan in telling Ekido to "just let it go" rather than sort through the details and implications of what happened? As a reasonable parallel, imagine a couple who comes in for therapy because one spouse did something that crossed a previously agreed-upon line and then refused to discuss it. Is there any therapist *anywhere* who would simply tell the concerned spouse to let it go without trying to talk it through toward some constructive resolution that would well serve the relationship? From this vantage point, Tanzan's reply to Ekido isn't enlightening—it is *avoidant*.

We see here again that there are differences we must acknowledge between a spiritual philosophy and a clinical context and between what is metaphorically elegant and pragmatically valuable. When someone cannot recognize those differences and respond to them meaningfully, they can too easily place abstract concepts ahead of concrete realities. The big picture is great, but problem solving is in the details of what one actually says and does. For example, teaching abstinence to teens is a great concept; the reality, though, is teens are sexual beings and they are going to behave sexually regardless of how we might feel about that fact. No wonder we have a rate of teenage pregnancy in America that is so high, despite the growth of religious conservativism and its incredibly unrealistic push toward celibacy.

Distinctions and Decisions

In the sky there is no distinction of east and west; people create distinctions out of their own minds and then believe them to be true.

Buddha

In the course of a single day, every one of us must make many choices, ranging from the mundane (e.g., what to wear) to the profound (e.g., what to believe about our responsibilities toward others). What we decide is important, but *how* we decide is even more important. This is what I call the art of discrimination, the ability to make a good choice in a given situation utilizing both insight and foresight. The ability to discriminate, or distinguish, between available alternatives to choose with insight and foresight is an exceptionally sophisticated multidimensional skill requiring an effective strategy. A discrimination strategy is a series of deliberate steps you follow in thinking and reacting that lead you to choose among available options to form an effective response to the circumstances at hand. A discrimination strategy helps one answer the question, "Should I do this or should I do that?" As we watch people live out the damaging consequences of poor decisions, whether made as individuals or societies, we can see how often discrimination skills are missing to the detriment of all of us.

In the simplest terms, our quality of life is hugely influenced by the quality of the decisions we make and the consequences that arise both directly and indirectly from those decisions. Remarkably, though, people do not necessarily sense that they *are* making decisions. Instead, they think that things just happen and don't sense any participation in the unfolding of what happens. Sometimes things do just happen, but more often than not, we are a moving part of the machinery driving what happens. It is a repetitive theme of therapy to help people who feel disconnected from the decision-making process, who feel utterly victimized by circumstances, to take some form of action that will help empower them. Whether the action is less or more direct in manner, it necessarily involves a sense of participation and, hence, ownership. But how does one choose one's course of action? Can mindfulness, with its emphasis on acceptance, and hypnosis, with its emphasis on empowerment, help with the next step of the process: making and implementing good choices for action? Being clear how things are, that is, accepting reality, is an essential first step in this endeavor.

Discrimination Strategies

An old man riding the subway catches the attention of a younger man who notices his lined and weathered face. He good-naturedly wonders about the old man's life and what it has been all about. As he surreptitiously studies the old man, he sees him reach into his coat pocket and pull out a pack of cigarettes. Then, he reaches into his other pocket for a lighter, and with a well-practiced motion, the old man lights his cigarette and begins to smoke it. The young man debates for a moment whether to tell the old man he can't smoke on the subway, but only a moment, before quickly deciding he must say something to get him to stop smoking. He approaches the old man and politely says, "Sir, do you see that sign there? It says, 'No smoking.'" The old man looks directly into the eyes of the younger man, pauses, and replies, "See that sign over there? It says, 'Eat Corn Flakes.' So, does that mean I have to eat Corn Flakes?"

The old man regards the sign that says "No Smoking" as no different than the sign that says, "Eat Corn Flakes." He may well know the difference and just wants to be obstinate, but let's assume, for the sake of discussion, that he really doesn't know the difference. How would you explain the difference to him?

Decisions, Decisions

Let's consider some fairly routine situations in which to start deepening our appreciation of discriminations and their role in decision making:

- Your new therapy client presents the problem of depression and asks you about the bewildering array of treatment options available, including antidepressant medications, mindful meditation, cognitive therapy, diet and exercise, and many others. How do you decide what to recommend as your treatment plan?
- Your boss politely asks you at the last minute to work overtime but you already had other plans. Should you maintain your plans and assertively refuse, or should you bend and accommodate the request?
- The person you are dating has some relatively minor habits that annoy you. Should you try and get him or her to change these irritating habits, or should you learn to be more tolerant?
- Your therapy client credits you with having helped improve her relationship with her daughter, and, months into her therapy, asks you to come to her daughter's wedding. Should you go and participate in an important and happy event in your client's life, or should you decline because it might suggest a dual relationship, that is, a conflict between personal and professional relationships?

These are typical decisions that all of us must make routinely in the course of everyday living. Some of the decisions we have to make each day have no long-lasting or potentially harmful effects and so can be made spontaneously or without much thought, simply on the basis of a whim. Other decisions, though, are huge and can carry serious consequences that will undoubtedly echo throughout the rest of our lives.

How do you determine what your response will be, or what course of action to take in the various situations you face each day? What factors do you need to take into account? Once you decide which factors to consider, how do you decide which ones to give greater or lesser weight? Different decisions require different qualities of decision making for us to make effective decisions in a given context.

At the end of each scenario above, a question is posed that represents the essence of the decision to be made, some variation of this one: How do you know whether you should do this or that? The qualities of your discrimination strategy will be a powerful determinant of whether you end up handling a situation well or badly. The quality of your life is a direct consequence of the choices you make. When someone makes choices according to ineffective discrimination strategies, the consequences will prove troublesome at least and disastrous at most. The value of self-hypnosis or mindful meditation as a means of "clearing yourself" to prepare yourself to make good decisions and take effective action is one of the best of all reasons to use these approaches.

Are People Motivated to Make Self-Damaging Decisions?

There's a line of thought in the psychology profession, which I don't subscribe to, that suggests people *want* to have their symptoms and problems because they serve some greater unconscious psychological need. Many clinicians are trained to immediately look for the secondary gain, that is, the payoff for maintaining the symptom pattern, in their interviews with clients. Too many of my colleagues, in my opinion, concentrate on issues of motivation and strive to resolve the client's "unconscious fear of success" or "unconscious need to suffer."

I don't believe that people want or need to suffer or that people are motivated to have symptoms and problems. When I ask my clients how they decide what to do, I almost invariably discover that they are either misinformed (i.e., using wrong information to make a decision) or uninformed (i.e., attempting to make a decision without the relevant information). Thus, I see my clients' problems as typically stemming from a lack of ability to make key discriminations, rather than an insufficient level of motivation or a pathological need to suffer. No amount of positive motivation is going to make up for a lack of the relevant ability. No matter how much you want to watch the glorious sunset, you are going to miss it if you face east.

Figure-Ground Relationships

The creative and wonderfully puzzling paintings of M. C. Escher have always been a favorite of mine for their perceptual challenge of seeing how subjects become backgrounds and backgrounds become subjects. The common visual illusion of the two faces that are also a vase, or the illusion of either a young woman or an old one, are familiar to most people. These illusions illustrate exceptionally well that when you focus on one aspect of the image you notice one thing, but you see another thing embedded within it when you simply change your focus. You don't see both the young girl and the old lady. You see only one or the other. One choice of focal point precludes the other.

What you notice is called the figure, and what recedes into the background is called ground. How does one determine what is figure and what is ground, whether in a painting, a visual illusion, or a life circumstance? Is this determination a conscious, deliberate choice, or is it mediated by unconscious factors?

One of the domains of automatic responses, discussed earlier, is the realm of figure-ground relationships. For a variety of reasons that have to do with the way the brain is "hardwired," what we notice in a given circumstance is a product of quite a few variables, including our previous experience with that type of situation (history), our expectations for what we are going to notice, our mood state, the intensity of whatever draws our attention, the novelty of what's going on, what we're motivated to notice, and the presence of competing events that may distract us or divide our attention.

In a simple but effective example, it is why 10 people can all witness the same event yet report 10 different versions of what happened. A huge gap separates what actually happened from what people subjectively notice and report. The same gap separates objectively available information and perspective from what little or irrelevant information people end up using in formulating their responses. This is the gap we want to bridge in learning effective discrimination strategies.

Figure-Ground Relationships and How Problems Develop

The previous points have profound implications for understanding how problems develop and the ways mindfulness and hypnosis may be applied. Here are some examples to help illustrate the consequences of a misdirected focus:

• Depressed people commonly feel helpless to improve their lives. They assume they have no control over situations and so do nothing proactively to improve them. They focus on their feelings of helplessness (figure) and miss the opportunities to make things better (ground). Such people need a discrimination strategy to help them determine when they have control and can make a positive difference by taking sensible action steps and when they are indeed helpless and no amount of effort will make a meaningful difference.

- Anxious people commonly worry about what might go wrong that will hurt them. They assume they will be overwhelmed and dread the prospect of facing whatever they fear. They focus on their overestimated sense of risk in uncertain situations (figure) and pay little or no attention to their personal resources for coping (ground). Such people need a discrimination strategy to help them determine which situations are high risk and which pose no real danger. They also need a discrimination strategy to distinguish which stressors might actually overwhelm their current style of coping and which are, in fact, simply unpleasant but manageable.

- People with relationship problems are often hurt by the actions of their partner and feel angry and disappointed. They focus on what they want (e.g., affection, loyalty) that they are not getting from their partner (figure) and not on evaluating realistically what this person is actually capable of providing in that regard (ground). Such people need a discrimination strategy for determining whether their expectations for the person are realistic or unrealistic.

- People who are perfectionistic and self-critical often belittle and berate themselves even when, by realistic standards, they have done well. They focus on what they (arbitrarily) decide represents perfection (figure) and ignore any other feedback that more objectively defines success in some context (ground). Such people need a discrimination strategy for knowing when something is (or whether it even can be) objectively perfect and when it is objectively good enough.

Socialization and Learning to See What Is Worth Seeing

A primary goal of mindfulness is to "fall into clarity" (Kabat-Zinn, 2006), that is, see things as they "really" are, and "realize our true nature" (Brach, 2004, 2007). Different influences on our experience, including entirely unconscious ones, make seeing clearly more difficult, perhaps even impossible. Human beings are not perfect processors of information, and no amount of meditation, hypnosis, or life experience can help them become so. For as long as we live in a human body and have a human brain, we will be subject to their inherent strengths and limitations. There are inevitable differences between the universe as it exists and what we are neurologically capable of processing, instantly making any truth a subjective one. The proof is irrefutable: there is light above and below the threshold of what we can see with our eyes. There is sound above and below the threshold of what we can hear with our ears. Our brains need some stimulation from the outside to function properly, but not too much, causing sensory overload, or too little, creating sensory deprivation.

Perception is necessarily a subjective phenomenon: Each person will react to and interpret different sensory experiences differently. We may expand possibilities, but not infinitely so. (Try to grow a new arm!) We want to distinguish between *realistic* hopefulness for increased possibilities, and *unrealistic* hopefulness for things no amount of optimism and hope will actually change. Hope can inspire, and hope can delude. When any philosophy or therapy promises living fully in eternal bliss, it might be wise to save your time and money.

Socialization is the process of learning to integrate into a culture by absorbing its rules, values, behaviors, and all the other aspects of living in groups that shape our perceptions and responses. Socialization is how we come to see the world, and literally shapes whether we hear music or noise, whether we see the art of a genius or the waste of good canvas. Socialization informs our goals and dreams and determines what we think is important. Yes, we are individuals, but no one escapes the forces of socialization. Learning to speak and think in English is just one example of how our thoughts are shaped by the very language we learn as toddlers. And every time we asked, "Why, Mommy? Why, Daddy?" while growing up, we learned why we do this but don't do that.

Your socialization has shaped you and your responses to an enormous extent. What you notice and, likewise, what you don't notice is easily traced to what you were taught, both directly and indirectly. For example, if you were taught to be punctual and respectful of other people's time and not inconvenience them by making them wait for you, then you will notice clocks and deadlines. If you were allowed to roll in anytime you darn well pleased and there was no consequence for doing so, you learned that clocks are irrelevant because you run on your own time, no one else's. The examples of how you come to notice what matters and what doesn't could fill a library. The main point is, your socialization history largely defines the quality of your discriminations and, ultimately, your responses. That includes your responses to hypnotic approaches.

Discriminations in Mindfulness and Hypnosis

When so much of the language associated with mindfulness is global in nature, how is the client to learn to make meaningful discriminations? Thinking globally precludes thinking in detail. The global philosophy of mindfulness is simple, but living it is hard. In fact, Jon Kabat-Zinn (2006) called it "the hardest work in the world . . . the challenge of a lifetime."

The importance of awareness, openness, acceptance, and evolving a mind-set of equanimity are beyond question. But there is no specific set of discrimination skills that provide someone with a clear sense of when to be aware, open, accepting, or calm. (To be open to everything means, paradoxically, being open to the idea that there are some things to which one should be closed.)

Although both mindfulness and hypnosis emphasize the importance of accepting reality for what it is, hypnosis generally pays more attention to *acceptance as a precursor to making deliberate and meaningful change*. Both mindfulness and hypnosis are clear that acceptance has to precede change, but in hypnosis a well-defined therapeutic target lies one step beyond acceptance. In hypnosis, there is an implicit or explicit suggestion to *do* something. The client is encouraged to make specific cognitive, behavioral, perceptual, sensory, or relational shifts toward a goal. Unlike mindfulness, which is often described as the intention to pay attention without directing the attention, a description that I have come to believe is at least partly self-deceptive, hypnosis is attention with direction. In the world of psychotherapy, this is especially appropriate, since therapy is itself necessarily—and appropriately—a goal-oriented process.

This is a vital discrimination for the clinician to make: Are you going to encourage clients who come to therapy with a goal (a hope, a wish, a desired outcome) in mind to "just be" and lead them to believe that by "just being" they will resolve their problems? If so, will you help them learn how specifically doing that makes a difference, or will it be offered as an undefined, global promise of "personal growth"? Alternatively, will you retain the essence of the message about the merits of focusing, meditating, and "just being" while encouraging clients to actively evolve specific skills for problem solving? The skill might even be to learn that some problems cannot be solved and the message to "accept and just be" is perfect.

Acceptance: The Challenge of a Lifetime

I was in Africa a few years ago and had the occasion to visit a small village in Zimbabwe. The people were economically terribly poor but spiritually rich, generous in sharing their way of life with my small group of visitors. Only a year before, the village had been lent a hand when an international relief organization dug a well for them. For the first time ever, they could go to the well at their leisure and pump clean water to drink. It was a daily ritual for the village women to take their containers, walk the long mile to the well in the heat and dust, pump vigorously to get water into the containers, then carry the heavy containers back to the village balanced on their heads. I imagined a sudden rise in neck problems among the village women, but saw no evidence of this.

I was amazed at the amount of hard work a woman had to go through to get a bucket of water back to her home. In talking with one young village woman about this, I asked with an expression of both awe and respect in my voice, "How can you walk a mile each way to get water?" It was really meant as a rhetorical question indirectly expressing admiration for her enduring the associated difficulties, but she looked at me with a gentle smile and replied simply, "Because that's where the water is."

This young African woman had no anger in her, no hint of sarcasm in her voice. She modeled equanimity—she was peaceful, compassionate, and accepting, both of me as a visitor and of her life conditions. When I think of what a powerful example of acceptance looks like in real-world terms, I invariably think of this young African woman. (She, of course, has no idea that I think of her often and in this special way.)

> [A] foundation of mindfulness is . . . acceptance. This one's really misunderstood by people all the time. Accepting what? Accepting that things are the way they are. It's not saying you should be passively resigned to how things are. If things are going to hell in a hand basket, then that knowing, that awarenessing of things . . . can give you a place to stand to act in the next moment. (Kabat-Zinn, 2006)

I agree. It's this moment of mindful acceptance that permits, even encourages, a sensible response:

All of a sudden it becomes possible to stand in this moment without it having to be any different. And that's freedom, that's liberation. . . . It's actually seizing hold of the actuality of things and then the next moment, if you have to act, act. But, you'll act out of mindfulness, out of heartfulness, out of some kind of emotional intelligence instead of hijacked by whatever your feelings are about what you can't accept. (Kabat-Zinn, 2006)

In the previous chapter, I described the paradox that acceptance itself is a change. When someone has been fighting against the reality of what is, then striving for acceptance and attaining it is a powerful therapeutic intervention. In clinical practice, though, the decision of whether to act and how to act in the next moment following mindful acceptance is critical in determining whether someone makes a good, bad, or irrelevant decision. In order to make better, more adaptive choices, and do so more automatically, the client does need to face reality, but must sense the ability to choose as well as taking the responsibility for choosing wisely. What, if anything, about reality suggests to someone the need to, as Kabat-Zinn said above, "act out of some kind of emotional intelligence?" Mindfulness can open the door, but some new idea or experience is necessary to lead you to a new possibility. GMM and clinical hypnosis sessions share the function of stimulating those new ideas and experiences.

Acceptance of how things are has been the basis for many different therapies. It's the next moment, though, when the person says, "So, now what do I do?" that changes lives for better or worse, depending on the answer.

The Most Important Discrimination: Controllability

The concept of acceptance, even radical acceptance, is unquestionably of critical importance in the processes of mindfulness and hypnosis. It inevitably gives rise to the salient discrimination question: How do you know when to accept something as it is, or when to mindfully accept then actively strive to change whatever is going on? Consider this moving passage from *Buddha's Brain*:

Life includes getting wounded. Accept as a fact that people will sometimes mistreat you, whether accidentally or deliberately. Of course, this doesn't mean enabling others to harm you, or failing to assert yourself. You're just accepting the facts on the ground. Feel the hurt, the anger, the fear, but let them flow through you. Ill will can become a way to avoid facing your deep feelings and pain. (Hanson & Mendius, 2009, p. 167)

It is realistic advice to point out that others may be hurtful at times and that accepting this as true will be empowering in deciding what to do when someone actually does inflict some harm. It is the next step, though, that defines how valuable the advice really is. Asserting yourself with people is a good idea, *generally*. More specifically, when is it a good idea to assert yourself, and when isn't it? Or is it a global recommendation to always assert yourself regardless of the outcome or the risks in doing so? And, by suggesting to people that they be assertive, does that empower them to be assertive now? Telling people what to do doesn't teach them how to do it.

This is a reason why experiential processes can have multiple functions that operate synergistically. Mindfulness provides a great foundation for focusing, attending, and evolving a spirit for growth as a person. But how much more powerful would such approaches be in a clinical context if they were more deliberately defined as goal-oriented, skill-building, educational processes tailored to the uniqueness of the person? Instead of the client coming to the philosophy and techniques of mindfulness as an ancient tradition, what about adapting the methods in a clinical context to the person?

Primary and Secondary Control Issues

In a clinical context, the above question is vital to the development of a realistic treatment plan. Specifically, each clinician must, together with the client, make a determination whether the most appropriate focus of treatment is to strive to address issues of primary or secondary control. Primary control refers to changing the circumstances in some beneficial way. Secondary control refers to changing one's reactions to the circumstances in some beneficial way. As a clinician interviews a client, gathering relevant information about the problems, the clinician attempts to define the boundaries or limits of what the client can and cannot change in his or her problem experience.

Consider an example: a client complains about a hypercritical and extremely difficult supervisor at work. Part of what any clinician would likely want to find out is whether it is possible to do something proactively to change the way the supervisor treats this client or, as an alternative, whether the client can change the circumstances, perhaps by requesting a transfer to another department or another supervisor. These are examples of primary control interventions. The clinician and client together weigh the option of doing something to change the external circumstances. But what if it is not possible to change the external circumstances? What if it is a small organization headed by one person who is in charge? Quitting the job may not be a viable solution, especially in today's uncertain economic times. So, in such an instance, the external circumstances cannot change. Thus, the focus in treatment will likely be on how to change the person's reaction to the circumstances. This is an intervention based on secondary control.

One can easily see the relevance across many different contexts. As another example, what happens when someone is dealing with a physical pain issue? Of course, the first-line approach is to seek a medical resolution. This is a primary control intervention. But, in a chronic pain situation in which no medical solution is available, helping someone adjust to the inevitability of pain is a sensible and desirable secondary control intervention.

Suggesting that someone develop acceptance as a mind-set and as a vehicle of becoming more realistic, compassionate, and open is a potentially valuable intervention. But before it makes sense to suggest acceptance as a means of obtaining some pain relief, it is first necessary to establish the perceptual frame that makes acceptance possible. If hypnosis can be used to transform the pain, creating a dissociation that leads to a subjective perception of analgesia and pain relief, then what language should we use to conduct the session? Should we say acceptance precedes transformation? Should we instead say, "You don't have to accept it when you can transform it?" Personal philosophy, clinical judgment, and what the client believes and will likely respond to will determine your approach.

Acceptance is the starting point for changing perspectives in helpful ways, and that includes accepting when someone cannot seem to accept something. Milton Erickson was widely acknowledged for his ability to utilize what others termed resistance. Erickson believed that so-called resistance was simply how people communicated their limitations (i.e., what they could or could not experience) and thus provided valuable information about them. This nonpathological viewpoint allowed him to develop a variety of strategic ways of suggesting possible solutions to people, prompting Jay Haley (1992/2010), at least, to consider him a Zen master in style, if not philosophy.

What makes people fight against accepting reality? When people don't like what's going on, naturally they want to change it. When they don't know what to do to change it, they feel victimized. If they simply react emotionally—globally and internally focused on their feelings of distress—they remain distressed. When the therapist, or spiritual guide, as the case may be, suggests putting some emotional distance between themselves and the problem, this is a huge first step in beginning to problem solve.

The next step, an exceedingly difficult one, is to determine one very specific factor: how much control one actually has over the circumstances. The well-known Serenity Prayer comes to mind:

> God, grant me the serenity
> To accept the things I cannot change;
> The courage to change the things I can;
> And the wisdom to know the difference.

Insightful clinicians would have to examine their beliefs about the issue of controllability and how they influence their style of clinical practice. Specifically, how do you determine what is and is not controllable in a given situation? How do you determine when a client is limited in some way and when those limits should be accepted and respected versus when those limits should be rejected by the client who, in your judgment, should instead strive to transcend them?

The potential for making errors in forming such subjective judgments about what is controllable should be obvious. Communicating such subjective judgments as the authority to a suggestible client is a potentially hazardous process. Clearly the clinician needs to have a good strategy, once again, for discriminating what is from what is not controllable in a given context.

Hypnosis and Secondary Control

The skilled application of clinical hypnosis is especially evident in enhancing secondary control. It could reasonably be said that enhancing secondary control by helping people change their perceptions of their difficulties is what hypnosis does best. Clinicians use hypnosis to help people manage pain, for example. When pain is chronic and incurable, the primary control strategy of developing a cure is not viable. The reality of pain requires effective adaptation (i.e., secondary control strategies), perhaps adjusting how one moves, structures time, manages pain medically, deals with family and friends, and learns to actively detach from (dissociate) and alter sensory awareness of the pain (hypnotic analgesia or anesthesia). As another example, clinicians use hypnosis to help people manage anxiety in situations where the perceived threats in the world will not change but their responses to them can. The airplane is still the airplane, but the reaction to flying in the airplane can be greatly modified with suggestions for viewing the experience differently.

The goal, therefore, is to use hypnosis as a vehicle for teaching the client how to proactively strive to identify what is controllable in a given context and then act sensibly on that knowledge. Or, conversely, use hypnosis to teach the client how to identify what is not controllable and facilitate an acceptance process before deciding what, if anything, to do next.

Assessing Controllability

In the context of psychotherapy, where mindfulness and hypnosis are increasingly being applied to a wide variety of clinical conditions, clinicians' views of what is controllable influence the advice they give and the treatment plans they establish. It is less about data gathered from large clinical populations and more about perspective imparted on a one-to-one basis. I have an entertaining but informative way of making this point at my clinical training sessions. I will ask attendees, all well-educated and experienced professionals, to assess the degree of controllability an individual has, ranging from zero (no control) to 100 (complete control), in a variety of real-life vignettes I present to them.

So I might say, "A woman who was recently diagnosed with breast cancer wants to use mindfulness and self-hypnotic methods of mind-body healing rather than chemotherapy or radiation to cure herself. Using such mind-body healing approaches, what degree of control do you think she has in curing herself?" Some in the group will say "no control" (zero) and others will say "total control" (100). In another vignette, I will describe an unemployed man urgently wanting a job who is going for a new job interview. The job would be perfect for him, considering his degree, expertise, and experience. When I ask, "What degree of control does he have over whether he will get the job?," again the audience responses range from zero to 100.

Can professionals get any farther apart in their perceptions of controllability than those replies indicate? One wonders what clinicians with such extreme perceptions are telling their clients in private, and whether it is helpful to them.

Try this exercise sometime with your colleagues. Create some vignettes in which a person has to make a judgment about what to do where the issue of perception of control is very much in play. When you find out directly how difficult it is, even for professionals, to make these judgments, you can better appreciate why clinicians have some obligations to go beyond global goals of acceptance and provide specific tools for what happens next. This is, arguably, what well-applied clinical hypnosis does best.

Conclusion

In this chapter, I have acknowledged the powerful and essential role of acceptance in both mindfulness and clinical hypnosis. Acceptance as a precursor to sensible, emotionally intelligent action is well considered in mindfulness. Likewise, acceptance and utilization are well considered in hypnosis. The salient question that this chapter addresses is: Once someone accepts what needs to be accepted as true, then how does he or she choose the emotionally intelligent course of action? This involves making discriminations, distinctions between possible options. How well we live is a product of those choices.

Striving to find empowering resources inside oneself is a value both hypnosis and mindfulness share. Hypnosis and GMM serve as vehicles of teaching clients, helping them put together (associate) ideas, feelings, and behavior in novel ways that can enhance their experience. They both relieve distress and build on client resources, amplifying and readying them for appropriate usage. Hypnosis, though, involves a greater open acknowledgment that the therapeutic relationship involves two people and is therefore interpersonal by definition. Mindfulness advocates speak to the issue of attunement, also emphasizing the importance of the relationship between clinician and client, but do so largely in biological terms, minimizing or ignoring altogether the social influence issues raised here. To think it is possible to guide someone with one's words and actions yet *not* be a cocreator of his or her experience is an unfortunate self-deception. It camouflages the truth of what we as clinicians are doing and why we are doing it. In my opinion, GMM is a form of hypnosis.

CHAPTER 8

Moving Forward Mindfully and Hypnotically

It may be a little extreme to rely completely on meditation techniques to train the mind, but I feel that it is just as extreme to completely rely on external methods. Humans have a wonderful intelligence that should be utilized to alleviate ill-nesses, especially mental problems.

The Dalai Lama

Hypnosis is not some mystical procedure, but rather a systematic utilization of experiential learnings—that is, the extensive learnings acquired through the process of living itself.

Milton H. Erickson, MD

As Terri walked slowly toward me, the effort she expended with each step showed as a flicker of tension across her face. Between flickers, she smiled a polite smile. She stopped in front of me and kindly looked into my eyes as she greeted me. She had called and asked to see me for help with managing pain in her knee, but began our session by confessing her embarrassment because the pain had disappeared in the interim. Asked whether there was more to discuss, Terri reported that where she most needed help was in walking; she said she had "a history of falling down." In her 70s and legitimately concerned about the prospect of breaking fragile bones in a fall, Terri had become anxious about walking. Predictably, her anxiety would lead her to fall, intensifying the vicious circle of more fear causing more falls, thereby increasing her fears. Anticipatory anxiety is the term clinicians commonly use in such instances, and it involves an obvious orientation to a future mishap that generates anxiety in the here and now.

Terri was invited to close her eyes and focus on her breathing, and this seemed to calm her relatively quickly. She was encouraged to begin to think of the steps involved in performing an activity, any activity. There is a sequence to follow, a beginning step and a next step and perhaps many next steps before reaching a last step in the sequence. She accepted this obvious truth easily. Next, Terri was invited to think about the steps involved in walking, from the lifting of a foot to the planting of a foot with each step. She was focused intently on the physical sensations of feeling her weight shift as she stepped, such as the feel of her foot—whether in a shoe or not—making contact with the ground and distributing her weight safely and the many other sensations of walking mindfully. She was gently reminded that she could maintain that immediate sensory awareness wherever she went, whether at home or someplace far away. She was invited to consider the importance of being deeply aware inside at times and the equal importance of being deeply aware of the surroundings at times. At any given moment, before she took a step in walking, she could comfortably take a preliminary step of noticing the environment and whether she would be walking an even or uneven surface, a hard or soft surface. She could comfortably take the next step of focusing on her body, her legs, her feet, and her well-practiced ability to walk with awareness with each footstep. Beyond the act of walking, she could also comfortably take each next step in her life with awareness and balance, moving forward mindfully and hypnotically. ("The Case of Terri," including long-term follow-up information, is available on DVD from Zeig Tucker Publishers, www. zeigtucker.com.)

Was this a GMM session? Was it a hypnosis session? Was it an integration of these two approaches? Given all I have said about the fluid boundaries between

GMM and clinical hypnosis to this point, there seems to be no correct answer. It now seems less important to focus on perceived differences, whether imaginary or real, and more beneficial to recognize the shared aspects of such absorbing and transformative experiences. Lynn et al. grasped this point perfectly when they wrote:

> The starting place for much of the work of clinical hypnosis, and the creation of new response sets, is acceptance. Erickson pioneered the utilization approach in hypnosis and psychotherapy—the radical acceptance of the client's current reality and responses, as a foundation on which to build new response sets by way of the following strategies: using permissive and indirect suggestions, subtle priming of therapeutic responses, accepting/utilizing client resistance as a springboard for change, noticing and capitalizing on small changes in the client, gently guiding the client's associations and stream of awareness to influence the outcomes they think about, and using paradoxical interventions and reframing to turn a client's deficits into assets (see Lynn & Hallquist, 2004). Each of these tactics implies a profound respect for clients' individuality and acceptance of their moment-to-moment experience. The use of many of these techniques is now widespread in the hypnosis field and reflected in a number of mindfulness-based approaches, including ACT (Hayes et al., 1999). . . . We suggest that it may be worthwhile to use hypnosis to catalyze mindfulness-based approaches. Meta-analyses and qualitative reviews have shown that hypnosis enhances the effectiveness of both psychodynamic and cognitive-behavioral psychotherapies (Kirsch, 1990; Kirsch, Montgomery, & Sapirstein, 1995; Lynn, Kirsch, Barabasz, Cardeña, & Patterson, 2000). In fact, the mean effect for adding hypnosis to cognitive-behavioral therapy (.48) rivals the effect size of psychotherapy itself (.52; Lipsey & Wilson, 1993). Accordingly, there is reason to believe hypnosis will enhance the effectiveness of mindfulness training as well. After all, basic instructions to practice mindfulness can be thought of as suggestions that, like other imaginative or attention-altering suggestions, can be augmented by means of hypnosis. (2006, pp. 154–155)

Suggesting Being Mindful of Suggesting

In this final chapter, I want to introduce some new ideas, expand on some of the points made previously, and then consider the next step. Clinicians routinely strive to expand their range of helping skills; given the attention I have paid to the suggestive language of GMM and clinical hypnosis, a sensible next step is to evolve a greater familiarity with such language. Beyond the structures and styles of suggestive language, it would also be valuable to appreciate how focused states, whether meditative or hypnotic, give rise to some of the more remarkable human capacities. Knowing how to help catalyze such potentially transformative experiences is certainly worth learning. As we have already seen, just because someone isn't consciously goal oriented doesn't mean he or she isn't unconsciously goal oriented. The notion that you are violating some rule of mindfulness if you meditate with deliberate intent should not diminish the therapeutic value of the experience. Some unnecessarily limiting rules are meant to be broken . . . or at least temporarily suspended.

Doing Hypnosis or Being Hypnotic? The Spirit of the Therapeutic Relationship

The qualities of the suggestions inherent in conducting GMM and clinical hypnosis sessions certainly matter (Barabasz et al., 1999). What matters more, though, is the interpersonal context in which the suggestions are offered.

I have already described how distinctly different it is to *do hypnosis* than to *be hypnotic*. Doing hypnosis is relatively easy compared to the complexity of being hypnotic. Being hypnotic means many things, but especially conveys a sensitive recognition of the power of words to heal and the power of relationships to inspire. It is living the compassionate acknowledgment of the uniqueness of each person.

Some clinical hypnosis practitioners use the older term *rapport* to describe the positive interrelationship between clinician and client. Rapport was—and still is—correctly considered a vital ingredient in successful treatments. Later, the phrase Carl Rogers advocated, "unconditional positive regard," was widely used to describe the power of acceptance in the therapeutic relationship. Next, the term *therapeutic alliance* became the standard for describing the joining of clinician and client in the treatment process, again emphasizing the healing power that can come from such joining. Most recently, the term *attunement* has become popularized, largely based on the remarkable neuroscientific findings that indicate when we talk about "having chemistry" with someone, it is more than a metaphor; there really are mutual physiological changes that take place when people are meaningfully attached.

As an example, one study of physical measures of therapists conducting treatment showed that during moments of high positive emotion, both clients and therapists had strikingly similar physiological responses (Marci, Ham, Moran, & Orr, 2007). This observation is fascinating in and of itself. More fascinating, though, was the finding that clients later gave higher ratings of perceived therapist empathy at those times. The researchers wrote, "This research supports brain imaging data that shows humans are literally 'wired to connect' emotionally. There is now converging evidence that, during moments of empathic connection, humans reflect or mirror each other's emotions, and their physiologies move on the same wavelength" (Marci et al., 2007, p. 109).

Mirror Neurons, Attunement, and the Value of Observation

Why do we react at a gut level to other people's actions or emotions? What did Marci et al. mean when they said, "humans are literally 'wired to connect' emotionally?" They refer to a most telling discovery that first launched inquiry into how relationships affect our brains. Like many important discoveries, this one was made by accident in the early 1990s by a team of Italian researchers led by neuroscientist Giacomo Rizzolatti. In an experiment, macaque monkeys' brains were "wired" to show which neurons were active while the monkeys engaged in different activities (Rizzolatti & Craighero, 2004). Specific neurons would fire when a monkey grabbed an object, which was expected. But, fascinatingly, the same neurons would fire when the monkey was passively watching another monkey grab an object. Neurologically, the monkey's brain reacted in the same way whether he was doing it himself or just watching another monkey perform the action. The brain cells would mirror each other in different individuals. These brain cells came to be called mirror neurons.

Humans also have mirror neurons. When we watch other people, a part of our brain actively registers what is going on and portions also actively relate to their experience. Some experts in neuroscience say we have "social brains" for this very reason. Interestingly, brain scans of people who show serious social deficits, such as an inability to show empathy for others, show significant differences from those of people who can engage meaningfully with others.

The chemistry, harmony, or attunement that takes place between people is a critical component of mental health. Psychotherapist Pilar Placone, in her valuable guide to mindful parenting, *Mindful Parent, Happy Child*, stated, "a parent's awareness of self and other is a primary ingredient in the establishment of a healthy parent-child connection. Increasing the strength and vitality of this connection is properly the goal of every good parent" (2011, p. 10).

> When we attune to others we allow our own internal state to shift, to come to resonate with the inner world of another. This resonance is at the heart of the important sense of "feeling felt" that emerges in close relationships. Children need attunement to feel secure and to develop well, and throughout our lives we need attunement to feel close and connected.... Empathy is the capacity to create mindsight images of other people's minds.... We sense the other's intentions and imagine what an event means in his or her mind. (D. Siegel, 2010b, pp. 27–28)

In a live presentation on the Web, Dan Siegel (2010a) further elaborated on the importance of empathy and the power of mindfulness to cultivate it. He suggested that mindful awareness builds empathy, prevents burnout, and keeps a clinician feeling well in order to be able to be more open and caring. He claimed that the more you are aware of your own internal states, the more you can be aware of others' internal states; the "circuits" we develop in ourselves are the ones we need to connect with others empathically.

Siegel certainly has supportive evidence for these claims. When therapists are more present with their clients, they may be more open and accepting and less reactive, fostering greater trust in the client and a better quality of interaction (Gehart & McCollum, 2008; Geller & Greenberg, 2002; McCollum & Gehart, 2010). What is perplexing, though, is the seeming contradiction between being more internally aware and more externally responsive. Is empathy an internally or externally oriented phenomenon—or both?

Is Knowing Yourself the Path to Knowing Others?

What a world of difference there is between the science of mirror neurons and *really knowing* what someone is experiencing internally. Consider Dan Siegel's statement, "We sense the other's intentions and imagine what an event means in his or her mind" (2010b, p. 28). It is the *imagining* of what is in someone else's mind that concerns me. To believe that you can better know someone else's experience by more closely examining your own is too often how people misconnect rather than connect, despite their matching rates of respiration. Other people may see things quite differently than we do. While being more internally, mindfully aware is considered the path to empathy, I see the process of imagining what is in someone else's mind as potentially hazardous.

In the language of mindfulness some use, the (idealistic) goal is to have people "clear" themselves and meditate to discover the "truth" of who they "really are" so they can "wake up to reality." I understand the metaphor that some mindfulness experts advocate of needing to "tune up your instrument" with meditation so you can "play well in the orchestra of life." In the real world, though, as far as I can tell, believed-in imaginings get in the way of clarity. When our feelings are so easily manipulated by others (e.g., Hollywood, terrorists, good writers) and our choices are primed by so many forces we can never be fully conscious of, it is potentially dangerous to believe your imaginary understandings accurately reflect someone else's internal experience. As we have learned in so many sensitive contexts, including iatrogenic therapies, people can be absolutely sure, and absolutely *wrong* (Barlow, 2010; Boisvert & Faust, 2002; Dimidjian & Hollon, 2010).

Observation as Another Path Toward Empathy

One of the foundational cornerstones of the field of clinical hypnosis is the importance of being observant. Those trained in clinical hypnosis regularly learn how to "get out of themselves" while conducting hypnosis sessions and keep the focus on the client's experience while doing all they can to *not* imagine what the client is experiencing. Instead of imagining or making projections about the meaning of the client's experience, the goals are to observe, support, amplify, associate, and expand. But if you really want to have some idea of what's going on in there, then ask! (Yapko, Barretta, & Barretta, 1998).

The primary lesson is to accept and utilize client experience, which presupposes first noticing it. Here is an example from one of my own training programs. I had just talked to the group about the importance of being observant. I had articulated that you cannot utilize someone's eye closure or shift in breathing (e.g., "and as your eyes close and you continue to breathe deeply you can become more comfortable") if you don't first notice it. The group was then assigned to practice some inductions on each other. As I walked around the room to offer feedback and support, I couldn't help but notice one fellow with his eyes closed swaying back and forth to his own words and rhythm as he performed his induction. Unbeknownst to him, his partner was not into the experience at all and had, in fact, already opened his eyes, ready to stop the exercise. But, because this fellow's eyes were closed and his focus was entirely internal, he had no idea. So, with a surge of mischievous feelings, I silently motioned to the man in the client role to get up and go, and I sat in his chair instead. It took some time, but when the hypnotist finally opened his eyes, he was startled to see me. Okay, perhaps that was slightly mean on my part, but I can promise you, he will never lose track of his client again. Keep your eyes open, observe, accept, utilize, and connect.

I love the idea of being clear enough to be an effective instrument with other people. Being observant seems a more objective, reality-based way to do that. Of course, it's not an "either-or" phenomenon—both matter. But, unless one is coached as a student in clinical training to be aware of the pitfalls of making assumptions and imaginings, it is too easy to become dogmatic. I much prefer the beginner's mind in that respect. So do many hypnosis practitioners, starting with Erickson. As psychologist Ronald Havens wrote in describing the genius of Milton Erickson:

> He developed his remarkable understandings of how people behave purely by observing them very, very closely, open-mindedly, and almost naively. He did not sit in his office reading or thinking about how people operate—he watched them. He did not become immersed in theories which he then tried to apply to various patients—he noticed what his patients did and modified his thinking in response. . . . But Erickson observed in a manner and with an intensity not typical of most people. First of all, he observed himself in incredible detail internally and externally. Secondly, he observed others with an intensity that surpassed even the most self-conscious analysis. (1985/2003, pp. 4–5)

Havens further described key domains of Erickson's observational skills: The influence of breathing patterns, learning about one's body, the multiple meanings of words, nonverbal communication, physiological and behavioral patterns, and cultural differences. It is curious how Havens described Erickson as open-minded, almost naive. He was a master who had mastered the beginner's mind. Erickson himself said, "And so, walk around with a blank face, your mouth shut, your eyes open and your ears open, and you wait to form your judgment until you have some actual evidence to support your inferences and your judgments" (Zeig, 1980, p. 234). That seems like very good advice.

What is it like to be the object of that level of attention from the clinician? When a clinician is open, nonjudgmental, and curious enough to ask lots of questions in an obvious effort to better understand the client's experience on as many levels as possible, the client can feel valued, appreciated, worthwhile. Asking questions that elicit his or her strengths, virtues, and unique attributes creates a context for the relationship to be open, warm, caring, and mutually responsive. The attunement that all clinicians strive for develops through this type of high-quality interaction.

Guided Mindfulness Meditation, Clinical Hypnosis, and Increasing Empathy

Let's consider the issue of timing in conducting GMM and clinical hypnosis sessions in regard to empathy. Should you, as a mindful therapist, build a certain level of attunement and empathy *before* providing GMM and hypnosis sessions, or might it be preferable to provide these hypnotic experiences as the *means for building* attunement and empathy? This is, as it must be, a matter of individual clinical judgment. Some clinicians are simply reluctant to engage with a client on experiential levels until they feel like they have an established relationship, whereas others feel comfortable engaging with people experientially to establish the relationship. The client obviously has a say in the matter, but is typically going to follow the lead of the clinician, who is the expert (Perrin, Heesacker, Pendley, & Smith, 2010).

I prefer to provide hypnotic experiences as early in the therapy context as is feasible, even in the first session. There are some compelling reasons for doing so:

1. GMM and hypnosis amplify aspects of personal experience and may make it easier to recognize how the client's patterns of perception, thinking, interpersonal relating, and so on are contributing to his or her distress.

2. Hypnotic suggestion is an effective method of achieving pattern interruption, vital for therapeutic success.
3. GMM and hypnosis stimulate experiential learning, generally the most powerful form of learning.
4. GMM and hypnosis help organize and contextualize desired responses (such as accessing compassion toward the self in response to inappropriate self-criticism).
5. Employing hypnotic approaches encourages and models flexibility within the therapeutic relationship, indirectly telling the client "we can relate to each other in a variety of ways and on a variety of levels," rather than only one, helping promote the positive use and integration of multiple dimensions of experience.
6. Experiential approaches help build focus and, in so doing, retrain the brain as well as the mind (stimulating neurogenesis, neuroplasticity, and even gene expression).
7. GMM and clinical hypnosis encourage positive expectancy, the single most important factor predicting treatment outcomes. Using these approaches, especially early in treatment, gives clients direct experiential evidence that their perceptions and experiences are malleable, not fixed. Catalyzing shifts in clients' perceptions of their body, time, general awareness, the meaning of past events, personal identity, relationships to others, and so much more is a vehicle for the powerful transformative experiences associated with both GMM and hypnosis.

When clients discover the malleability of subjective experience firsthand through these positive guided experiences, they can begin to redefine not only self-perceptions, but also perceptions of the clinician. When the clinician uses permissive language that fully respects the autonomy of clients and their ability to choose whether to respond and how to respond to particular suggested ideas or images, the potential for attunement and empathy increases. When process suggestions are used that invite clients to participate in the experience by cocreating its qualities, they can feel more connected to both the flow of the session and the flow of the relationship with the therapist. When the therapist checks in (i.e., talks) with clients during the course of the GMM or hypnosis session to explore their experience, the therapist thereby deepens the sense of presence on multiple levels of interpersonal engagement. Rather than just talking "at" the client, the therapist's interest in and willingness to join with the client's experience further defines the relationship as close and mutually responsive. When the clinician has tiptoed through the client's conscious and unconscious experience with GMM and hypnosis, and done so respectfully, compassionately, and helpfully, attunement and empathy are maximized.

Does Changing One's Brain or Feeling Better Mean Being Better?

The domain of psychotherapy has faced a challenge throughout its entire history: proving that it works. The evidence for the merits of psychotherapy has now grown sufficiently to be able to say with confidence that, for most disorders, people who receive treatment are generally better off than those who do not. But it is difficult to predict to what degree, if any, a specific individual is likely to be helped.

Adopting a biological framework for demonstrating the value of a treatment has become more compelling for many clinicians. In a highly informative Webinar presentation by Rick Hanson (2010), author of *Buddha's Brain*, he offered his insights as to why a neurobiological framework employed specifically for describing the merits of mindfulness can be valuable. He suggested it provides an organizing framework for treatment, motivates clients to view their problems as physical (thus providing a concrete reason that people who prefer concrete reasons can more easily accept), increases the likelihood that policymakers and insurance companies will find related treatments more plausible and worthy of financial support, encourages a more integrated approach by dealing with body and mind, and inspires more innovative methods of treatment, such as neurofeedback.

In the same presentation, Hanson also pointed out some potential liabilities of adopting the neurobiological framework. He acknowledged the potential for oversimplifying people's problems by defining them in only physical terms (what I referred to earlier as bioreductionism). He pointed out the danger of overlocalizing brain functions, which happened a couple of decades ago when people stated that the left hemisphere of the brain did certain things and the right hemisphere did certain other things. This cerebral asymmetry hypothesis, as it was known, was subsequently shown to be largely inaccurate. Hanson also acknowledged the danger of neuroscientists defining the field simply by claiming the right to do so as holders of biological truth. Given how this has already happened in the realm of psychiatry, where equivocal evidence has skewed perceptions of mental health issues in the direction of liberally and questionably medicating people, Hanson's concern does not seem misplaced.

The biology of mindfulness has received considerable attention and has already accumulated more and better information than has the biology of hypnosis. This research includes oft-cited evidence that meditation experience is associated with increased cortical thickness (Lazar et al., 2005), increased myelinization of nerves, synaptic changes, neurogenesis (Treadway & Lazar, 2009), and electroencephalogram (EEG) patterns of synchronicity (Lutz, Greischar, Rawlings, Ricard, & Davidson, 2004). As Dan Siegel (2010a) pointed out, the "close paying of attention" appears to change brains in measurable ways and in ways that may activate neural pathways for promoting greater integration and may even alter gene expression in ways that will be epigenetically beneficial to oneself and even one's offspring. The suggestion is that mindfulness changes the brain wiring, which changes the brain firing and thereby helps move us from chaos and rigidity to integration, presumably manifesting harmony, flexibility, compassion, and connection to a larger world.

What remains to be shown, though, is that increased cortical thickness or greater nerve myelinization developed through long-term meditation translates into specific therapeutic gains. In fact, the findings have to be considered equivocal: Did you know that increased cortical thickness has also been associated with *autism* (Hardan, Muddasani, Vemulapalli, Keshavan, & Minshew, 2006)?

There is already evidence from the domains of both clinical hypnosis and mindfulness that these processes help people recover from depression (Alladin, 2006, 2010; Williams et al., 2007). What we do not yet know, though, is whether this is because of presumed brain changes (because therapists do not regularly conduct brain scans), the acquisition of a new cognitive framework for thinking about depression, the specific experiential or behavioral activation strategies employed, specific new coping or problem-solving skills acquired through GMM and hypnosis, or something else.

There was a rush to attribute improvements in depressed people taking antidepressants to the medications. Now there is good reason to doubt that attribution in light of more recent evidence suggesting a significant placebo effect may be the greater factor in improvement (Kirsch, 2010; Whitaker, 2010). Similarly, while I do not dispute the neuroscientific findings regarding mindfulness, and find them intriguing, I am openly questioning whether the biological framework is necessarily the best framework for clinicians to adopt. Can people show greater EEG synchronicity and still be lousy decision makers in their personal lives? Can people engage their prefrontal cortex more and still be symptomatic? We do not really know yet. To highlight the complexity of this issue further, what should we make of *single* hypnosis sessions that have lasting therapeutic impact, as years of follow-up demonstrate?

Hanson's point that biology provides an organizing framework is true. So does a sociocognitive framework, a neodissociative framework, a cognitive-behavioral framework, a behavioral activation framework, and an interpersonal systemic framework. His point that motivating the client to think in physical terms, a kinder variation of the well-known brain disease model which suggests that a neurochemical defect causes the disorder (e.g., depression), may, in fact, motivate some people to accept the need to practice mindfulness in order to change their brains. We currently have no idea for how many people it has the opposite effect: demotivating them because they now see themselves as a victim of a brain anomaly. In the world of psychotherapy, perception is everything and people's viewpoints are not always rational or do not reflect what you would expect them to understand based on what you actually said.

I remember how in the 1970s it was routine to blame people's problems and bad behavior on poor self-esteem. Many clinicians and social commentators still do so. In California, where I live, legislators actually formed a government task force on self-esteem, giving it the mandate to establish self-esteem-building programs in schools. Third graders were encouraged to jump up on their desks and loudly proclaim, "I am special!" The irony seemed to escape the experts that if everyone was special, was *anyone* special? Psychologist Jean Twenge (2007) wrote a superb book called *Generation Me: Why Today's Young Americans Are More Confident, Assertive, Entitled—and More Miserable Than Ever Before*. She also wrote, along with W. Keith Campbell, *The Narcissism Epidemic: Living in the Age of Entitlement* (Twenge & Campbell, 2010). Both of these books highlight the longer-term detriments of attributing problems to poor self-esteem and striving to build self-esteem, only to fuel a damaging sense of entitlement instead. What are the long-term detriments of (over) attributing problems to faulty biology and the desirability of brain changes as evidence of improvement? Will people who show greater myelinization be considered more enlightened?

There is no evidence that people with higher self-esteem are better people. (When you consider the inflated self-esteem of sociopaths, there is even some evidence against it.) There is no evidence that people with thicker cortices are better or more enlightened people. Thus, the expanded mindfulness approaches that emphasize acceptance, compassion, loving-kindness, gratitude, forgiveness, and other *relational* elements may hold greater therapeutic potential. These qualities are inherent in the suggestions found in mindfulness approaches, and they encourage better values in relating to both oneself and others. Emphasizing these qualities helps ensure that not only do people feel better, they *are* better. The character strengths and virtues described earlier, such as kindness, generosity, and compassion (Peterson & Seligman, 2004), are most often evident in the interpersonal domain. In no small way, it is deliberate on my part to draw attention to interpersonal aspects as the key aspects of GMM and hypnosis. I have made the point in many ways that when you serve as a guide for these highly suggestive experiential processes, the interpersonal components, especially empathy and suggestibility, play a dominant role in what happens.

The Inevitability and Power of Suggestion in Transforming Experience

Empowering people to lead better lives is the calling of the clinical arts and sciences. Many have responded to the call, especially in the field of psychotherapy, in which it is estimated that over 400 theories and models of treatment have been developed (Consoli & Jester, 2005). There are those who have focused on identifying the differences between these many approaches, and those who have focused on the similarities. Some of the research lending support to the similarities suggests that nearly half of the changes reported in therapy are attributable to common factors (such as the therapeutic alliance) but only about one-tenth of the changes are attributable to specific techniques (Brown, 2010; Lambert, 1992; Lambert & Simon, 2010).

It is difficult to know what exactly accounts for a therapeutic shift when people are more dedicated to the content of an approach than to its process. When people advocate for the concepts, terminology, and methods (including rituals) of each of the hundreds of forms of therapy, there is a loyalty to the approach that makes it harder to be objective about its essence. This unquestioning allegiance to a particular theory or method is a primary motivator for writing this book: the philosophy and methods of mindfulness are rapidly growing in popularity but, until now, the common denominators (e.g., suggestion, power, expectancy) have received too little attention. We have seen how these factors are dealt with in the mindfulness literature, which has placed great emphasis on the power of mindfulness to transform lives, change brains, improve physical health, cultivate kindness and compassion, and attain enlightenment. The parallels to the many religions and psychotherapies that make similar promises and provide compelling empirical evidence for their claims may be obvious. Subscribers to the faith, the true believers, whether religiously or psychotherapeutically faithful, are notoriously adherent to the teachings and convinced of their truth. Whether it is reaching nirvana by dancing feverishly or by reenacting the crucifixion, the belief is self-reinforced that the action provides benefit.

Suggestion, Psychotherapy, and Deceptive and Nondeceptive Placebos

The building of the appropriate frame of mind through suggestion, carried out to encourage the self-reinforced belief that action provides benefit, is the essence of hypnosis. Many research and clinical approaches, especially drug studies in which the research subjects are misled into believing they are being given an active drug when they are actually being given an inert placebo, involve deception. Our knowledge of the placebo effect has grown quite substantially in recent years, largely due to the willingness of researchers to provide sham drugs, sham surgeries, and other forms of sham treatment in order to assess how much derived benefit is actually due to an active treatment.

These studies affirm and reaffirm the power of suggestion to transform not only subjective experience, but physiology as well. Consider as just one example a study that reported findings from the UCLA Neuropsychiatric Institute regarding the relationship between EEG changes and clinical outcome in patients taking the commonly prescribed antidepressants Effexor and Prozac (Hunter, Leuchter, Morgan, & Cook, 2006). Research subjects were tested for quantitative EEG cordance during a placebo lead-in phase, often conducted before randomization of the research subjects (receiving either drug or no treatment) in clinical trials is performed, as well as during treatment. Remarkably, significant changes in EEG patterns became evident in responders *before the active drugs were administered*, purely on the basis of the subjects expecting their brains to change by taking the drugs. The authors stated: "Some neurophysiological changes that are associated with endpoint antidepressant outcome reflect non-pharmacodynamic factors. . . . Future studies should examine how brain changes during the lead-in period may be associated with patient expectations, the therapeutic relationship, and treatment history" (Hunter et al., 2006, p. 1429). Brain changes have been shown to arise in response to other psychotherapy interventions as well (Schwartz & Begley, 2003) and, when placebos work, they may do so by changing brain chemistry (Mayberg et al., 2002).

When therapists promise great benefits of treatment to their clients, they do so with sincerity and conviction. But is there a relationship between the magnitude of the promise and the magnitude of the result? The evidence says yes. Two factors are involved: The strength of the expectancy (how confident one is the response will occur) and the magnitude of the expected response. When a person has a strong expectancy for a relatively small change in response, the expectancy is more likely to be confirmed. A weak expectancy for a large change in response is less likely to be confirmed (Kirsch, 1999).

Kirsch (1999; Lynn & Kirsch, 2006) made a distinction between deceptive and nondeceptive placebos and characterized hypnosis as the utilization of nondeceptive placebos. Giving people suggestions during a hypnosis session in the context of therapy is generally a nondeceptive intervention. For example, saying, "You may notice your symptoms diminishing this week," suggests *a possibility*. It isn't a command, it isn't a lie, and it isn't a promise. It is a suggestion that something might change in a beneficial direction. Similarly, suggesting to someone in pain, "You may notice your body becoming more numb and seemingly detached, allowing you a deep sense of relief" isn't a command, lie, or promise. The suggestion creates the possibility of a response by activating some still-unknown changes in both the brain and body that provide a transformative experience of symptom or pain relief. Clients use their brain and body to fulfill the suggestion, an empowering, exhilarating experience they get to fully own.

Similarly, when you suggest, "You can cultivate kindness and compassion toward yourself and others," or "You can picture your thoughts as signs on a road you're traveling, noticing them only with a sense of curiosity and comfortable detachment," these are not commands, lies, or promises, either. But, through the vehicle of suggestion, you create the possibility that clients can discover a path that changes them in profound ways. Both GMM and hypnosis share the power of suggestion and use it to help strengthen people in ways far more profound than mere words can capture. *The right words, in the appropriate context, can transform lives.*

Compelling Reasons to Study Clinical Hypnosis

As I see it, there are compelling reasons why training in clinical hypnosis should be a mandatory part of every advanced academic program that produces health care professionals. After all, every therapeutic intervention one can name, whether medical or psychological in nature, will necessarily involve some degree of skilled—and suggestive—communication with an individual within the context of a therapeutic alliance. Hypnosis is the study of skillfully applied suggestion. The psychotherapy context in particular invites a more careful consideration of therapeutic communication: How does a psychotherapist define the therapeutic relationship and establish the all-important therapeutic alliance? How does he or she build a positive expectancy for the benefits of the therapeutic interventions to be employed, such as mindfulness? How does he or she package and present valuable ideas and experiences (i.e., conduct GMM) in such a manner that the client can relate to them meaningfully and use them to improve?

These basic issues of clinical practice simply open the door to much deeper questions that have been the focus of the field of hypnosis for decades: How does a clinician's influence catalyze shifts in patterns of thinking, feeling, or behaving that are objectively detectable with brain scans? How can a clinician suggest a profound shift in sensory experience such that someone can detach from normal sensory processing and, as an example, experience a natural anesthesia sufficient to have major surgery painlessly? How does a clinician's use of carefully worded suggestion help transform someone's experience in therapeutic ways?

These are difficult questions to answer, of course. Someone unfamiliar with hypnosis might be more than a little surprised to discover that hypnosis has been subjected to a wide variety of empirical investigations, attempting to better understand how a clinician's words can become the basis for seemingly remarkable experiences. But anyone who thinks of people as having more resources than they consciously realize will, hopefully, be interested in how to help mobilize those resources.

Hypnosis engenders an entirely optimistic appraisal of people: Therapy is organized around the belief that people can discover and develop the very resources within themselves that they need. Hypnosis creates an amplified, energized, high-powered context for people to explore, discover, and use more of their innate abilities. As you now know, hypnosis is not the therapy, and hypnosis itself cures *nothing*. Rather, hypnosis is the vehicle for empowering people with the abilities and realizations that ultimately serve to help them. It is not the experience of hypnosis itself that is therapeutic; it is what happens *during* hypnosis in terms of developing new and helpful associations. The study of hypnosis, then, involves a process of discovering what latent capacities are accessible—and what new ones can be developed—in the experience of hypnosis, and how to bring them forth at the times and places they will best serve the client. It truly is a positive psychology in practice.

Hypnosis allows for therapeutic possibilities simply not likely to occur through other means. Mindfulness shares that great potential and is also heavily reliant upon suggestive factors to help that potential unfold in a meaningful direction. That alone warrants serious consideration of the dynamics of hypnotic influence.

If Hypnosis Is So Great, Why Isn't Everyone Using It?

To the experts in hypnosis, there are few more puzzling questions. Perhaps the biggest obstacles to hypnosis becoming a well-developed skill in each clinician's repertoire are the outdated, myth-based views I hope I have helped to correct here. Hypnosis has a strange history, replete with scare stories and controversies that have lingered in many professionals' minds. Consider this: Mindfulness is symbolized by the Buddha, whereas hypnosis is (mis)represented by Svengali. Mindfulness is practiced in spiritual retreats; hypnosis is practiced in nightclubs. This state of affairs is terribly unfortunate, of course, because both therapists and their clients miss out on a tool of huge potential benefit for enhancing the potentials of whatever approach they may employ.

What is encouraging, though, is how the clinical world is moving toward

washington centerville
PUBLIC LIBRARY
www.wclibrary.info

Items that you checked out

Title: All things must pass [sound
recording] / George Harrison.
ID: 33508010270208
Due: Tuesday, September 19, 2023

Title: Beginnings [sound recording] / the
Allman Brothers Band.
ID: 33508009540124
Due: Tuesday, September 19, 2023

Title: Journeyman [sound recording] /
Eric Clapton.
ID: 33508013566891
Due: Tuesday, September 19, 2023

Title: Mindfulness and hypnosis : the
power of suggestion to transform
experience / Michael D. Yapko.
ID: 33508012464288
Due: Tuesday, September 19, 2023

Title: Mindfulness meditation and the art
of reiki : the road to liberation /
Steve Gooch.
ID: 38181000019566
Due: Tuesday, September 19, 2023

Total items: 5
Account balance: $0.00
8/29/2023 4:22 PM
Checked out: 5
Overdue: 0
Hold requests: 0
Ready for pickup: 0

***You have completed a self-checkout
transaction with WCPL. Thank you for
using your local public library!***

Check out Vega Discover, WCPL's new
library catalog. Try out the new user-
friendly design and improved
accessibility. wclibrary.info/catalog/vega/

hypnosis rather than away from it. Techniques like mindfulness, focusing, guided imagery, mind-body healing, and the like are skyrocketing in popularity, riding the wave of empirical support for their effectiveness. All of these techniques, and many others, are undeniably hypnotically based in their use of focusing, suggestion, and dissociative methods to achieve their aims. When it serves people's purposes, they employ hypnotic and mindful methods by calling them something else. Ronald Siegel (2010) directly suggested to listeners they avoid "the B word," referring to Buddhism, when it might offend someone with a negative view. He further suggested avoiding the word *mindfulness* with people who may be prone to dismissing it as esoteric, instead saying something more acceptably scientific sounding, such as "systematic attentional training." A rose, a trance, a meditation by any other name.

The literature of hypnosis can provide deeper insights into how and why such methods are valuable in therapeutic practice, literally identifying their suggestive and interpersonal mechanisms of action and clinical utility. This book has, hopefully, provided a step in this direction. If you want to understand more about the nature of unconscious processes and how they become accessible and amenable to therapeutic influence, then studying the clinical hypnosis literature and developing skills in the use of hypnosis makes good sense.

Final Thoughts

In life we may keep looking for the right answer, but there is no right answer. Everything is relative rather than absolute. That's the answer.

Lama Surya Das

I hope to have made it abundantly clear that I am a strong proponent of experiential learning, powerfully enhanced through GMM and clinical hypnosis. Encouraging people to focus, either narrowly or broadly, internally or externally, concretely or abstractly, as a means of becoming more aware, open, and accepting is not unique to either hypnosis or mindfulness, however. Suggestion is inherent across *all* treatments. I am considerably less interested in being right and more concerned with being effective, which helps me appreciate the wise words of Lama Surya Das (1997, p. 20) above. It also helps me focus more on the essence of something rather than its packaging.

Deep questions remain. How do we create the conditions that encourage knowing and growing the best parts of ourselves and others? How can we make the merits of mindfulness, hypnosis, and other such opportunities for experiential learning more understandable, usable, and available to the clients we serve? How can we selflessly share knowledge that makes the whole greater than the sum of the parts?

I think Buddha's answer to such questions is perfect: "Mind comes first. Before deed and words comes thought or intention."

Hypnosis Organizations and Journals for Professionals

American Psychological Association, Division 30, The Society of Psychological Hypnosis

The American Psychological Association (APA) is the national organization for psychologists in America, with a large membership well exceeding 100,000 members. It is divided into dozens of components, each with a specialized focus within the domain of psychology. Division 30 is called the Society of Psychological Hypnosis. Once a member of APA, you are eligible to join the component division branches of your choice. When you join Division 30, you will receive an informative bulletin three times per year about events within the field in general and within Division 30 in particular. Clinical issues, news updates, literature reviews, and other informative and helpful information is included. Furthermore, at the large annual meetings of APA, the Society of Psychological Hypnosis holds specialized programs with prominent members sharing their latest research and clinical insights. For membership information, you can contact APA directly.

Website:www.apa.org.
For Division 30 information write:
The American Psychological Association
P.S.O./Division 30
750 First Street NE
Washington, DC 20002-4242
Phone numbers in the U.S.: (800) 374-2721; (202) 336-5500

American Society of Clinical Hypnosis (ASCH)

ASCH is the largest of the national professional hypnosis societies in the world. ASCH holds smaller, more topically focused regional workshops several times a year around the United States, and a large annual meeting with an impressive array of topics and presenters. ASCH also has component branches in most of the major cities across the United States. Components vary in their level of local activity. Many hold monthly meetings and annual workshops.

Website: www.asch.net

E-mail: info@asch.net

Journal: *American Journal of Clinical Hypnosis* (*AJCH*)—published quarterly and included with membership in the organization along with a quarterly newsletter.

For membership information write:
American Society of Clinical Hypnosis
140 North Bloomingdale Road
Bloomingdale, IL 60108-1017
Phone number in the U.S.: (630) 980-4740

International Society of Clinical Hypnosis (ISH)

ISH, headquartered in Rome, is the umbrella organization for dozens of component society branches all over the world. ISH holds triannual meetings, each time in a different location somewhere around the world, that feature many of the world's premier researchers and clinicians presenting their latest findings.

Membership includes an informative newsletter containing articles, interviews, and conference information.

Website: www.ISH-hypnosis.org

E-mail: contact@ish-hypnosis.org

Newsletter: ISH quarterly newsletter featuring informative articles, interviews, meeting information, and component activity updates is included in membership.

For membership information write:

ISH Central Office

Via Tagliamento, 25-00198

Rome, Italy

Phone number in Rome: +39.06.8548205

Society for Clinical and Experimental Hypnosis (SCEH)

SCEH is a prominent American organization for hypnosis professionals, both clinical and research oriented, that places especially heavy emphasis on research. The *International Journal of Clinical and Experimental Hypnosis* is one of the most respected and most frequently cited scientific journals in all the behavioral sciences, and reflects the high standards of SCEH. SCEH holds an annual conference that features papers, workshops, and panels on latest developments within the field, presented by many of the most well-known and respected people in the field.

Website: www.sceh.us

E-mail: info@sceh.us

Journal: *International Journal of Clinical and Experimental Hypnosis* (*IJCEH*), published quarterly and included with membership in the organization along with a quarterly newsletter.

For membership information write:

Society for Clinical and Experimental Hypnosis

P.O. Box 252

Southborough, MA 01772

Phone number in the U.S.: (508) 598-5553

For journal subscriptions only, write to:
Taylor and Francis, LLC
325 Chestnut Street
Philadelphia, PA 19106
Phone number in the U.S.: (215) 625-2940

The Milton H. Erickson Foundation

This organization is very active in advancing psychotherapy in all its forms, but is especially dedicated to the advancement of Ericksonian approaches to hypnosis and psychotherapy. The foundation is not a society and does not have a membership. They organize major internationally attended annual meetings, most often on Ericksonian approaches but also on brief therapy and the evolution of psychotherapy. These meetings are held over 4 to 5 days and feature stellar faculties conducting workshops, clinical demonstrations, and other presentation formats. The foundation also holds many smaller meetings throughout the year around the United States. The foundation is the core of an international network of Erickson Institutes around the world (more than 120 to date) that also strive to advance the work of Dr. Erickson. Each institute sets its own length and frequency of training. Contact the foundation for institute locations.

Website: www.erickson-foundation.org
E-mail: office@erickson-foundation.org
Newsletter: published three times a year
For general information write:
The Milton H. Erickson Foundation, Inc.
3606 N. 24th Street
Phoenix, AZ 85016-6500
Phone number in the U.S.: (602) 956-6196

APPENDIX B

Mindfulness Resources

Lama Surya Das: www.surya.org

Rick Hanson: www.rickhanson.net

Tara Brach: www.tarabrach.com

Mindfulness-Based Stress Reduction: www.umassmed.edu/cfm

Duke Integrative Medicine: www.dukeintegrativemedicine.org

Cambridge Insight Meditation Center: www.cimc.info

Zen Center of San Diego: www.zencentersandiego.org

Dzogchen Foundation: www.dzogchen.org

Deer Park Monastery: www.deerparkmonastery.org

Mindfulness (Journal Editor: Nirbhay N. Singh): www.springer.com

Sounds True (Self-Help Materials): www.soundstrue.com

References

Alladin, A. (2006). Experiential cognitive hypnotherapy: Strategies for relapse prevention in depression. In M. Yapko (Ed.), *Hypnosis and treating depression: Advances in clinical practice* (pp. 281–313). New York: Routledge.

Alladin, A. (2010). Evidence-based hypnotherapy for depression. *International Journal of Clinical and Experimental Hypnosis, 58*(2), 165–185.

American Psychological Association, Division of Psychological Hypnosis. (1985, August). *A general definition of hypnosis and a statement concerning its application and efficacy* (report submitted to the Council of Representatives of the American Psychological Association). Washington, DC: APA.

Aronson, E., Wilson, T., & Akert, R. (2009). *Social psychology* (7th ed.). New York: Prentice Hall.

Barabasz, A. (2000). EEG markers of alert hypnosis: The induction makes a difference. *Sleep and Hypnosis, 2*, 164–169.

Barabasz, A., Barabasz, M., Jensen, S., Calvin, S., Trevisan, M., & Warner, D. (1999). Cortical event-related potentials show the structure of hypnotic suggestions is crucial. *International Journal of Clinical and Experimental Hypnosis, 47*, 5–22.

Barabasz, A., & Watkins, J. (2005). *Hypnotherapeutic techniques* (2nd ed.). New York: Brunner/Routledge.

Dietrich, A. (2003). Functional neuroanatomy of altered states of consciousness: The transient hypofrontality hypothesis. *Consciousness and Cognition, 12*, 221–256.

Dimeff, L., & Koerner, K. (Eds.). (2007). *Dialectical behavior therapy in clinical practice: Applications across disorders and settings.* New York: Guilford.

Dimidjian, S., & Hollon, S. (2010). How would we know if psychotherapy were harmful? *American Psychologist, 65*, 21–33. doi:10.1037/a0017299

Elkins, G., Jensen, M., & Patterson, D. (2007). Hypnotherapy for the management of chronic pain. *International Journal of Clinical and Experimental Hypnosis, 55*(3), 275–287.

Epley, N., Savitsky, K., & Kachelski, R. A. (1999). What every skeptic should know about subliminal persuasion. *Skeptical Inquirer, 23*(4), 40–46.

Erickson, M. (1954). Special techniques of brief hypnotherapy. *Journal of Clinical and Experimental Hypnosis, 2*, 109–129.

Erickson, M. (2009). Further clinical techniques of hypnosis: Utilization techniques. *American Journal of Clinical Hypnosis, 51*(4), 341–362. (Original work published 1959)

Erickson, M., & Rossi, E. (1979). *Hypnotherapy: An exploratory casebook.* New York: Irvington.

Erickson, M., & Rossi, E. (1981). *Experiencing hypnosis: Therapeutic approaches to altered states.* New York: Irvington.

Erickson, M., Rossi, E., & Rossi, S. (1976). *Hypnotic realities: The induction of clinical hypnosis and forms of indirect suggestion.* New York: Irvington.

Flammer, E., & Alladin, A. (2007). The efficacy of hypnotherapy in the treatment of psychosomatic disorders: Meta-analytical evidence. *International Journal of Clinical and Experimental Hypnosis, 55*, 251–274.

Gehart, D., & McCollum, E. (2008). Teaching therapeutic presence: A mindfulness-based approach. In S. Hick & T. Bien (Eds.), *Mindfulness and the therapeutic relationship* (pp. 176–194). New York: Guilford.

Geller, S., & Greenberg, L. (2002). Therapeutic presence: Therapists' experience of presence in the psychotherapy encounter. *Person-Centered and Experiential Psychotherapies, 1*, 71–86.

Gibbons, D., & Lynn, S. (2010). Hypnotic inductions: A primer. In S. Lynn, J. Rhue, & I. Kirsch (Eds.), *Handbook of clinical hypnosis* (2nd ed., pp. 267–291). Washington, DC: American Psychological Association.

Gladwell, M. (2005). *Blink: The power of thinking without thinking*. New York: Little, Brown.

Gorassini, D., & Spanos, N. (1999). The Carleton Skill Training Program for modifying hypnotic suggestibility: Original version and variations. In I. Kirsch, A. Capafons, E. Cardeña-Buelna, & S. Amigó (Eds.), *Clinical hypnosis and self-regulation: Cognitive-behavioral perspectives* (pp. 141–178). Washington, DC: American Psychological Association.

Graci, G., & Hardie, J. (2007). Evidence-based hypnotherapy for the management of sleep disorders. *International Journal of Clinical and Experimental Hypnosis, 55,* 288–302.

Green, J. (2010). Hypnosis and smoking cessation: Research and application. In S. Lynn, J. Rhue, & I. Kirsch (Eds.), *Handbook of clinical hypnosis* (2nd ed., pp. 593–614). Washington, DC: American Psychological Association.

Green, J., Barabasz, A., Barrett, D., & Montgomery, G. (2005). Forging ahead: The 2003 APA Division 30 definition of hypnosis. *International Journal of Clinical and Experimental Hypnosis, 53,* 259–264.

Haley, J. (1986). *Uncommon therapy: The psychiatric techniques of Milton H. Erickson, M.D.* New York: Norton. (Original work published 1973)

Haley, J. (1992). Zen and the art of therapy. In J. Zeig (Ed.), *The evolution of psychotherapy: The second conference* (pp. 24–36). New York: Brunner/Mazel. Reprinted in M. Richeport-Haley & J. Carlson (Eds.) (2010). *Jay Haley revisited* (pp. 315–335). New York: Routledge.

Hammond, D. (2007). Review of the efficacy of clinical hypnosis with headaches and migraines. *International Journal of Clinical and Experimental Hypnosis, 55,* 207–219.

Hanh, T. N., & Cheung, L. (2010). *Savor: Mindful eating, mindful life*. New York: Harper One.

Hanson, R. (2010, October 13). *Neurodharma: How to train the brain toward mindfulness*. Live Web seminar sponsored by the National Institute for the Clinical Application of Behavioral Medicine.

Hanson, R., & Mendius, R. (2009). *Buddha's brain: The practical neuroscience of happiness, love & wisdom*. Oakland, CA: New Harbinger.

Hardan, A., Muddasani, S., Vemulapalli, M., Keshavan, M., & Minshew, N. (2006). An MRI study of increased cortical thickness in autism. *American Journal of Psychiatry, 163,* 1290–1292.

Harrer, M. (2009). Mindfulness and the mindful therapist: Possible contributions to hypnosis. *Contemporary Hypnosis, 26*(4), 234–244.

Hassin, R., Uleman, J., & Bargh , J. (Eds.) (2005). *The new unconscious: Social cognition and social neuroscience*. New York: Oxford University Press.

Havens, R. (2003). *The wisdom of Milton H. Erickson, M.D.: The complete volume*. Norwalk, CT: Crown House. (Original work published 1985)

Hayes, S. C. (1987). A contextual approach to therapeutic change. In N. S. Jacobson (Ed.), *Psychotherapists in clinical practice: Cognitive and behavior perspectives* (pp. 327–387). New York: Guilford.

Hayes, S. (2004). Acceptance and commitment therapy and the new behavior therapies: Mindfulness, acceptance, and relationship. In S. Hayes, V. Follette, & M. Linehan (Eds.), *Mindfulness and acceptance: Expanding the cognitive-behavioral tradition* (pp. 1–29). New York: Guilford.

Hayes, S., Strosahl, K., & Wilson, K. (1999). *Acceptance and commitment therapy: An experiential approach to behavior change*. New York: Guilford.

Healy, D. (2004). *Let them eat Prozac: The unhealthy relationship between the pharmaceutical companies and depression*. New York: New York University.

Heap, M., Brown, R., & Oakley, D. (Eds.). (2004). *The highly hypnotizable person: Theoretical, experimental and clinical issues*. New York: Brunner-Routledge.

Hick, S. (2010). Cultivating therapeutic relationships: The role of mindfulness. In S. Hick & T. Bien (Eds.), *Mindfulness and the therapeutic relationship* (pp. 3–18). New York: Guilford.

Hilgard, E. (1965). *Hypnotic susceptibility*. New York: Harcourt, Brace, and World.

Hilgard, E. (1977). *Divided consciousness: Multiple controls in human thought and action*. New York: John Wiley.

Holroyd, J. (2003). The science of meditation and the state of hypnosis. *American Journal of Clinical Hypnosis, 46*(2), 109–128.

Hunter, A., Leuchter, A., Morgan, M., & Cook, I. (2006). Changes in brain function (quantitative EEG cordance) during placebo lead-in and treatment outcomes in clinical trials for major depression. *American Journal of Psychiatry, 163*(8), 1426–1432.

Jacobson, N., Dobson, K., Truax, P., Addis, M., Koerner, K., Gollan, J., et al. (1996). A component analysis of cognitive-behavioral treatment for depression. *Journal of Consulting and Clinical Psychology, 64*, 295–304.

Kabat-Zinn, J. (1990). *Full catastrophe living: Using the wisdom of your body and mind to face stress, pain, and illness.* New York: Delta.

Kabat-Zinn, J. (2002). *Guided mindful meditation: Series 1.* Boulder, CO: Sounds True.

Kabat-Zinn, J. (2006). *Mindfulness for beginners* [audio CD]. Boulder, CO: Sounds True.

Kabat-Zinn, J. (2007, March 8). Mindfulness [lecture for Google employees]. Retrieved from http://www.youtube.com/watch?v=3nwwKbM_vJc.

Kabat-Zinn, J., Lipworth, L., & Burney, R. (1985). The clinical use of mindfulness meditation for the self-regulation of chronic pain. *Journal of Behavioral Medicine, 8,* 163–190.

Kabat-Zinn, J., Massion, A. O., Kristeller, J., & Peterson, L. G. (1992). Effectiveness of a meditation-based stress reduction program in the treatment of anxiety disorders. *American Journal of Psychiatry, 149*(7), 936–943.

Kabat-Zinn, J., Wheeler, E., Light, T., Skillings, A., Scharf, M., Cropley, T., et al. (1998). Influence of mindfulness meditation-based stress reduction intervention on rates of skin clearing in patients with moderate to sevre psoriasis undergoing phototherapy (UVB) and photochemotherapy (PUVA). *Psychosomatic Medicine, 60,* 625–632.

Kay, A., Wheeler, S., Bargh, J., & Ross, L. (2004). Material priming: The influence of mundane physical objects on situational construal and competitive behavioral choice. *Organizational Behavior and Human Decision Processes, 95*(1), 83–96.

Kirsch, I. (1990). *Changing expectations: A key to effective psychotherapy.* Pacific Grove, CA: Brooks/Cole.

Kirsch, I. (Ed.). (1999). *How expectancies shape experience.* Washington, DC: American Psychological Association.

Kirsch, I. (2010). *The emperor's new drugs: Exploding the antidepressant myth.* New York: Perseus.

Kirsch, I., Montgomery, G., & Sapirstein, G. (1995). Hypnosis as an adjunct to cognitive behavioral psychotherapy: A meta-analysis. *Journal of Consulting and Clinical Psychology, 63,* 214–220.

Kornfield, J. (2008). *Meditation for beginners.* Boulder, CO: Sounds True.

Kosslyn, S., Thompson, B., Costantini-Ferrando, M., Alpert, N., & Spiegel, D. (2000). Hypnotic visual illusion alters color processing in the brain. *American Journal of Psychiatry, 157,* 1279–1284.

Lambert, M. (1992). Psychotherapy outcome research: Implications for integrative and eclectical therapists. In J. Norcross & M. Goldfried (Eds.), *Handbook of psychotherapy integration* (pp. 94–129). New York: Basic Books.

Lambert, M., & Simon, W. (2010). The therapeutic relationship: Central and essential in psychotherapy outcome. In S. Hick & T. Bien (Eds.), *Mindfulness and the therapeutic relationship* (pp. 19–34). New York: Guilford.

Lawrence, J., & Lee, R. (2003). *Inherit the wind.* New York: Ballantine. (Original work published 1951)

Lazar, S., Kerr, C., Wasserman, R., Gray, J., Greve, D., Treadway, M., et al. (2005). Meditation experience is associated with increased cortical thickness. *NeuroReport 16*(17), 1893–1897.

Lazarus, A. (2010). A multimodal framework and clinical hypnosis. In S. Lynn, J. Rhue, & I. Kirsch (Eds.), *Handbook of clinical hypnosis* (2nd ed., pp. 239–264). Washington, DC: American Psychological Association.

Linehan, M. (1993). *Cognitive-behavioral treatment of borderline personality disorder.* New York: Guilford.

Lipsey, M. W., & Wilson, D. B. (1993). The efficacy of psychological, educational, and behavioral outcomes: Confirmation from meta-analysis. *American Psychologist, 48*, 1181–1209.

Lutz, A., Greischar, L. L., Rawlings, N. B., Ricard, M., & Davidson, R. J. (2004). Long-term meditators self-induce high-amplitude gamma synchrony during mental practice. *PNAS, 101*, 16369–16373. doi: 10.1073/pnas.0407401101

Lynn, S., Barnes, S., Deming, A., & Accardi, M. (2010). Hypnosis, rumination, and depression: Catalyzing attention and mindfulness-based treatments. *International Journal of Clinical and Experimental Hypnosis, 58,* 202–221.

Lynn, S., Das, L. S., Hallquist, M., & Williams, J. (2006). Mindfulness, acceptance and hypnosis: Cognitive and clinical perspectives. *International Journal of Clinical and Experimental Hypnosis, 54,* 143–166.

Lynn, S., & Green, J. (2011). The sociocognitive and dissociation theories of hypnosis: Toward a rapprochement. *International Journal of Clinical and Experimental Hypnosis, 59, 3,* 277–293.

Lynn, S. J., & Hallquist, M. N. (2004). Toward a scientifically based understanding of Milton H. Erickson's strategies and tactics: Hypnosis, response sets and common factors in psychotherapy. *Contemporary Hypnosis, 21,* 63–78.

Lynn, S., & Kirsch, I. (2006). *Essentials of clinical hypnosis.* Washington, DC: American Psychological Association.

Lynn, S., Kirsch, I., Barabasz, A., Cardeña, E., & Patterson, D. (2000). Hypnosis as an empirically supported adjunctive technique: The state of the evidence. *International Journal of Clinical and Experimental Hypnosis, 48*, 343–361.

Lynn, S., Neufeld, V., & Mare, C. (1993). Direct versus indirect suggestions: A conceptual and methodological review. *International Journal of Clinical and Experimental Hypnosis, 41*, 125–152.

Ma, S., & Teasdale, J. (2004). Mindfulness-based cognitive therapy for depression: Replication and exploration of differential relapse prevention effects. *Journal of Consulting and Clinical Psychology, 72*, 31–40.

Marci, C., Ham, J., Moran, E., & Orr, S. (2007). Physiologic correlates of perceived therapist empathy and social-emotional process during psychotherapy. *Journal of Nervous and Mental Diseases, 195*(2), 103–111.

Marlatt, G. A. (2002). Buddhist philosophy and the treatment of addictive behavior. *Cognitive and Behavioral Practice, 9*, 44–49.

Mayberg, H., Silva, J., Brannan, S., Tekell, J., Mahurin, R., McGinnis, S., & Jerabek, P. (2002). The functional neuroanatomy of the placebo effect. *American Journal of Psychiatry, 159*, 728–737.

McCollum, E., & Gehart, D. (2010). Using mindfulness meditation to teach beginning therapists therapeutic presence: A qualitative study. *Journal of Marital and Family Therapy, 36*(3), 347–360.

McQuillan, A., Nicastro, R., Guenot, F., Girad, M., Lissner, C., & Ferrero, F. (2005). Intensive dialectical behavior therapy for outpatients with borderline personality disorder who are in crises. *Psychiatric Services, 56*, 193–197.

Mellan, O. (2010, March 28). *Getting mindful about money.* Workshop presented at the Psychotherapy Networker Symposium, Washington, DC.

Mellinger, D. (2010). Hypnosis and the treatment of anxiety disorders. In S. Lynn, J. Rhue, & I. Kirsch (Eds.), *Handbook of clinical hypnosis* (2nd ed., pp. 359–390). Washington, DC: American Psychological Association.

Moore, M., & Tasso, A. (2008). Clinical hypnosis: The empirical evidence. In M. Nash & A. Barnier (Eds.), *The Oxford handbook of hypnosis* (pp. 697–726). Oxford, UK: Oxford University Press.

Nash, M., & Baker, E. (2010). Hypnosis in the treatment of anorexia nervosa. In S. Lynn, J. Rhue, & I. Kirsch (Eds.), *Handbook of clinical hypnosis* (2nd ed., pp. 453–466). Washington, DC: American Psychological Association.

Néron, S., & Stephenson, R. (2007). Effectiveness of hypnotherapy with cancer patients' trajectory: Emesis, acute pain, and analgesia and anxiolysis in procedures. *International Journal of Clinical and Experimental Hypnosis, 55,* 336–354.

Oakley, D. (2008). Hypnosis, trance, and suggestion: Evidence from neuroimaging. In M. Nash & A. Barnier (Eds.), *The Oxford handbook of hypnosis* (pp. 365–392). Oxford, UK: Oxford University Press.

Oakley, D., & Halligan, P. (2010). Psychophysiological foundations of hypnosis and suggestion. In S. Lynn, J. Rhue, & I. Kirsch (Eds.), *Handbook of clinical hypnosis* (2nd ed., pp. 79–117). Washington, DC: American Psychological Association.

Orne, M. (1959). The nature of hypnosis: Artifact and essence. *Journal of Abnormal and Social Psychology, 58,* 277–299.

Otani, A. (2003). Eastern meditative techniques and hypnosis: A new synthesis. *American Journal of Clinical Hypnosis, 46*(2), 97–108.

Palsson, O., Turner, M., Johnson, D., Burnett, C., & Whitehead, W. (2002). Hypnosis treatment for severe irritable bowel syndrome: Investigation of mechanism and effects on symptoms. *Digestive Diseases and Sciences, 47,* 2605–2614.

Patterson, D. (2010). *Clinical hypnosis for pain control.* Washington, DC: American Psychological Association.

Patterson, D., Jensen, M., & Montgomery, G. (2010). Hypnosis for pain control. In S. Lynn, J. Rhue, & I. Kirsch (Eds.), *Handbook of clinical hypnosis* (2nd ed., pp. 521–549). Washington, DC: American Psychological Association.

Perrin, P., Heesacker, M., Pendley, C., & Smith, B. (2010). Social influence processes and persuasion in psychotherapy and counseling. In J. Maddux & J. Tangney (Eds.), *Social psychological foundations of clinical psychology* (pp. 441–460). New York: Guilford.

Peterson, C., & Seligman, M. (2004). *Character strengths and virtues: A handbook and classification.* New York: Oxford University Press.

Placone, P. (2011). *Mindful parent, happy child: A guide to raising joyful and resilient children.* Palo Alto, CA: Alaya Press.

Posner, M., & Peterson, S. (1990). The attention system of the human brain. *Annual Review of Neuroscience, 13,* 25–42.

Random House college dictionary. (1973). New York: Random House.

Raz, A. (2005). Attention and hypnosis: Neural substrates and genetic associations of two converging processes. *International Journal of Clinical and Experimental Hypnosis, 53,* 237–258.

Raz, A., Fan, J., & Posner, M. (2005). Hypnotic suggestion reduces conflict in the human brain. *Proceedings of the National Academy of Sciences of the United States of America, 102*, 9978–9983.

Reps, P., & Senzaki, N. (1998). *Zen flesh, Zen bones: A collection of Zen and pre-Zen writings.* Boston: Tuttle.

Richeport-Haley, M., & Carlson, J. (Eds.). (2010). *Jay Haley revisited.* New York: Routledge.

Rizzolatti, G., & Craighero, L. (2004). The mirror-neuron system. *Annual Review of Neuroscience, 27*, 169–192.

Rogers, C. (1986). Client-centered therapy. In I. Kutash & A. Wolf (Eds.), *Psychotherapist's casebook: Theory and technique in practice* (pp. 197–208). San Francisco: Jossey-Bass.

Schwartz, J., & Begley, S. (2003). *The mind and the brain: Neuroplasticity and the power of mental force.* New York: Harper Perennial.

Segal, Z. V., Williams, S., & Teasdale, J. (2002). *Mindfulness-based cognitive therapy for depression: A new approach to preventing relapse.* New York: Guilford.

Segal, Z., Bieling, P., Young, T., MacQueen, G., Cooke, R., Martin, L., et al. (2010). Antidepressant monotherapy vs. sequential pharmacotherapy and mindfulness-based cognitive therapy, or placebo, for relapse prophylaxis in recurrent depression. *Archives of General Psychiatry, 67*(12), 1256–1264.

Seltzer, L. (1986). *Paradoxical strategies in psychotherapy: A comprehensive overview and guidebook.* New York: John Wiley.

Shor, R. (1959). Hypnosis and the concept of the generalized reality-orientation. *American Journal of Psychotherapy, 13*, 582–602.

Siegel, D. (2010a, October 27). *The mindful therapist.* Live Web seminar sponsored by the National Institute for the Clinical Application of Behavioral Medicine.

Siegel, D. (2010b). *Mindsight: The new science of personal transformation.* New York: Bantam.

Siegel, R. (2009). *The mindfulness solution: Everyday practices for everyday problems.* New York: Guilford.

Siegel, R. (2010, September 22). *Harnessing mindfulness: Fitting practice to person.* Live Web seminar sponsored by the National Institute for the Clinical Application of Behavioral Medicine.

Silvia, P., & Gendolla, G. (2001). On introspection and self-perception: Does self-focused attention enable accurate self-knowledge? *Review of General Psychology, 5*, 241–269.

Simpkins, C., & Simpkins, A. (2010). *Neuro-hypnosis: Using self-hypnosis to activate the brain for change.* New York: Norton.

Solberg, E., Halvorsen, R., Sundgot-Borgen, J., Ingjer, F., & Holen, A. (1995). Meditation: A modulator of the immune response to physical stress? A brief report. *British Journal of Sports Medicine, 29,* 255–257.

Spanos, N., & Chaves, J. (1989). *Hypnosis: The cognitive-behavioral perspective.* Amherst, NY: Prometheus.

Spanos, N., Robertson, L., Menary, E., & Brett, P. (1986). Component analysis of cognitive skill training for the enhancement of hypnotic susceptibility. *Journal of Abnormal Psychology, 95,* 350–357.

Spiegel, D. (2008). Intelligent design or designed intelligence? Hypnotizability as neurobiological adaptation. In M. Nash & A. Barnier (Eds.), *The Oxford handbook of hypnosis* (pp. 179–199). Oxford, UK: Oxford University Press.

Spiegel, D. (2010). Hypnosis in the treatment of posttraumatic stress disorders. In S. Lynn, J. Rhue, & I. Kirsch (Eds.), *Handbook of clinical hypnosis* (2nd ed., pp. 415–432). Washington, DC: American Psychological Association.

Spiegel, D., White, M., & Waelde, L. (2010). Hypnosis, mindful meditation, and brain imaging. In D. Barrett (Ed.), *Hypnosis and hypnotherapy: Vol. 1, Neuroscience, personality, and cultural factors* (pp. 37–52). Santa Barbara, CA: Praeger.

Spinelli, E. (1994). *Demystifying therapy.* London: Constable.

Suzuki, S. (1988). *Zen mind, beginner's mind: Informal talks on Zen meditation and practice.* New York: Weatherhill.

Szasz, T. (2010). *The myth of mental illness: Foundations of a theory of personal conduct.* New York: Harper Perennial.

Tacón, A. (2003). Meditation as a complementary therapy in cancer. *Family & Community Health, 26*(1), 64–73.

Teasdale, J., Segal, Z., Williams, J., Ridgeway, V., Soulsby, J., & Lau, M. (2000). Prevention of relapse/recurrence in major depression by mindfulness based cognitive therapy. *Journal of Consulting and Clinical Psychology, 68,* 615–623.

Tellegen, A. (1978/1979). On measures and conceptions of hypnosis. *American Journal of Clinical Hypnosis, 21,* 219–237.

Thompson, K. (1985). Almost 1984. In J. Zeig (Ed.), *Ericksonian psychotherapy, Vol. 1: Structures* (pp. 89–99). New York: Brunner/Mazel.

Thompson, K. (2004). An introduction to hypnosis. In S. Kane & K. Olness (Eds.), *The art of therapeutic communication: The collected works of Kay F. Thompson* (pp. 9-28). Bancyfelin, Carmarthen, Wales: Crown House.

Tobis, I., & Kihlstrom, J. (2010). Allocation of attentional resources in posthypnotic suggestion. *International Journal of Clinical and Experimental Hypnosis, 58*(4), 367–382.

Treadway, M., & Lazar, S. (2009). The neurobiology of mindfulness. In F. Didonna (Ed.), *Clinical handbook of mindfulness* (pp. 45–57). New York: Springer.

Twenge, J. (2007). *Generation me: Why today's young Americans are more confident, assertive, entitled—and more miserable than ever before.* New York: Free Press.

Twenge, J., & Campbell, W. (2010). *The narcissism epidemic: Living in the age of entitlement.* New York: Free Press.

Uleman, J. (2005). Introduction: Becoming aware of the new unconscious. In R. Hassin, J. Uleman, & J. Bargh (Eds.), *The new unconscious: Social cognition and social neuroscience* (pp. 3–18). New York: Oxford University Press.

Vermetten, E., Bremner, J., & Spiegel, D. (1998). Dissociation and hypnotizability: A conceptual and methodological perspective on two distinct concepts. In J. Bremner & C. Marmar (Eds.), *Trauma, memory and dissociation* (pp. 107–161). Washington, DC: American Psychiatric Press.

Wagstaff, G. F. (2004). High hypnotizability in a sociocognitive framework. In M. Heap, D. Oakley, & R. Brown (Eds.), *The highly hypnotizable person* (pp. 85–114). London: Brunner-Routledge.

Watts, A. (1961). *Psychotherapy east and west.* New York: Random House.

Watts, A. (1999). *The way of Zen.* New York: Vintage. (Original work published 1957)

Watzlawick, P. (1985). Hypnotherapy without trance. In J. Zeig (Ed.), *Ericksonian psychotherapy, Vol. 1: Structures* (pp. 5–14). New York: Brunner/Mazel.

Wegner, D. (2003). *The illusion of conscious will.* Cambridge, MA: MIT Press.

Wegner, D. (2005). Who is the controller of controlled processes? In R. Hassin, J. Uleman, & J. Bargh (Eds.), *The new unconscious: Social cognition and social neuroscience* (pp. 19–36). New York: Oxford University Press.

Weinberger, J., & Eig, A. (1999). Expectancies: The ignored common factor in psychotherapy. In I. Kirsch (Ed.), *How expectancies shape experience* (pp. 357–382). Washington, DC: American Psychological Association.

Weitzenhoffer, A. (2000). *The practice of hypnotism* (2nd ed.). New York: John Wiley.

Whitaker, R. (2010). *Anatomy of an epidemic: Magic bullets, psychiatric drugs, and the astonishing rise of mental illness in America.* New York: Crown.

Williams, J., Hallquist, M., Barnes, S., Cole, S., & Lynn, S. (2010). Hypnosis, mindfulness, and acceptance: Artful integration. In S. Lynn, J. Rhue, & I.

Kirsch (Eds.), *Handbook of clinical hypnosis* (2nd ed., pp. 319–338). Washington, DC: American Psychological Association.

Williams, L., Bargh, J., Nocera, C., & Gray, J. (2009). The unconscious regulation of emotion: Nonconscious reappraisal goals modulate emotional reactivity. *Emotion, 9*(6), 847–854.

Williams, M., Teasdale, J., Segal, Z., & Kabat-Zinn, J. (2007). *The mindful way through depression: Freeing yourself from chronic unhappiness.* New York: Guilford.

Wilson, T. (2004). *Strangers to ourselves: Discovering the adaptive unconscious.* Cambridge, MA: Belknap/Harvard University Press.

Yapko, M. (1983). A comparative analysis of direct and indirect hypnotic communication styles. *American Journal of Clinical Hypnosis, 25,* 270–276.

Yapko, M. (1992). *Hypnosis and the treatment of depressions: Strategies for change.* New York: Brunner/Mazel.

Yapko, M. (1994). *Suggestions of abuse: True and false memories of childhood sexual abuse.* New York: Simon & Schuster.

Yapko, M. (1997). *Breaking the patterns of depression.* New York: Random House/Doubleday.

Yapko, M. (1999). *Hand-me-down blues: How to stop depression from spreading in families.* New York: St. Martin's.

Yapko, M. (2001a). *Treating depression with hypnosis: Integrating cognitive-behavioral and strategic approaches.* New York: Brunner-Routledge.

Yapko, M. (2001b). Jay Haley on Jay Haley. In J. Zeig (Ed.), *Changing directives: The strategic therapy of Jay Haley* (pp. 183–202). Phoenix, AZ: Milton H. Erickson Foundation Press.

Yapko, M. (2003). *Trancework: An introduction to the practice of clinical hypnosis* (3rd ed.). New York: Routledge.

Yapko, M. (2005/2006). Some comments regarding the Division 30 definition of hypnosis. *American Journal of Clinical Hypnosis, 48*(2–3), 107–110.

Yapko, M. (Ed.). (2006). *Hypnosis and treating depression: Applications in clinical practice.* New York: Routledge.

Yapko, M. (2007). The case of Carol: Empowering decision-making through metaphor and hypnosis. In G. Burns (Ed.), *Healing with stories: Your casebook collection for using therapeutic metaphors* (pp. 67–78). New York: John Wiley.

Yapko, M. (2009). *Depression is contagious: How the most common mood disorder is spreading around the world and how to stop it.* New York: Free Press.

Yapko, M., Barretta, N., & Barretta, P. (1998). Clinical training in Ericksonian hypnosis. *American Journal of Clinical Hypnosis, 41*(1), 18–28.

Zeig, J. (Ed.). (1980). *A teaching seminar with Milton H. Erickson, M.D.* New York: Brunner/Mazel.

Zeig, J. (Ed.). (1982). *Ericksonian approaches to hypnosis and psychotherapy.* New York: Brunner/Mazel.

Zeig , J. (Ed.) (1992). *The evolution of psychotherapy: The second conference.* New York: Brunner/Mazel

Zeig, L. (2010). An interview with Marsha Linehan. *Milton H. Erickson Foundation Newsletter, 30*(1), 1–24.

Index